Municipal Management Series

Housing and Local Government

Mary K. Nenno
Paul C. Brophy

with contributions by
Michael Barker
Douglas S. Ford
Frank Keefe
G. Terry McNellis
William A. Witte

International
City
Management
Association

Municipal Management Series

David S. Arnold, Editor   *5 74 9 83*

Housing and Local Government
Developing the Municipal Organization
Effective Supervisory Practices
The Essential Community: Local Government in the Year 2000
Local Government Police Management
Management Policies in Local Government Finance
Managing Fire Services
Managing Human Services
Managing the Modern City
Managing Municipal Leisure Services
The Practice of Local Government Planning
Public Relations in Local Government
Small Cities Management Training Program
Urban Public Works Administration

Library of Congress Cataloging in Publication Data
Nenno, Mary K., 1923–
    Housing and local government.
    (Municipal management series)
    Bibliography: p.
    Includes index.
    1. Housing policy—United States. 2. Local
government—United States. I. Brophy, Paul C. II.
Title. III. Series.
HD7293.N44   1983   363.5'8'0973   82-9174
ISBN 0-87326-025-2   AACR2
ISBN 0-87326-026-0 (pbk.)

HD
7293
. N44
1982

Printed in the United States of America.
12345 • 8988878685848382

Foreword

Housing in the United States was strictly a private-sector activity (with the exception of building codes and other safety measures) until the early thirties. Under the pressures of the Great Depression, the National Housing Act of 1934 created the Federal Housing Administration, which guaranteed mortgages for families that could not obtain private market financing. In the half century since, housing has broadened to include many other kinds of governmental actions—urban renewal, slum clearance, neighborhood conservation, relocation services, housing codes, publicly assisted housing for low- and moderate-income families, rent controls, and rent supplements.

Housing and Local Government, a new title in the ICMA Municipal Management Series, is a book for local government managers—housing authority directors, community development directors, housing managers, city and county managers, planning directors, finance officers, and development specialists. It is a book for both the policy issues and the day-to-day problems of housing for the eighties.

For almost forty years, housing in this country meant largely a panoply of federal government programs, often administered through local housing authorities. Cities, counties, and other general-purpose local governments were involved only on the periphery through zoning ordinances, subdivision regulations, property purchases and sales, land purchases and sales, and the location and relocation of schools.

From the mid-seventies on, this situation changed rapidly as federal programs were constantly changed, reduced, or transferred to state and local governments. In addition, many local governments, especially larger cities, took on new activities in housing rehabilitation and mortgage financing. The dynamics of housing have changed radically, and the focal point is the city hall or the county courthouse. This book covers these emerging local government responsibilities for housing provided by the public sector, the private sector, and a mix of the two.

The Municipal Management Series, published by the International City Management Association, is a series of training manuals that go back to the mid-thirties. Many of the titles in the series, including this one, have been prepared for correlative use by the ICMA Training Institute, which offers in-service training courses designed specifically for local government managers.

It is a pleasure to acknowledge the fine work of the primary authors of this book: Mary K. Nenno and Paul C. Brophy. Their extensive experience in housing, planning, community development, and neighborhood revitalization is reflected in these pages.

Special appreciation is expressed to the Ford Foundation, in particular, Louis Winnick, for the individual grant to Mary K. Nenno for assistance in preparation of the manuscript. Also, a special word of thanks is due John A. McCauley, Deputy Commissioner of the Baltimore Department of Housing and Community Development, and Bernard L. Tetreault, Executive Director of the Housing Opportunities Commission of Montgomery County, Maryland, for their cooperation in preparing material for the final chapter.

Mark E. Keane
Executive Director
International City
   Management Association

Preface

The emergence of housing as a growing function of local government comes at a critical juncture in the evolution of housing policies and housing institutions, both private and public, in the United States. The demands of the 1980s are stimulating new housing approaches to meet changing household requirements, shifting patterns of economic growth and development, and increasing competition for investment capital. These demands are also causing a new examination of housing responsibilities of all levels of government.

While it is estimated that the population of the nation as a whole will grow by less than 10 percent in the decade of the 1980s, the number of households is expected to rise sharply at a rate of more than 16 percent, with a declining household size and a higher proportion of single and nonfamily units. The spreading out of population and employment toward the West and the South, and to suburban and nonmetropolitan areas, will likely continue. Housing demand will vary considerably by geographic region and by type of community. Poor and minority households will likely continue to be concentrated in central cities.

An increase in the number of households will create pressure for an expansion of the housing supply, but high interest rates caused by inflation will tend to constrain housing construction and increase the price of new housing. This, in turn, could further reduce the availability and increase the cost of housing in the existing supply, particularly for lower-income families seeking rental housing. At the same time, the demands for investment capital by all sectors of the national economy will place housing in a competitive market, requiring major transformations in housing finance policies and financing instruments.

Under pressure to reduce housing costs and to conserve energy, the trend to preserve existing housing and neighborhoods will continue. New housing construction is likely to favor more compact forms of development, particularly in multifamily construction of condominiums and cooperatives, at higher densities than for detached dwellings. There also will be a growing trend toward mixed-use developments, combining industrial/commercial expansion or revitalization with residential development.

All these demands and trends will directly affect public policies and actions for housing at all levels of government. The 1980s will likely witness a new "sorting out" of government responsibilities for federal, state, and local governments. Already, at the federal level, there is a new exploration of the influence of national macroeconomic policies on housing—credit allocations, tax subsidies, and income support for poverty-level families. The more direct programs of federal housing assistance for lower-income families are subject to severe budget constraints, raising questions about the level of future federal support. Increasingly, state and local governments are moving to take housing actions designed to fill the gap between private housing resources and more limited direct federal assistance. These "gap-filling" local housing initiatives are often linked directly to neighborhood conservation or economic development.

It is our hope that *Housing and Local Government* will provide a useful perspective for local and state governments in assessing how their housing responsibilities are evolving, how some jurisdictions are organizing and managing their housing functions, and—most important—how state and local housing initiatives can fit into the major shifts in housing policy being generated on a national level. The growing maturity of local and state housing activity holds promise that it will be a vital force in helping to shape the national housing policies that are now in formulation. This is our hope and our objective.

Mary K. Nenno
Paul C. Brophy

Contents

Housing
and
Local
Government

Chapter 1

Evolution of local housing involvement

Housing and the local community are bound together in a complex web of individual choices and community structure. Unlike food and clothing, which are consumed in a short time, the third basic human need of shelter has a long-term influence on the individual household as it goes through various stages of life, and on the individual community as it matures and changes.

The focus of this book is on the direct housing functions of local government, which are still evolving from the federal programs that began in the early 1930s—that is, housing for low-income families and slum clearance. These direct housing functions, however, can best be understood in relation to all of the local government interventions affecting housing, especially land use controls, building codes, housing codes, and the local property tax. In addition to their regulatory functions, local governments provide the services on which residential areas depend—schools, recreation, health and social services, police and fire protection, and waste collection. They also build and maintain the infrastructure and provide for utilities.

Given the overpowering effect of local government on housing, the direct local function in housing must be viewed in the context of local government. It is the thesis of this book that a permanent local housing function is evolving as the end product of both local interventions and federally assisted initiatives over the past fifty years. The final section of this chapter identifies "clusters" of local activity, and subsequent chapters describe their current status and potential for the future.

HOUSING IN THE LOCAL COMMUNITY

Sorting out the various components of housing is not easy. Glenn Beyer characterizes housing as both "a highly complex product" and "an economic and a social process." As a product, it is "bulky, durable, and permanent." In the economic system, Beyer points out that builders, materials manufacturers, and bankers rely on housing for their livelihoods, and housing programs provide employment opportunities. Further, "housing has highly significant social implications because it provides the shelter for our basic unit—the family."[1]

In its comprehensive review of urban needs and programs in 1968, the Douglas Commission listed three primary functions of housing in its community setting: "to provide (1) comfortable shelter; (2) a proper setting, both within the structure and in its neighborhood, for the day-to-day activities of families and households, of small, informal groups of children and adults, and of the individuals who make them up; and (3) the locus or location of families and other groups within the larger physical pattern of the locality. This is simply saying a little more explicitly—a decent home and a suitable living environment."[2]

The intricate relationship of housing to goals and planning, both by families and by communities, was set forth by an American Bar Association report in 1978. The report pointed out that housing represents a major expenditure for most American families, that a high proportion (over 40 percent) of developed land is devoted to residential use, and the availability of housing "both affects and is affected by a wide variety of public and private actions, and must therefore be coordinated with all forms of planning and implementation activities" at all levels of government.[3]

While it may be impossible to set forth all of the interrelationships among housing and other community concerns, it is essential for an understanding of the public function of housing to identify some of the major ones:

1. Housing is a durable, physical product in a neighborhood setting.
2. Housing is a major user of community land.
3. Housing is a generator of local public facilities and services.
4. Housing is the object of local real estate taxes.
5. Housing is a major influence on its physical and social environment.
6. Housing is an essential supporter of business and industry.
7. Housing is a major source of employment.
8. Housing is a major investment or expenditure for individual families.
9. Housing is a major investment for the private financial community.
10. Housing is a major ingredient in family satisfaction or dissatisfaction and in a community's sense of well-being.

It is not too much to state that housing is the physical, economic, and social backbone of community structure.

HOUSING AS A PUBLIC FUNCTION:
HISTORICAL PERSPECTIVE

As early as 1917, the historian Charles A. Beard pointed out that such significant questions as overcrowding, unemployment, and low standards of living could not be solved by municipal action alone.[4] Authorities in public administration observe that slums developed for decades, but municipal action was restricted by legal and financial limitations on local government ventures into low-income housing; moreover, American public opinion regarded construction and operation of low-rent housing by government as one of those socialistic experiments suitable to European experience but a method apart from the American way of life.[5]

Given this environment, it is not surprising that housing was generally regarded in the United States solely as a function for private enterprise rather than as a responsibility of municipal government.

Public housing, redevelopment of slum areas, and rehabilitation of blighted areas constitute municipal activities assisted by federal aid and were virtually nonexistent until 1933. It took the economic and social disturbances of the Great Depression to spawn the first major, direct intervention in housing in the United States. The Federal Home Loan Bank System was created by legislation in 1932. The Public Works Administration (PWA), created under the National Industrial Recovery Act of 1933, authorized the first federally assisted construction of low-income housing. The National Housing Act of 1934 created the Federal Housing Administration (FHA), which guaranteed mortgages for families who could not obtain private market financing. In 1937 the United States Housing Act solidified and made permanent a federally assisted public housing program. In the same year the National Resources Planning Board summarized the condition of cities.

Dislocations, maladjustments, and other defects and deficiencies in the urban structure; congestion, excessive land prices, slums, blighted residential areas and deteriorating business sections, as well as premature and unnecessary sub-divisions—and the economic losses and social ills resulting therefrom; are the price of inadequate attention to the development and welfare of the community as a whole—of not planning—and may be found in almost every large urban area.[6]

When the conditions of the Great Depression stimulated a public response to housing needs, the initiative was federal, but the delivery was local. The public powers and authority of local government to undertake the new housing activities had to be justified under powers granted by the states, and these powers vary considerably from state to state. From the late 1930s through the 1950s, local public activities in low-rent housing and slum clearance were tested in the courts and upheld in nearly every state.[7]

The division of housing responsibilities among levels of government in the U.S. federal system is constantly changing, but certain components of the federal role seem clear and are stated succinctly in a report of the American Bar Association:

At the outset it must be noted that many of the most fundamental issues concerning housing are beyond the control of state and local governments. Only the federal government has the resources and authority to affect capital formation, interest rates, the availability of mortgage capital, and to infuence the distribution of incomes. Moreover, federal policies designed to slow inflation, lower unemployment, and encourage increased rates of economic growth all profoundly influence levels of housing production. In short, the federal government has the primary resources for strengthening and facilitating the private sector's efforts in providing housing to those able to afford it and providing assistance for those forced to spend too much for housing.[8]

State governments traditionally have played minor roles in housing by passing enabling legislation that allowed local governments to establish housing authorities or urban renewal agencies or by delegating police powers over zoning, building, and housing codes to cities. But this has changed (see Tables 1-1 and 1-2). States have taken on new initiatives that include using their superior taxing power, fiscal stability, and greater access to national bond markets to stimulate housing through a variety of financing

Table 1-1   Number of state-assisted housing units built prior to 1960 for low- and middle-income families, 1980.[1]

State[2]	Single family	Multi-family	Total
New York	. . .	76,000	76,000
Massachusetts	. . .	21,390	21,390
Connecticut	6,400	12,420	18,820
New Jersey	. . .	7,730	7,730
Pennsylvania	. . .	3,200	3,200
Total	6,400	120,740	127,140
	(5%)	(95%)	(100%)

Source: National Association of Housing and Redevelopment Officials, *Housing and Urban Renewal Directory, 1961–1962* (Washington, D.C.: National Association of Housing and Redevelopment Officials, 1961), pp. 23–32.
Leaders (. . .) indicate data inapplicable.
1 Includes public housing, veterans housing, and elderly housing.

2 Typically, state-assisted housing prior to 1960 was developed and managed by local housing authorities. Multifamily housing developed by state housing finance agencies after 1960 involved financial assistance to private sponsors.

Table 1–2 Number of state-assisted housing units assisted after 1960 for low-, moderate-, and middle-income families, 1981.[1]

State[2]	Single family	Multi-family	Total
New York	29,900	67,546	97,446
New Jersey	11,937	29,475	41,412
Michigan	10,210	30,251	40,461
Massachusetts	3,335	34,584	37,919
Connecticut	29,670	7,034	36,704
Virginia	18,089	11,468	29,557
Rhode Island	19,411	7,258	26,669
Minnesota	11,295	14,891	26,186
Missouri	9,000	14,848	23,848
Alaska	22,393	. . .	22,393
Illinois	. . .	20,907	20,907
California	14,203	5,910	20,113
Kentucky	16,300	1,833	18,133
Wisconsin	6,886	9,287	16,173
Pennsylvania	. . .	14,020	14,020
South Dakota	11,086	1,996	13,032
West Virginia	6,761	6,030	12,791
Maryland	5,513	6,864	12,337
Oregon	7,814	2,534	10,347
25 other states[3]	114,024	28,144	142,168
Total	305,171	296,195	601,366
	(51%)	(49%)	(100%)

Source: Council of State Housing Agencies, *1981 Survey of Housing Finance Agencies* (Washington, D.C.: Council of State Housing Agencies, 1981).
Leaders (. . .) indicate data inapplicable.
1 Includes mortgages purchased and projects receiving permanent state financing.

2 Most of the multifamily units developed by state housing finance or mortgage agencies after 1965 received federal assistance under the rent supplement or Section 236 below-market interest rate programs, and after 1974 from the Section 8 rental assistance program.
3 Less than 10,000 units in any state.

and taxation programs. Federal and state involvement in local government functions have intensified the traditional tensions that exist among levels of government. On one side of the spectrum are those who contend that if federal or state assistance is to be given, it should be given without conditions under a system of "revenue sharing" or "block grants" for broad purposes. At the other side of the spectrum are those who contend that federal or state assistance should be given only with specific objectives for important, narrowly defined public purposes.

Whatever the mode of assistance, most observers of current urban problems see no alternative to jointly initiated and implemented efforts. Housing is a function of such scope and complexity that the participation and cooperation of federal, state, and local levels of government are viewed as necessary to provide the resources to meet demands for housing and related services. The local government cannot do it alone.

HOUSING AS A PUBLIC FUNCTION: EVOLVING INFLUENCES

In upholding the delegation of power to undertake the public housing program, the New York State Court of Appeals declared in 1936:

> The fundamental purpose of government is to protect the health, safety, and general welfare of the public. . . . Its power plant for the purpose consists of the *power of taxation, the police power,* and *the power of eminent domain.* Whereas there arises, in the state, a condition of affairs holding substantial menace to the public health, safety, general welfare, it becomes the duty of the government to apply whatever power is necessary and appropriate to check it. . . . It seems to be constitutionally immaterial whether one or the other sovereign powers is employed.[9]

This 1936 decision sets forth the basic framework for all local activities affecting housing. Direct public regulation of land and construction of buildings is carried on under the police power through which a government assures the health, safety, and general welfare of its citizens. Generally speaking, the courts have determined that such regulation is a matter of state, rather than federal, police power under the Constitution; within the states this power has been delegated within specified statutory limits to municipal governments. Local building codes are the most direct and obvious example of local police power regulation in the housing field; housing and health codes are focused on maintaining minimum standards of fitness for human occupancy.

Land use controls and housing

The two principal mechanisms utilized by municipalities since the 1920s to control land use are zoning and subdivision regulations. With experience, local governments devised variations of these basic instruments. Two of the most important variations are architectural or design control ordinances and planned unit development (PUD) ordinances, the latter being a hybrid of zoning, subdivision regulation, and design control. In some communities, these innovations are incorporated as a part of the zoning ordinance; in others, they are separate documents.

A third important element in land use development is indirect control of land use planning. The pioneer law was a Massachusetts statute of 1913.

Evolution of zoning and land subdivision The distinguishing characteristic of zoning is the division of jurisdictional areas into *zoning districts* or *zones* with uniform regulations throughout each district but with differing regulations for different types of zones: the control is exercised through the specification of minimum or maximum limits, as appropriate, on lot size; on size and height or placement of structures; and through the permission, prohibition, or specific requirement of the uses to which land or buildings may be put. *Land subdivision regulations* are applied through specification or approval of street alignment and width; water supply, sewerage, drainage, and roadway design and construction; grading plans; and lot size and configuration.

The states began to confer comprehensive zoning authorizations on municipalities early in the 1920's. Most of these early statutes were patterned after a model published in 1924 by the U.S. Department of Commerce, the *Standard State Zoning Enabling Act.* By 1926, when the U.S. Supreme Court established the constitutionality of comprehensive zoning, there were 564 cities with such ordinances.

As applied in the United States, zoning grew out of the law of nuisance and became a device for protecting individual property owners from adverse actions by their neighbors. Subdivision control, on the other hand, was based on the need to protect the public investment in the creation of capital improvements, especially streets and highways. Zoning was for the protection of private interests in already developed land; subdivision control was for the protection of the public interest in servicing land to be developed in the future.

Source: Excerpted from: American Society of Planning Officials, *Problems of Zoning and Land Use Regulation,* prepared for the National Commission on Urban Problems, Research Report No. 2 (Washington, D.C.: Government Printing Office, 1968), p. 4; and James G. Coke and John J. Gargan, *Fragmentation in Land-Use Planning and Control,* prepared for the National Commission on Urban Problems, Research Report No. 18 (Washington, D.C.: Government Printing Office, 1969), pp. 5, 7.

Quasi-independent city planning commissions multiplied during the 1920s as their method of organizing local planning became entrenched in state after state. The U.S. Department of Commerce gave additional impetus to the use of planning commissions in its 1928 model law, the Standard City Planning Enabling Act. In 1968, 65 percent of the 7,609 local governments in the nation's SMSAs (standard metropolitan statistical areas) had planning agencies in operation. Section 701 of the 1954 Housing Act greatly stimulated activity by providing federal funds for local, regional, and state planning.[10]

Despite the rapid development of land use controls, the effort suffered from fragmentation of responsibility: "There is no necessary connection between zoning and subdivision control, and . . . these functions, as well as land use planning itself, may be performed by entirely separate organizations. The end result is not only that planning and controls may be frag-

mented territorially but also dispersed organizationally within a single jurisdiction."[11]

An early trend in the development of land use controls was a tendency to
utilize them to help solve public financial problems—to reduce or avoid
local government expenditures—with generally negative effects on housing
development. These are some of the results:

1. The search for additional revenue has led communities to overzone
   for industry and commercial development.
2. The desire to avoid additional public expenditures has been a
   primary reason for large lot zoning, for the limitation or prohibition of
   apartments, for the restriction or prohibition of mobile homes, and for
   excessively high zoning, subdivision, and building code standards
   that have impeded the provision of low- and moderate-income
   housing.
3. The desire to avoid school costs has favored single-family housing
   over apartments, particularly low- and moderate-income
   developments, influenced by the local governing body's belief that
   apartments generate more school costs than they return in taxes.[12]

The exclusionary nature of much zoning practice in relation to minority
and low-income persons has been documented by Mary Brooks in *Exclusionary Zoning.*[13]

When the federally assisted programs of slum clearance and public
housing began in the 1930s, they were subject to local zoning and land use
regulations. In addition, under most state enabling laws, new sites for public
housing development were subject to prior approval by local governing
bodies. Because of their low-income objectives and character, slum clearance and public housing were particularly vulnerable to exclusionary and
fiscal zoning and local land use practices. As these housing efforts grew,
there ensued over the years a series of judicial tests and remedies that
incorporated special zoning and land use techniques for advancing low-
and then moderate-income housing.[14]

One of the newer techniques is "inclusionary" development, under
which local ordinances require that most new housing developments include a minimum number of units for sale or rent to low- and moderate-
income families. Among the local jurisdictions testing this mechanism have
been Montgomery County, Maryland (1974); the city of Los Angeles (1974);
and Fairfax County, Virginia (1961—this ordinance was subsequently invali-
dated by the courts in Virginia). Some states have also taken special measures to stimulate housing development: Massachusetts (1969), which provides for state review of local zoning petitions that adversely affect the
development of low- and moderate-income housing; California (1974) and

Florida (1975), which require that every general plan have a housing element; and New Jersey (1976), where, under an executive order of the governor, priorities for state-controlled assistance for planning, finance, and development are given to those localities providing housing opportunities under their land use regulations. The unique power of New York state's Urban Development Corporation (UDC), created in 1968, to develop housing projects without complying with local zoning ordinances, building codes, or other laws or regulations, was partially revoked in 1973.

Expanding urbanization forced changes in zoning and land use regulations, especially in rapidly expanding metropolitan areas, to meet the spillover consequences of actions by individual localities. This led to the growth of "advisory reviews" of proposed actions by areawide planning agencies and, in some states, to increased state control of local land use planning. Many of these reforms were stimulated by federal assistance programs—in particular, the encouragement of state, regional, and metropolitan comprehensive planning under the Section 701 programs established by the Housing Act of 1954 and the A-95 review process established under the Inter-Governmental Cooperation Act of 1968. In addition, the Section 701 planning program was amended in 1968 to require the preparation of a housing element as part of the overall work program of any agency receiving federal urban planning assistance funds. Regulations of the U.S. Department of Housing and Urban Development (HUD) included coordination of housing plans with other regional plans, identification of housing needs, and delineation of strategies for meeting housing needs. The housing element of the Section 701 planning program, the A-95 review process, and judicial pressure to disperse federally assisted housing (subsequently codified in HUD's project selection criteria) catalyzed efforts to implement regional housing allocation plans.[15]

In the 1960s and 1970s, under the pressures of expanding development and rising costs, many communities streamlined or consolidated their zoning and land use approvals. A 1978 survey of the American Planning Association (APA) documented that over two hundred local communities had taken these actions. APA found, however, that "when it comes to commercial or industrial development, many local governments have created 'fast tracks' to expedite permit approval. . . . But few communities have been as willing to push for residential development. Housing has become a stepchild in many local communities in the 1960's and 1970's."[16]

Planning and housing

Land use planning by local government has gradually evolved into a more sophisticated framework, including not only the administration of zoning ordinances and subdivision regulations but also growth management techniques that link land use controls to operating budgets and capital improvement programs. The development of growth management in the 1970s has been termed "the coming of age of planning":

[It] brings together the plan and the tools of implementation. Growth management programs have designed and implemented new ways to control growth—new ways to use the traditional powers of zoning and capital investment. The interest in growth management has enhanced the status of the city plan. It is the plan that forms the foundation for political acceptance. The public, the builder, and political leaders will accept the restrictions of a growth management program if they can be certain that it has been soundly conceived.[17]

The major instrument of comprehensive development planning, growing out of the adoption in 1975 of the American Law Institute's *Model Land Development Code,* is the "local land development plan" that sets forth long-term policies and goals for land use and development. The plan sets guidelines for short-term programs and decisions. The organizational location of planning in local government is not specified in the model code, but the client for the plan is the local governing body of the municipality; adoption by that body gives the plan legal status. The merits of the plan are in the close and comprehensive relationship between long-term planning and short-term land use regulations, including zoning.[18] The city of Atlanta was a pioneer in the use of comprehensive development. A 1974 city charter amendment declared that the city's operating and capital budgets must be based on the comprehensive development plan, thus tying planning and implementation together to direct the growth of the city.

Another significant trend in comprehensive development planning is the growth of planning or planning/development departments to supersede independent planning commissions. Although the institutional arrangements for local government planning are varied, most involve close ties to the chief executive of the city, including appointment of the planning director.

A parallel trend in the 1970s has been the reduction of planning assistance from the federal government. Despite the major reform of Section 701 in the 1980 Housing and Community Development Act, federal funding has declined steadily since 1975 and increasingly is restricted to areawide planning agencies involved in planning coordination. The HUD budget for fiscal 1983 submitted by the Reagan administration would eliminate this program, and this termination could have significant effects on areawide planning, A-95 reviews of federally assisted development proposals, and areawide housing opportunity plans.

In any event, the comprehensive planning function is rapidly becoming, if it is not already in fact, a full-fledged, permanent local government function, directly integrated with the office of the local government chief executive.

Overall, the relationship between comprehensive planning and the programming of housing and community development has been slow to evolve. An analysis in 1969 described the shifting emphasis from a "project" orientation in the 1930s (where each new public housing development had to be located within reasonable access of schools, shopping, and transportation) to a citywide comprehensive development approach (beginning with the urban renewal program initiated in 1949, the Community Renewal Program [CRP] in 1959, and the growth of housing rehabilitation and preservation under the concentrated housing codes programs of 1965).[19]

As land use and comprehensive planning have evolved, new opportunities have emerged to make housing a more integral part of the total community development process. Because housing depends on infrastructure—transportation, public facilities, utilities—any improvement in comprehensive development planning provides new opportunities for housing in optimum locations relative to future city development. Relationships with the total community have multiplied as the direct housing functions evolving from the federal assistance programs of the 1930s have matured to incorporate neighborhood conservation and rehabilitation, physical renewal and redevelopment, and economic revitalization. The housing dimension also has expanded, particularly in relation to the federal requirements that all of these federally assisted efforts give priority or be targeted to lower-income families or neighborhoods. The requirement for a Housing Assistance Plan (HAP) under the Community Development Block Grant (CDBG) program of the Housing and Community Development Act of 1974 provided a new, stronger link between assisted housing and community development.

As of 1981 the instruments to link housing to comprehensive planning had been fully developed in only a few instances. A study by the National Association of Housing and Redevelopment Officials (NAHRO) proposed two basic instruments: (1) the Comprehensive Development Guide (providing the long-range policies, systems, and programs—the framework within which physical development activity, such as housing, can take place); and (2) the Comprehensive Community Development Program (the short-term, implementing mechanism, required under the 1974 Housing and Community Development Act, for carrying out both private and public development activity).[20]

Few local jurisdictions have a Comprehensive Development Guide; a prime example is the one developed by the Metropolitan Council of the Twin Cities of Minneapolis–St. Paul, which was used as the model in the NAHRO study.

Only a handful of communities have fulfilled the expectations of the Comprehensive Local Community Development program envisioned in the 1974 act: Baltimore, Atlanta, and Pittsburgh might be cited among larger cities attempting such comprehensive approaches.

Building codes and housing

The first building regulations in the United States were enacted in New Amsterdam as early as 1625 to govern the types, locations, and roof coverings of houses. Other cities gradually passed similar ordinances, but the early philosophy of the country, oriented to private initiatives and rights, was not conducive to the enactment of comprehensive public building codes. It was only following a series of disastrous fires in such major cities as Chicago and San Francisco that regulations began to appear. The first national model building code was promulgated in 1905. There was a rapid expansion in the adoption of local codes, particularly after a building code was made a requirement for federal urban renewal assistance under the "workable program" requirement of 1954.

Evolution of building codes A building code is a series of standards and specifications designed to establish minimum safeguards in the erection and construction of buildings, to protect human beings who live and work in them from fire and other hazards, and to establish regulations to further protect the health and safety of the public. Building codes are formulated and enforced through the police powers of State governments, ordinarily delegated to and exercised by local governments, usually municipalities.

The National Board of Fire Underwriters (now the American Insurance Association) is credited with providing the first model "National Building Code" which could be used by communities to regulate construction. From 1905 to 1927 it was the only code of its kind, and was geared primarily to protecting the interests of insurance companies which had suffered heavy losses because of fires originating in unregulated buildings. Local building officials began to organize in 1915, and they produced a series of new model codes: the Pacific Coast Building Officials (later the International Conference of Building Officials) produced the "Uniform Building Code" in 1927; the Southern Building Code Conference produced a separate code in 1945; and the Building Officials Conference of America developed the "Basic Building Code" in 1950.

Source: National Commission on Urban Problems, *Building the American City* (Washington, D.C.: Government Printing Office, [1968]), p. 254; Robert E. O'Bannon, *Building Code Administration* (Whittier, Calif.: International Conference of Building Officials, 1973), p. 106; and Allen D. Manvel, *Local Land and Building Regulations,* prepared for the National Commission on Urban Problems, Research Report No. 6 (Washington, D.C.: Government Printing Office, 1968), pp. 3–23.

The lack of uniformity among building codes brought increasing criticism, beginning as early as the 1920s.[21] In 1966 the U.S. Advisory Commission on Intergovernmental Relations (ACIR) reported great variation in the administration and enforcement of building codes among local jurisdictions. This variation can "limit initiative and innovation in the development of new construction materials and techniques. Such diversity also results in excessive requirements adding to the cost of construction; narrows the market for such products; and increases the cost of research, testing, maintenance, and servicing of the many building codes."[22]

Independently the same year, the National Commission on Technology, Automation, and Economic Programs urged the federal government to promote the modernization of building codes and the removal of impediments to new technology. ACIR corroborated that code diversity hindered development of such production techniques as prefabrication, use of components, mechanical cores, prefinished materials, and modular construction.

Another problem in building code administration was the dispersion of responsibility for administering the various codes within the local government structure, adding to the complexity and costs of the process. A survey of the International City Managers' Association in 1963 found that only about 40 percent of all cities of over 100,000 population combined administration of six basic regulations (building, plumbing, heating, electricity, housing codes, and zoning ordinances) under one department.[23]

Building codes clearly have state and federal as well as local government dimensions. The primary state involvement has been in mechanical codes and regulations. ACIR reported that four-fifths of all states had one or more of the following: statewide plumbing, electrical, boiler, and elevator codes or regulations. Almost half the states had a statewide fire code or regulations, but only five states had enacted statewide building construction codes, and none was mandatory for all construction. Federal government involvement in building codes traditionally has been influential in four areas: (1) direct construction; (2) direct operating and regulatory impact of federal insurance or assistance programs (the Minimum Property Standards of the Federal Housing Administration were particularly influential); (3) research on building specifications, standards, and testing techniques; and (4) building code standards and testing procedures.[24]

One of the most influential federal actions was the "workable program" requirement of the Housing Act of 1954; it conditioned urban renewal assistance on the preparation of a workable program for meeting problems of slums and urban blight. The workable program required that cities and other local public bodies develop positive renewal programs through the adoption of housing, zoning, *building* and other local laws; codes and regulations for land use; and adequate standards of health, sanitation, and safety for buildings. It was estimated that over 3,000 localities adopted building codes as a result of this requirement.[25] This rapid expansion of building codes led to further lack of uniformity in requirements and implementation.

Both ACIR in 1966 and the National Commission on Urban Problems in 1968 made strong cases for expanded state and federal government roles in reforming the administration of building codes, including national perform-ance criteria and testing procedures, a model national construction code, a state model building code, and statewide standards and review proce-dures.[26]

Following the release of these two influential reports, several develop-ments occurred to move building code administration toward these reform goals: (1) the resurgence of a forceful state role in building codes; (2) the stimulus of HUD's "Operation Breakthrough," initiated in 1969, in devel-oping state performance codes for industrialized housing; and (3) intensi-fied activity by associations of building officials to develop two specialized national codes—for one- and two-family housing and for rehabilitated hous-ing. A 1973 HUD survey documented that fifteen states had statewide build-ing codes, twenty-eight had preemptive laws governing factory-built hous-ing components, and thirty-eight had preemptive mobile home construction regulations.[27]

A further action toward reform of building code administration took place under the Housing and Community Development Act of 1974 with the creation of the National Institute of Building Sciences (NIBS), which is spe-cifically directed to develop performance criteria, standards, and testing procedures suitable for adoption by code regulatory agencies—in essence an authoritative product-testing agency. NIBS is only beginning to undertake its role, but even if it is fully implemented, its recommendations are only persuasive, not binding.

Substantial progress has been made in achieving a more orderly pro-cess of building regulation, but much remains to be done to meet the hous-ing demands of the eighties. A 1977 report by the Urban Consortium, a coalition of thirty-four major urban goverments, examined the inhibiting ef-fects of codes on low- and moderate-income housing, and the chronic prob-lems of lack of code uniformity, lack of flexibility, and institutional rigidity were still cited as major issues.[28] The 1978 report of the American Bar Association summarizes the current status of building codes as follows:

The trend is clearly toward uniformity, but whether the uniformity will come through federal intervention or through the adoption by individual states of a uniform code remains to be seen. In summary, what building codes really do is to make inexpen-sive housing illegal to build. . . . these code standards ought to be drastically re-vised . . . to prevent direct threats to health and safety, and that is all. At present these codes, along with such regulations as those for minimum lot size, help to make housing too expensive for a growing number of our people. The states, having delegated these regulatory powers to local governments, have the respon-sibility to supervise their use. Alternatively, they should reassert their authority and promulgate statewide codes that will preempt unsatisfactory local codes.[29]

While not all of the interests concerned with building code administra-tion would accept this American Bar Association recommendation, there probably is general agreement that the current pace of building code reform is not brisk enough to permit aggressive action by local governments, with state and federal government support, to meet their rapidly escalating local housing demands.

Occupancy standard codes and housing

The origin of minimum housing standards in the United States dates back to the mid-nineteenth century and grew out of concern for unsanitary housing as a cause of illness. Local and state health agencies have a long history of involvement in the hygiene of housing. This concern for unsanitary living conditions was joined with the housing reform movement in the late 1890s and early 1900s with the passage of tenement house legislation in New York and other large cities. Spencer Parratt in 1970 identified five distinct phases in the development of local housing codes:

1. The tenement laws in New York and other major cities following the Civil War
2. The growth of housing regulations as part of public health sanitary codes
3. The development of the minimum standards housing code, beginning in the 1940s, and the publication of the American Public Health Association (APHA) minimum code in 1952
4. The entry of federal government assistance, particularly in the urban renewal program of 1949, and the Housing Act of 1954, which placed more emphasis on housing and neighborhood rehabilitation and established the "workable program" requirement
5. The resurgence of the state role.[30]

Despite the rapid adoption of codes after 1954, the Douglas Commission found that "most housing codes are not administered effectively enough to achieve full compliance even with minimum requirements for health and safety."[31]

Two areas were sources of particular problems in the early administration of housing codes: (1) the dispersion of responsibility for the administration of the various health and safety codes among various city agencies; and (2) the climate of "enforcement" and "penalties" that characterized the implementation. In a 1960 survey the International City Managers' Association identified several organizational patterns for administration of housing standards, including the building inspector's office, the health department, and a separate housing or renewal department.[32]

In a study for the National Commission on Urban Problems in 1969, Joseph S. Slavet and Melvin R. Levin described the increasing influence of

Evolution of housing occupancy codes A housing code is an application of State police power put into effect by a local ordinance setting the minimum standards for safety, health, and welfare of the occupants of housing. It covers three main areas: (1) the supplied facilities in the structure, that is, toilet, bath, sink, etc., supplied by the owner; (2) the level of maintenance, which includes both structural and sanitary maintenance, leaks in the roof, broken banisters, cracks in the walls, etc.; and (3) occupancy, which concerns the size of dwelling units and of rooms of different types, the number of people who can occupy them, and other issues concerned on the whole with the usability and amenity of interior space.

In 1914, the Russell Sage Foundation published "A Model Housing Law" by Lawrence Veiller, which gave the first concrete form to minimum housing standards. The growth of housing codes, however, was an extremely slow process until the mid-1950s. As late as 1956, 100 or fewer of larger cities had housing codes. The National Commission on Urban Problems reported in 1968 that until the "workable program" requirement was introduced in 1954 conditioning urban renewal assistance on the existence of a housing code, relatively few cities had housing codes. The number of housing codes rapidly increased in the period from 1956 to 1968; in this latter year, 4,904 out of 17,993 cities surveyed had housing codes.

Source: Excerpted from National Commission on Urban Problems, *Building the American City* (Washington, D.C.: Government Printing Office, [1968]), pp. 274, 276–77.

local public agencies (LPAs), which operated within a community to plan and implement renewal projects.[33]

The recasting of housing code administration into a major tool to rehabilitate and conserve neighborhoods was stimulated by a series of provisions in federal housing acts:

1964—Section 312 rehabilitation loans: direct federal grants to assist property owners or tenants in urban renewal or code enforcement programs to rehabilitate their residential or business structures

1965—Section 115 rehabilitation capital grants to assist poor homeowners in urban renewal and code enforcement areas to cover the cost of necessary repairs and rehabilitation

1965—Section 116 demolition grants to provide local communities with up to two-thirds of the cost of demolishing structures determined to be structurally unsound or unfit for human habitation

1965—Section 117 federally assisted code enforcement (FACE) grants to cities and counties to assist them in carrying out programs of concentrated code compliance, including street improvements, to arrest the decline of deteriorating areas.

These federally assisted programs were a major force in turning the urban renewal program in U.S. cities toward conservation and rehabilitation of neighborhoods. They prepared the way for the Community Development Block Grant (CDBG) program of the 1974 Housing and Community Development Act under which local communities received federal grants to carry out community development activities. It is not surprising that over the first five years of CDBG experience, involving over 3,300 communities, "conservation of the housing stock" grew from 16 percent of funds spent to achieve national objectives in 1975 to 31 percent in 1979; it was second only to "elimination of slums and blight" as a CDBG activity.[34]

Experience under the federally assisted code enforcement activities of the late 1960s and early 1970s also provided experience leading to an expanded concept of code enforcement that moved away from the punitive nature of earlier code administration. Roger Ahlbrandt summarized this evolution in 1976 as follows:

As one of the inputs into a neighborhood preservation program, code enforcement needs to be implemented in a manner consistent with the goals and objectives of the over-all strategy, i.e., to upgrade investment attitudes toward the neighborhood. Accordingly, one of the assumptions . . . is that the primary objective of code enforcement is to achieve voluntary compliance. . . . A comprehensive approach toward stemming decline, no matter how ingeniously devised, will not accomplish the stated task unless the residents of the neighborhood are committed to remaining there . . . to invest in the maintenance of their homes.[35]

As demonstrated in Chapter 2, "Conserving and Rehabilitating Existing Housing and Neighborhoods," housing code enforcement is now poised to enter still a further phase in its evolution—that of giving the community the techniques to maintain its existing housing inventory.

The property tax and housing

Despite increasing federal and state financial assistance, the real property tax continues as the major source of income for general local government; taxation of residential property contributes the largest single portion of revenues from these taxes. In fiscal 1978–79, the U.S. Bureau of the Census reported that property taxes made up 32 percent of all the revenues of counties, municipalities, and townships—a total of $33.4 billion. Property taxes accounted for 63 percent of all locally derived revenues.[36]

In a 1968 study of land use in 106 large cities, Allen D. Manvel found that only two-thirds of the land area of cities was devoted to ordinary private land holdings; the balance was devoted to public streets and other public and semipublic uses. Nearly half of the private land holdings—32 percent of all land in the average large city—was devoted to residential use. Commercial, industrial, and railroad uses altogether occupied about one-third as much land as residential property.[37]

Given this pattern of land use, it is not surprising that the 1977 Census of Governments showed that residential properties make up 59 percent of both the number of taxable properties and the gross assessed value of taxable properties. The residential share of assessed values subject to taxation varies significantly by state, by metropolitan area, and by central city. The Census of Governments data show a range from 30 percent in North Dakota to 72 percent in Maryland.[38]

An earlier study by Dick Netzer documents the variation among and within nineteen selected metropolitan county areas. Housing in the central city made up 62 percent of assessed value subject to taxation in San Antonio, Texas; outlying portions, 93 percent; and the metropolitan county area as a whole, 69 percent. In contrast, the housing portion made up only 22 percent of assessed value in the central city of Atlanta, Georgia; only 15 percent of outlying portions, and only 21 percent of the total metropolitan county. Netzer points out that in 1968 most central cities had substantially heavier concentrations of business activity within their boundaries than did the outlying parts of their metropolitan areas; also, central cities had relatively more low-quality housing than the suburbs and more multifamily housing (generally less valuable per unit). Some differences are related to the legal coverage of the tax, a function of state laws; other differences may be traced to the frequently favorable treatment of housing by central city assessors.[39] These relationships probably have undergone substantial changes since 1968, particularly because of (1) the trend of industry and business to locate in the suburbs; (2) the loss of industry and business in many large central cities; (3) the increasing volume of multifamily housing, including condominiums; and (4) the decline in housing quality and value in large urban centers.

The first salient point to be made about the property tax and housing is that housing represents a substantial and sometimes dominant source of community wealth and tax revenue. Trends in housing volume, condition, and value have a direct impact on the community's fiscal welfare. Housing is a resource to be protected and conserved.

Beyond its importance as a source of municipal revenue, the residential property tax and the way it is administered can have both *negative* and *positive* impacts on a local community's efforts to improve its housing supply and condition, to eliminate blight, and to revitalize neighborhoods. Six elements of the property tax have a detrimental effect on policies to stimulate construction, maintenance, and rehabilitation of housing: (1) the tax has a regressive effect on housing consumers; (2) it acts as a sales tax on housing; (3) it acts as a tax on capital invested in housing; (4) it reduces the cash available for maintenance and improvements; (5) it contributes to the "locking in" of current owners; and (6) it promotes fiscal competition and exclusionary zoning.[40]

Beyond these specific housing impacts are the broader effects of property taxes as a cause of urban blight and an obstacle to urban redevelopment. The foreword to *Property Taxes, Housing and the Cities,* published in 1973, concludes that a basic factor in assessing impacts is the quality of tax administration:

Poor property tax administration (1) is a contributing factor in urban blight; (2) is an obstacle to the upgrading of poor-quality housing; and (3) discourages minority ownership of urban property. . . . The study reveals that in five of the ten cities studied, the median effective tax rate in blighted neighborhoods is many times higher than that in stable or upward transitional neighborhoods. In most cases . . . such inequities are principally a result of confused reassessment policies which often bear no relation to actual market values and trends. . . . The report provides an important case study in how outmoded property tax systems can contribute directly to severe tax inequities, and, indirectly, to urban decay.[41]

In another study, George Peterson adds that the overassessment of properties in low-income neighborhoods stems from failure to readjust valuations as market values decline.[42]

Cities are using the property tax to encourage reinvestment in existing housing stock by property tax exemptions and/or abatements for rehabilitation activity. As of 1979, some twenty-five states had passed legislation to enable localities to establish property tax relief programs for housing rehabilitation, and twenty-eight cities had an active property tax exemption and/or abatement program for housing rehabilitation.[43] Despite the growing interest of cities in using property tax relief to advance housing rehabilitation, there is incomplete and mixed evidence as to its effectiveness. First, participation has been limited in cities with data, and officials in participating cities question whether much additional investment has been stimulated. Further, a policy of frequent reassessment of all policies could well be more effective in eliminating aspects of the property tax that discourage rehabilitation.[44]

Despite the caveats about the effectiveness of tax exemptions and/or abatements as spurs to housing rehabilitation, such programs can be useful if the tax measures are linked to the total package of rehabilitation activities in the local community.[45]

Another way in which localities have attempted to use the property tax to spur housing activity is to provide tax exemptions or tax abatement for new lower-income housing development. Traditionally, federally assisted public housing requires local tax exemption and makes a "payment in lieu of taxes" related to rental revenue. At least seven states authorize tax exemptions or abatements for privately owned federal- and state-assisted housing: Alaska, Colorado, Connecticut, Massachusetts, Minnesota, New York, and Vermont.

Other examples of tax abatement in connection with housing development are found in the states of Missouri and New York. In Missouri, private urban redevelopment corporations operating in designated blighted areas have access to tax abatement—the real property tax is measured solely by the assessed value of the land, exclusive of improvements, and for the next fifteen years taxes on both land and improvements are assessed at one-half of full value. These provisions have the potential of reducing rents for new apartments within the redevelopment plan. Also, developers may pass the tax abatement through to individual home buyers, thus reducing the monthly payment.

Two New York statutes are relevant: (1) the Limited Profit Housing Companies (Mitchell–Lama) Law of 1955 provides tax exemption and below-market interest rate financing to private sponsors of new construction or rehabilitation of rental housing; and (2) Section 421 of the Real Property Tax Law of 1971 provides for a declining rate of tax exemption for new or rehabilitated multiple dwellings of six or more units. Both of these statutes have generated significant new housing, particularly in New York City.

Tax increment financing is another way in which the property tax has been used to advance local housing interests. In this process monies are borrowed for urban renewal activities. Property values after redevelopment must be sufficiently higher than the property values before redevelopment to pay off the redevelopment agency's debt obligation. Application of the tax increment method to finance or subsidize low- and moderate-income housing alone is therefore problematic. However, the provision of such housing may be facilitated to some extent in mixed-use projects with intensive and highly leveraged office and commercial building development. Twelve states have some form of tax increment financing: Alaska, California, Colorado, Iowa, Minnesota, Nevada, Ohio, Oregon, Utah, Washington, Wisconsin, and Wyoming.

A unique, though indirect, method of assisting housing development is the Minnesota Regional Tax Allocation Plan. Under this plan, 40 percent of the increase in assessed valuation throughout the metropolitan Minneapolis–St. Paul area for all commercial–industrial valuation subsequent to 2 January 1971 is allocated among the local jurisdictions. This allocation has the effect of removing fiscal competition and thus makes lower-income housing development more acceptable. The Minnesota plan was adopted in 1971 and implemented in 1974. Since then there has been a steadily growing interest in tax-base sharing for a wide variety of purposes (in California, Maine, Maryland, New Jersey, Pennsylvania, and Washington).

Municipal services and housing

Until recent years, decisions by local public officials to approve or disapprove new development or land use, particularly new housing development, have been based on crude data and unproved assumptions. It has been particularly difficult to judge the fiscal impact of new development. Although analysis of municipal costs related to development dates back to the 1930s, the first intensive efforts to assess the fiscal impact of housing development came in the early 1970s.[46] Seminal work has been contributed by the Center for Urban Policy Research of Rutgers University and by the state of New Jersey.[47] The state of New Jersey Study Commission discounted the commonly accepted opinion that multifamily housing development always brings higher municipal service costs. Individual localities also began to take a closer look at cost impacts in the 1970s. Since these early works,

continued inflation and consequent strain for municipal budgets [have made local officials more] aware of the public costs associated with private development, major rezonings, annexations, or alternative land use plans. They need to project resident and school-age children populations attributable to development, the numbers of public employees—policemen, firemen, teachers, etc.—who must be hired, and the kinds of municipal facilities needed to serve the changing population.[48]

It was in response to this need that the Rutgers Center for Urban Policy Research prepared the *Fiscal Impact Handbook* to provide methodology to estimate both the costs and revenues associated with development. A major emphasis in the *Handbook* is alternative forms of housing development.[49] While this methodology has not yet been extensively used in practice, it provides for the first time an approach that is both orderly and comprehensive. However, there is still substantial methodological work to be done in this complicated exercise; analysis to date covers only the direct fiscal impact, not the indirect impacts on the local economy. Further, "cost–revenue analysis, which focuses on municipal revenues and services, should not be confused with cost–benefit analysis, which tries to assess nonmonetary issues as well, or with cost-effective analysis, which tries to assess the most economical way of carrying out a particular public service."[50] In any event, more accurate calculation of fiscal impact does not remove the local responsibility to judge the total public interest.

A related concern is the "pricing" of municipal services related to residential development, including development charges paid by residential developers, fees for sewer or waterline extensions and hookups, construction permits, and other charges for the provision of municipal services. The pricing policies adopted by cities can be an important influence on the rate and pattern of development; they can also have an important effect on the fiscal position of the city. Here again, the methodology is in an early stage of development. Increased capability in pricing city services for new development may also affect special assessments for streets, sanitary sewers, and water mains that benefit particular properties and fees and charges for ongoing city services for housing already in place. Such an application would be in line with the revived interest in user charges as a source of municipal revenue.

Welfare and housing

Public welfare payments to cover housing costs for families receiving public assistance constitute a little recognized but significant local function affecting housing. On a national basis, in fiscal year 1979, the U.S. Department of Health, Education and Welfare (HEW) spent at least $5 billion on these housing payments. This was larger than the $4 billion that HUD allocated to assisted housing and community development. A high proportion of these housing payments to public assistance families pays for substandard rental housing located in the older transitional neighborhoods of urban and rural communities, thus frustrating local efforts to improve housing conditions and neighborhoods.

A report to Congress by HEW in 1969 had documented that at least one-half of all assistance recipients lived in housing that was deteriorating, dilapidated, unsafe, unsanitary, or overcrowded. This same report found that only ten states had housing standards defining minimum adequate housing requirements for recipient households, and only thirteen states had shelter allowances generally equivalent to the actual cost of housing.[51] Despite the reforms proposed in the report, housing payments in public assistance programs were reduced during the 1970s. During this period most states consolidated welfare assistance payments into *flat grants* paid to recipients, eliminating a special allocation for housing costs.

The impact of these welfare housing policies on the local housing stock and on the living conditions of low-income families is predictable. In 1979 Westchester County, New York, documented that it spent over $45 million annually on behalf of approximately 42,000 persons for shelter and shelter-related expenses; up to 50 percent of these individuals lived in substandard housing. While the Westchester County Department of Social Services did not have any housing mandate, it had a substantial local housing market impact.[52] In New York City the welfare shelter allowance budget equals 48 percent of public assistance payments, or $530 million a year, and poses a major policy question as to how to direct these funds to stimulate improvements rather than to foster decline in the housing stock.[53]

An innovative effort to alleviate the adverse effect of welfare housing payments on families and neighborhoods, and to combine the resources of the public welfare department with those of the county's housing and redevelopment agencies, was launched in Westchester County in 1976. The results were promising, and the county has proposed a Comprehensive Welfare Housing Demonstration, supported by both HUD and the U.S. Department of Health and Human Services (HHS), to test a national application of the Westchester experience.[54]

To reform welfare housing assistance payments will require the resolution of the relative responsibilities of HHS and HUD in providing housing assistance for low-income families.

SLUM CLEARANCE AND HOUSING FOR LOWER-INCOME FAMILIES

As early as 1892 Congress had expressed concern about the slums in larger American cities by appropriating $20,000 to investigate these conditions. Other than some emergency housing for World War I factory workers, this was the sum of direct housing activity by the federal government until the Great Depression of 1929 brought together the economic circumstances— unemployment, decline of the housing industry, and loss of family homes— to generate support for more direct public action.

At the local level, a similar pattern prevailed. Although Charles A. Beard in 1912 pointed to concern over tenement conditions in large cities as a "newer tendency" in American city government, local government action was confined to a few cities that established health and safety codes for existing housing.[55]

Early federal government efforts to cope with depression-related housing conditions were directed at assisting individual homeowners to avoid foreclosures and stimulating activity for the badly hit home building industry. In the early 1930s, the federal government established the Federal Home Loan Bank System (1932), the Home Owners' Loan Corporation, including chartering the Federal Savings and Loan Association (1933), the Federal Housing Administration (1934), and the Federal National Mortgage Association (1934).

All these institutions were directed to private industry and individual homeowners. Of particular importance was the Federal Housing Administration (FHA), which became the major force in stimulating new housing for middle-income families by insuring home mortgages. Rural housing was addressed with the creation by executive order in 1935 of the Rural Housing Program under the Emergency Relief Appropriation Act and the passage in 1937 of the Bankhead–Jones Farm Tenant Act authorizing federal loans to farm tenants, laborers, and sharecroppers to finance the purchase of farms, repairs, and improvements, including housing.[56]

Community development and assisted housing are comparatively recent additions to the functions of local and state governments. Significant activity began in the early 1930s as a result of federal government initiatives. Although concern about slums and blight can be traced back to far earlier origins, such as the federally supported investigations of city slums in 1892 and 1908, and while there was a surge of activity related to publicly assisted housing for war workers during World War I, major ongoing activity began as a result of the Great Depression. Following is a listing of significant federal legislation that has spurred the expansion of local and state functions.

1933 The National Industrial Recovery Act of 1933 (Public Law 73–67) authorized federal funds to finance low-cost and slum clearance housing and subsistence homesteads. It resulted in 50 low-rent housing projects containing 21,600 units in 37 cities as well as 15,000 units in resettlement projects and "greenbelt" towns. This law stimulated the creation of local housing authorities with powers to receive federal assistance and to finance, develop, and manage low-income housing.

1937 The United States Housing Act of 1937 (Public Law 75–412) established a permanent public housing program and led to the expansion of local housing authorities and their activities.

1949 The Housing Act of 1949 (Public Law 81–171) established the national housing policy of "a decent home and a suitable living environment for every American family." To implement this broad commitment, it established federal assistance to local communities for slum clearance and redevelopment programs. The act also greatly expanded rural housing programs to include direct and insured loans for homes and farm buildings, rural rental and cooperative housing, and grants for domestic farm labor housing.

1954 The Housing Act of 1954 (Public Law 83–560) expanded federal assistance by changing the name of the 1949 "slum clearance and redevelopment program" to "slum clearance and urban renewal" while extending its focus to the prevention of slums and blight through rehabilitation and conservation of blighted and deteriorating areas. Federal assistance for comprehensive planning by local, regional, and state jurisdictions (Section 701) was authorized. New contracts for federal urban renewal assistance could not be approved until the locality had an approved "workable program," including the adoption, administration, and enforcement of housing, zoning, building, and other local codes. This act also authorized a new FHA mortgage insurance program to assist in the development of housing in urban renewal areas (Section 220) and a new FHA insurance program for those displaced by urban renewal (Sections 221 [d][3] and 221 [d][4]).

1955 The Housing Amendments of 1955 (Public Law 84–345) established a new federal public facilities loan program for a broad range of eligible states, general-purpose local jurisdictions, and local public agencies.

Figure 1–1 Chronology of major federal housing and community development laws.

1956   The Housing Act of 1956 (Public Law 84–1020) authorized relocation payments to persons and businesses displaced by urban renewal. Also, General Neighborhood Renewal Plans (GNRPs) were authorized for urban renewal.

1959   The Housing Act of 1959 (Public Law 86–372) authorized federal grants to assist local communities to prepare Comprehensive Community Renewal Plans (CRPs). It is also created the Section 202 direct below-market interest rate loan program for elderly persons.

1961   The Housing Act of 1961 (Public Law 87–70) expanded Section 221 (d)(3) to a below-market interest rate mortgage insurance rental housing program for moderate-income families and extended eligibility in the Section 202 direct loan program for housing for the elderly to public agencies. This same act established loans, planning assistance, and demonstration grants to local public bodies for urban mass transportation.

1964   The Housing Act of 1964 (Public Law 88–560) authorized Section 312 direct low-interest loans for eligible families to enable them to rehabilitate their residential or business structures.

1965   The Housing Act of 1965 (Public Law 89–4) established federal assistance, administered through local public agencies, to provide rehabilitation grants (Section 115) for home repairs and rehabilitation, demolition grants (Section 116) covering the demolition of unsound structures, and federally assisted code enforcement (FACE) (Section 117). In this same year, matching federal grants were authorized to local public bodies to finance basic water and sewer facilities and neighborhood facilities. This act also authorized the leasing of existing private housing by local housing authorities for occupancy by low-income families (Section 23). In addition, the "rent supplement" program was authorized for low-income families to enable them to occupy FHA-insured rental housing and the Section 202 direct loan program for elderly housing. The federal Department of Housing and Urban Development was also created in 1965.

1966   The Demonstration Cities (later Model Cities) and Metropolitan Development Act of 1966 (Public Law 89–754) authorized federal grants and technical assistance to local communities to plan, develop, and carry out comprehensive city programs for rebuilding or restoring entire sections and neighborhoods of slums and blighted areas by the concentrated and coordinated use of all available federal aids, together with local private and governmental resources. This act also authorized the FHA Section 221(h) insurance program for rehabilitation of housing by nonprofit groups.

1968   The 1968 Housing and Urban Development Act (Public Law 90–448) authorized the Neighborhood Development Program (NDP) under which urban renewal activities could be carried out in annual increments. It removed the unit restrictions on the number of residential units a local urban renewal agency could acquire and rehabilitate. It required that a majority of housing units in a community's future residentially developed projects be for low- and

Figure 1–1   (continued).

moderate-income families. This act also created the Section 235 (home ownership) and Section 236 (rental) mortgage insurance program (replacing the Section 221 [d][3] program) with below-market interest rates down to 1 percent. This act established a ten-year national housing goal of 26 million housing units, including 6 million units for low- and moderate-income families. Also authorized were federal guarantees of borrowings of private developers of new communities and the creation of National Housing Partnerships to encourage the greater use of private financial resources in low- and moderate-income housing.

1974 The Housing and Community Development Act of 1974 (Public Law 93–383) consolidated five major "categorical" assistance programs into a new community development block grant (CDBG) program. General purpose state and local governments were authorized as the direct recipients of assistance, and funds were allocated under a formula allocation to eligible communities and, under a "discretionary" application process, to other communities not eligible under formula entitlement. Eligible activities for use of CDBG funds included a broad range of physical improvement activities. The act also created a new federally assisted housing program—Section 8—which authorized federal "housing assistance payment contracts" to sponsors, including local and state public agencies, for the development or rehabilitation of housing or leasing of existing housing for lower-income families. Also, the act required a local Housing Assistance Plan as a condition of CDBG assistance.

1977 The Housing and Community Development Act of 1977 (Public Law 95–128) authorized federal urban development action grants (UDAGs) to severely distressed cities and urban counties to help alleviate physical and economic deterioration through coordination with private investment and reinvestment opportunities.

1978 The Housing and Community Development Amendments of 1978 (Public Law 95–557) established a new "moderate rehabilitation" category under the Section 8 existing housing program. It also authorized a new system of operating subsidies for Federal Housing Administration–assisted "troubled" multifamily projects. Two special programs were enacted: the "neighborhood self-help development program" (to provide grants and other assistance to qualified neighborhood organizations) and the "livable cities program" (to enhance the artistic, cultural, or historic resources of neighborhoods). The Neighborhood Reinvestment Corporation, designed to promote reinvestment in older neighborhoods, was established as a public corporation.

1980 The Housing and Community Development Act of 1980 (Public Law 96–399) established national standards for condominium and cooperative conversions, enforceable through civil action in state or federal courts. States and localities were granted three years to exempt themselves from these standards.

Figure 1–1 (concluded).

The evolution of direct public action in housing stemmed from the National Industrial Recovery Act (NIRA) of 1933 and its implementing entity, the Public Works Administration (PWA). This act authorized federal funds to finance low-cost housing, slum clearance, and subsistence homesteads. Under NIRA, low-income housing was built by direct federal construction in thirty-seven cities; however, the courts ruled that the federal government did not have the right to exercise the power of eminent domain (taking private property for public use) for the purpose of slum clearance and low-cost housing. Subsequently, a court decision in New York state in April 1935 upheld the constitutionality of the Municipal Housing Authorities Law and low-cost housing and slum clearance as a public use.[57] The direct public function of slum clearance and development of low-income housing was established as a local government function through enabling legislation passed by the states. Thus a path was opened for slum clearance and housing, which would be rapidly expanded over the next four decades.

Public housing as a pioneer local function

Much of the housing activity at the local level in the early 1980s can be traced to the early precedents of the public housing program, in particular: (1) direct assistance from the federal government to local public agencies, and (2) the initiation of "slum clearance" activity, which ultimately became full-fledged "community development" assistance. The pioneering Housing Act of 1937, which set up a permanent system for housing assistance to local housing authorities, was based on multiple objectives:

It is the policy of the United States to promote the general welfare of the Nation by employing its funds and credit, as provided in this Act, to assist the several States and their political subdivisions to alleviate present and recurring unemployment and to remedy the unsafe and unsanitary housing conditions and the acute shortage of decent, safe and sanitary dwellings for families of low income in rural or urban communities, that are injurious to the health, safety, and morals of the citizens of the Nation.[58]

The enactment of the 1937 act was not easy, involving at least three years and arousing controversies about the public role in housing that continued in the succeeding decades; in many quarters, public housing was considered a dangerous threat to private enterprise in real estate.[59]

When the PWA wound up its activities in late 1937, twenty-nine states had passed enabling legislation; forty-six local housing authorities had been established; and 21,000 PWA-developed low-income housing units were in place as a beginning inventory for the newly enacted housing act. Over the next forty years, public housing expanded and contracted, coinciding with the public and political support it could generate: it would experience the emergency of defense housing in World War II, the postwar housing demand, responses to families displaced by urban renewal, cutbacks due to national economic policies, and expansion to meet new housing needs such as those of elderly citizens.

Early public housing development, prior to the Housing Act of 1949, provided 204,872 units, of which 21,640 (10 percent) were under the original public works program, 118,507 (58 percent) under the Housing Act of 1937, and 64,725 (32 percent) under various defense and war housing programs.[60] In the 1950s, following the passage of the 1949 act, some 351,612 new units were placed under contract; in the 1960s an additional 464,514 new units were developed; and in the 1970s a total of 385,511 new units were placed under contract.[61] The high-level years in public housing were 1950 and 1951 (78,000 and 89,000 new units placed under contract), and 1967–1970 (when 70,000, 78,000, 109,000, and 101,000 new units were placed under contract). At the end of fiscal 1980 (30 September 1980), HUD reported that a total of 1.2 million units were owned and managed by local housing authorities. Public housing families during the twelve months ending 30 September 1979 had a median income of $4,475; with 41 percent of households categorized as elderly, the average monthly rent was $89.[62]

The distribution of local public housing agencies and federally assisted housing units across the nation reveals both a dispersed pattern (in terms of some 2,900 local authorities) and a more concentrated pattern (in terms of the geographical location of the housing units). Studies by the National Rural Housing Alliance and the Housing Assistance Council document the dispersal of housing authorities and housing projects.[63] Raymond J. Struyk, in his 1980 book, *A New System for Public Housing*, documents the fact that twenty-nine cities with 1975 populations of 400,000 or more are responsible for 373,500 public housing units, 31 percent of the national program.[64]

The local housing authority, as a public agency authorized under state law, typically is headed by a board of citizen commissioners appointed by the chief executive of the general-purpose local government that has responsibility for the authority, with delegation of day-to-day operation to an executive director or administrator. The financial formula under which public housing operates is threefold: (1) issuance of housing development bonds, which are exempt from the federal income tax (at a below-market interest rate); (2) an annual federal contribution to cover debt service over the life of the bonds; and (3) exemption from local property taxes, with a payment made "in lieu of taxes" equal to 10 percent of shelter rents received by the authority.

The chief instrument in a local authority operation is the annual contributions contract (ACC) under which the federal government pledges annual contributions toward debt service, and the local government and the authority make commitments for public housing operations. The second major instrument is the local "cooperation agreement" under which the local government and the local housing authority set forth city services and local authority payments.

Raymond Struyk has pointed out the complexity of the "institutional arrangement" of the local public housing authority, specifically the relationships among the housing authority, the local government, and HUD. Although the housing authority is usually politically independent of the municipal government, actions by both the local government and HUD affect its operation. To obtain HUD funding for projects, the local government must agree to provide services and not to tax the property. The local government also has a major voice in the location of housing projects. HUD, in turn, imposes its own constraints: (1) financial (provision of development funds, operating subsidies, and modernization funds) and (2) regulatory (establishment of accounting procedures, tenant admission and eviction policies, and rent levels). Congress and the courts, too, affect the public housing authority through legislative and judicial actions.[65]

Prior to 1961, local authorities received only debt service assistance from the federal government. However, the housing act of that year authorized monthly payments of ten dollars for each elderly family. With the press of rising costs in the 1960s, this operating assistance was gradually expanded until the adoption of the "Performance Funding System" in 1975, under the provisions of the 1974 Housing and Community Development Act.[66] A major factor in the widening gap between public housing revenues and rising operating costs was the Brooke amendments under the Housing Acts of 1969, 1970, and 1971, which set a cap on tenant contributions for rent, provided deductions from tenant income, and adjusted rent payments for families receiving welfare assistance.

The fiscal crisis in public housing operations was still a major issue in 1981, when Congress mandated a study of potential alternatives to the Performance Funding System to be prepared by 1 March 1982.

Since the passage of the Community Development Block Grant (CDBG) program under the Housing and Community Development Act of 1974, local communities have been authorized to use their local CDBG assistance funds for public housing modernization; from 1975 through 1979, over 27,000 public housing units in sixty-seven localities were rehabilitated with CDBG funds; one-fourth of the upgraded units in large cities (500,000 to 1 million population) and 13 percent in cities in the North Central region were in public housing complexes.[67]

A major issue in some localities is the declining level of payments in lieu of taxes (PILOT) by housing authorities to general local governments. As rent revenues were reduced under the various Brooke amendments, PILOT payments (based on 10 percent of shelter rents) also declined.

In recent years, the chronic shortage of operating revenue has tended to dominate the public housing program; the number of new units scheduled for development has been at a minimal level (21,500 units for fiscal 1982). The Reagan administration initiated major efforts to trim back national expenditures for all housing assistance programs and explored the feasibility of an expanded role by general-purpose local government in the public housing program. For the immediate future, it seems unlikely that any major expansion of public housing will take place. In the meantime, however, a standing inventory of about 1.2 million low-income public housing units is in place.

Leasing private housing

A major new resource was added to local housing assistance in 1965 when local housing authorities were authorized to lease private existing housing units for occupancy by lower-income families. This was originally cited as the Section 23 private leasing program under the Housing Act of 1937. In 1974 the Section 8 lower-income housing program was created and the Section 8 existing housing program superseded the Section 23 program. Under this program, HUD makes assistance payments to cover the difference between tenant rents and "fair market rents" set in each community. The administering agents for the Section 8 program are predominantly local housing authorities. State agencies also receive and administer some assistance under this program.

Eligible families can look for dwellings on the local market or remain in their own dwellings. Upon meeting program requirements relating to housing quality and rents, the owner and family sign a lease subject to the approval of the housing authority. A housing assistance payments contract is then executed between the PHA and the owner so that the owner is paid the difference between the rent actually paid by the family and the approved rent for the unit. As of 30 September 1979 there were 582,923 units occupied under the Section 8 existing housing program: 5 percent were administered by state agencies, 24 percent by HUD for FHA loan management programs, and 71 percent by local housing authorities.[68] The Section 8 existing housing program is becoming increasingly popular at all levels of government, because it uses existing housing and requires less federal subsidy. As of 1981 federal assistance is supporting 844,000 Section 8 leases. The Reagan administration proposes in the budget for 1983 to replace this program with a modified Section 8 housing certificate program and to convert Section 8 units to the new program as leases expire.

Housing, slum clearance, and urban renewal

The Housing Act of 1937 linked slum clearance and public housing together by requiring the elimination of one slum dwelling for every new unit of low-rent public housing that was built. Twelve years later a broader and more flexible program was adopted by Congress under Title I of the Housing Act of 1949, the Urban Redevelopment Program. The preamble of this act established the goal of "a decent home and a suitable living environment for every American family."[69] This legislation for the first time authorized federal financial assistance to local communities to be used exclusively for clearing slums and blighted areas and preparing sites for redevelopment. Capital grants were provided to help communities meet the net loss from acquiring and clearing a slum or blighted area and disposing of the land for redevelopment in accordance with local plans. Title I also, in effect, limited an urban redevelopment project area to one that was predominantly residential before redevelopment, or which was to be redeveloped for predominantly residential use; this provision was subsequently altered to provide a specific proportion of federal funds to be used for nonresidential projects (from 10 percent specified in the Housing Act of 1954 to 35 percent in the Housing Act of 1965).

The Housing Act of 1954 broadened slum clearance and urban redevelopment by authorizing federal assistance for rehabilitation and conservation of blighted and deteriorating areas and changing the program identification from "urban redevelopment" to "urban renewal." The 1954 act also established the "workable program" requirement which, as described earlier, stimulated local communities to adopt zoning ordinances, building codes, and housing codes. As a condition of receiving federal urban renewal or housing assistance, the local community was required to prepare a workable program for meeting its overall problem of slum and blight, including the adoption, modernization, administration, and enforcement of housing, zoning, building, and other local laws, codes, and ordinances. As noted earlier, the provisions of the 1954 act were influential in joining the previous "housing code" efforts to neighborhood improvement and housing rehabilitation.

The Housing Act of 1954 also authorized two new FHA mortgage insurance programs for housing development in urban renewal areas: Section 220 authorized FHA insurance for rehabilitation of existing housing or construction of new dwellings in urban renewal areas, and Section 221 authorized FHA insurance on low-cost rental housing for families displaced by urban renewal and other governmental action.

From 1961 to 1968, Congress adopted a number of measures to expand earlier legislation for housing and urban renewal, including provisions for federal interest subsidies to reduce rents for low-income families; extension of eligible housing sponsors to nonprofit organizations, limited dividend corporations, and public agencies (excluding housing authorities); special mortgage insurance for for-profit sponsors in urban renewal areas; rent supplements; special insurance programs for lower-income families, with interest rate reductions down to 1 percent; low-interest loans and grants for housing rehabilitation; demolition grants; and other measures to provide more housing in conjunction with urban renewal.

In addition, the Housing Act of 1968 removed the restriction on the number of residential units a local renewal authority could acquire and rehabilitate and required that a majority of the housing units in future residentially developed projects be available for low- and moderate-income families. The act also set ten-year national housing goals for both private and assisted housing of 26 million new or rehabilitated units, 6 million of which would be for low- and moderate-income families.

A similar pattern had been emerging under housing and neighborhood rehabilitation from 1964 through 1966 with the enactment of direct low-interest loans for housing rehabilitation in 1964; rehabilitation grants for low-income families and demolition grants to localities in 1965; and the federally assisted code enforcement (FACE) program in 1966.

The controversy in the urban renewal program over its "housing" focus and, in particular, over whether the program was creating more housing units than it was demolishing and providing housing for families it was displacing became increasingly strident. The label "urban removal" was used by program opponents. A whole literature evolved around this controversy.[70] As a result, a new local public function evolved—relocation of displaced families.[71]

The local administrative structure of local public agencies—LPAs—to carry out urban renewal activity in almost one thousand local communities was centered largely in independent local redevelopment authorities or in joint housing and redevelopment authorities, depending on state enabling legislation. Some LPAs (about 30 percent) were consolidated local departments of housing and community development or the city itself.[72]

Only recently have some efforts been made to take a look back at the urban renewal experience and the positive lessons learned from it.[73]

HOUSING AND COMMUNITY DEVELOPMENT

The Model Cities Program (adopted in 1966 as the "Demonstration Cities Program") was the first major effort to develop a comprehensive local improvement program to turn around and revitalize the most deteriorated sections of cities. This ambitious program, ultimately involving over 150 local communities, combined economic, physical, and social assistance into one concentrated program package; its very complexity was undoubtedly a major cause of its demise after 1974. Charles Haar notes that the lessons learned about how to reform and improve the system of federal assistance may well have been the greatest contribution of the program.[74]

Model Cities and the changing urban renewal program

Despite the termination of Model Cities, it was clear that housing, slum clearance, and urban renewal were gradually evolving into a more comprehensive process. With the 1968 Housing and Urban Development Act, the early efforts to stimulate private housing initiatives, clear slums, and build low-income public housing evolved into a forward-looking community planning and development program encompassing land clearance for new uses, neighborhood conservation, and acquisition of open space for community use, as well as housing.[75]

The urban renewal program itself was gradually changing. In 1956 Congress had authorized General Neighborhood Renewal Plans (GNRPs) for urban renewal areas of such scope that the activities had to be carried out over a period of years, rather than as a single project. In 1959 federal grants were authorized to assist local communities in preparing Community Renewal Plans (CRPs) for entire cities. The 1968 Housing and Urban Development Act authorized the Neighborhood Development Program (NDP) under which certain renewal project undertakings in one or more urban renewal areas could be planned and carried out on the basis of annual increments. These shifts in national legislative provisions were reflected in local planning and were a prelude to the basic restructuring that took place in 1974.

Housing and community development under the 1974 act: CDBG

The 1974 Housing and Community Development Act brought together two evolutionary streams: (1) the growing and more comprehensive nature of community development; and (2) the growing movement to decentralize federal government programs and place them with state and local governments. The idea of decentralization had arisen in the mid-1960s under the title of "Creative Federalism."[76] When the Nixon administration took office in 1969, it adopted the title of the "New Federalism." The 1974 act authorized block grants of community development funds (the community development block grants—CDBGs) to consolidate all previous categorical activities under urban renewal, Model Cities, neighborhood facilities, open space, water and sewer, and public facility loans.

The only program to retain separate status was the Section 312 rehabilitation loan program. The same act created a new federally assisted housing program—the Section 8 housing assistance program with separate components for existing housing and for new construction and substantial rehabilitation. This replaced Section 235 and 236 assistance programs and became the major vehicle for federal housing assistance. Under the new Section 8 program, assistance payments would be made to owners or prospective owners covering the difference between a lower-income family's required rent payment and a "fair market rent" for standard but modest housing in the local community. The Section 8 existing housing program, largely administered by local housing authorities, has been discussed previously. In the case of new construction, eligible sponsors (owners) included private builders, developers, cooperatives, and public agencies. These sponsors were eligible for FHA mortgage insurance, but otherwise they would secure their own financing on the private market.

The 1974 act provided for a new method of allocating federal housing assistance, based on a formula related to population, poverty, housing overcrowding, housing vacancies, substandard housing, and similar measures. Also, a new link was forged between housing assistance and community development by requiring the preparation of a local Housing Assistance Plan (HAP) as a condition of receiving community development assistance. The HAP became an instrument for involving general local governments more deeply in the housing assistance process and, in effect, created a new function in local government—not only to prepare the plan but also to review all housing assistance proposals.[77] Under this plan, the community was required to document its housing needs and the condition of its housing stock, identify general localities for proposed assisted housing, and develop an annual goal for assisted housing units. Over the first five years of the CDBG program, the HAP proved one of the most difficult areas to administer. The HUD *Fifth Annual Community Development Block Grant Report* concludes that the usefulness and effectiveness of HAPs varied among cities: "In some cities the HAP is used to develop a coordinated local housing strategy whose implementation is actively pursued. . . . In other cities, it is a mechanical exercise that sets goals that cannot be achieved."[78]

On the positive side, the HUD report found that, as communities and HUD gained experience in implementing HAPs, more realistic goals were being incorporated into the plans.

Another significant finding was the tendency of cities to use an increasing proportion of CDBG funds for housing purposes and to take other action to support housing. The report concluded that the HAP process had advanced the involvement of local communities in housing:

Except for the administration of housing and building codes, most cities did not play an important role in the housing development process before the advent of the CDBG program. Cities did little comprehensive planning and tended to be passive and rely on private developers or independent public housing for lower income families. Housing development occurred independently of city physical improvement activities. . . . Cities [now] seem to be increasing their involvement in assisted housing development.[79]

As the CDBG program evolved, it was also clear that new organizational patterns were developing. In contrast to the urban renewal program with 975 communities, CDBG after 1974 expanded rapidly to include over 3,000 communities, of which about 40 percent were direct entitlement communities of 50,000 population or more. The total number of participating communities remained stable over the first five years of CDBG—3,259 communities in fiscal 1975 and 3,305 communities in fiscal 1979.[80] Some shifts in local administrative responsibilities took place. In its third-year CDBG report, NAHRO reported that 27 percent of its sample communities had phased out redevelopment authorities, but the organizational responsibility was diffused. Whereas local development activity had previously been the responsibility of independent agencies (primarily redevelopment authorities), NAHRO found that under block grants community development directors reported directly to the mayor in 35 percent of cities surveyed, to the city council in 11 percent, and to the city manager in 36 percent. These officials generally turned over increased responsibility for the program to existing departments or agencies—notably planning departments. Planning departments had responsibility for HAP preparation in 35 percent of the sample cities. Community redevelopment authorities, where they exist, tended to retain responsibility for land acquisition and clearance and housing rehabilitation.[81]

The housing goals record

The end result of the decade of housing activity under the national housing goals set in the 1968 Housing Act was that total new production (excluding mobile homes) reached about two-thirds of the projected goal of 26 million housing units. The biggest shortfall in reaching the goal, however, was in assisted housing for low- and moderate-income families: the total of 2.7 million assisted units for the decade was less than half of the projected 6 million housing units.[82] A major reason was the erratic and changing nature of federal housing assistance mechanisms: from 1954 through 1974, the mechanisms (excluding the public housing program) were changed or added to at least ten times! There was little time or opportunity to gain local experience and to develop a well-administered federal oversight program. This led in turn to increasing program criticism, particularly in Congress. In January 1973 the Nixon Administration imposed a moratorium on all new federal housing assistance; it was not lifted until the creation of the Section 8 program in the 1974 Housing and Community Development Act. As the cost of operating housing (particularly the cost of utilities) increased with inflation, requests mounted for federal assistance in order to keep assisted housing within the reach of lower-income families, first in the public housing program and then in the Section 236 moderate-income rental program created in 1968.

As of 1981 the inventory of HUD-assisted housing units completed or leased for lower-income families totaled over 3.5 million; public housing and

Table 1–3 HUD-assisted housing units completed or leased for low- and moderate-income families, by housing category, as of 30 September 1981.

Housing category	No. of occupied units[1]	% of total
Section 8 (rental housing)	1,319,000	37
Existing leases	844,000	
New construction and substantial rehabilitation	475,000	
Public housing (rental housing)	1,200,000	34
Section 236 (rental housing)	537,000	15
Section 235 (home ownership)	241,000	7
Rent supplement (rental housing)	158,000	4
Section 202 elderly or handicapped (rental housing)	97,000	3
Total units	3,552,000	100

Source: U.S., Department of Housing and Urban Development, *FY 1983 Budget Summary* (Washington, D.C.: U.S. Department of Housing and Urban Development, February 1982), p. H-20.
1 Rounded to nearest thousand.

existing Section 8 leases made up 58 percent of this total (see Table 1-3). The total of 3.5 million assisted units made up 4 percent of the 80 million housing units in the United States.

Locally funded housing

In the 1970s several factors stimulated cities to take a more active role in assisted housing development. First was the moratorium on subsidized housing development declared by HUD in early 1973, followed by a leveling off in federal housing assistance. Second was the rising cost of housing development and management, as well as chaotic changes in the housing financial markets. These events are reflected in the growing number of communities that began financing housing through their own resources or through partnerships with private enterprise. These efforts include local general obligation bond issues or general revenues in such places as Dade County, Florida; Denver, Colorado; and Raleigh, North Carolina. Other innovations included housing allowances supported by general funds and/or rent supplements for elderly tenants. A still further technique is the use of municipal pension funds to finance low-interest residential mortgages.[83]

A major new mechanism for local financing of housing was the 1968 amendment to the U. S. Internal Revenue Code, which made "residential real property for family units" an eligible use for financing by municipalities using tax-exempt industrial revenue bonds. In July 1978, the city of Chicago issued $100 million in tax-exempt bonds to finance low-interest home mortgages for families with incomes up to $40,000. By the end of 1978, nineteen localities in seven states had issued about $550 million in tax-exempt bonds to finance home mortgages. In the first three months of 1979, another $1 billion in local bonds was issued.[84] This flurry of action prompted the federal administration to seek tax legislation to place some limitation on this use of federal tax exemptions. In December 1980 Congress passed the Revenue Adjustments Act of 1980, which placed limitations on these housing issuances; some of the key provisions, however, are considered unworkable by key participants, and amendments are proposed for congressional consideration.

If compromises can be reached on key amendments, the use of tax-exempt revenue bonds for housing, if used in conjunction with a community development program, could become a major mechanism for local governments to meet the needs of families priced out of the private housing market. According to a NAHRO policy statement, "Housing as a rapidly-evolving, locally-based concern and function, is a legitimate area for the issuance of local tax-exempt mortgage bonds, providing such issues are structured to enhance housing opportunities for low and moderate income families or to support comprehensive neighborhood and community improvement."[85]

Housing and economic development: UDAG

Economic development is another emerging housing relationship. The potential has been brought to light under the Urban Development Action Grant (UDAG) program adopted by Congress in 1977. The UDAG program is administered by HUD to help severely distressed cities and urban counties revitalize their stagnant economies and reclaim deteriorating neighborhoods. Its basic mechanism is a federal grant to capture and leverage private investment. Early experience with UDAG highlights the innovative ways in which front-end capital grants by a local government can, in conjunction with private enterprise, spur housing development, rehabilitation, and other housing activities. In the first two years, UDAG projects with housing components proposed to construct or rehabilitate 46,000 housing units; three-quarters of these units are in neighborhood projects, about a fifth in commercial projects, and only a small number in industrial projects.[86] Of the 521 UDAG projects receiving awards through the two years, 160 involved housing.[87]

Local government officials, developers, bankers, and others have devised a variety of ingenious ways to leverage front-end capital grants and private investment to stimulate housing, neighborhood improvement, and commercial development. Here are some examples:

Denver: an action grant to help in the revitalization of the city's oldest neighborhood, the cultural center of its Hispanic community, with construction and rehabilitation of 1,900 housing units, a new shopping center, and various public improvements

Pittsburgh: funds for rehabilitation, construction, and purchase of 750 houses in five neighborhoods and for such amenities as street lighting, parking, and small parks

Birmingham, Alabama: interest subsidy for buyers of 300 single-family houses

Norwalk, Connecticut: a loan to a private developer for construction and permanent second mortgage financing for 31 units of low- and moderate-income condominiums in conjunction with commercial development

Baltimore: a write-down of the initial cost to buyers of 89 townhouses to be built in an urban renewal area, recycling an industrial building into 47 townhouse units, and providing a second mortgage for 89 new townhouses

Lansing, Michigan: equity assistance to the developer for 116 new rental units

La Grange, Georgia: defraying the costs of infrastructure and write-down of the initial sales price of 35 single-family homes

SHIFTS IN HOUSING MARKETS AND NEIGHBORHOODS

Over the last two decades, local housing markets, particularly in large urban centers, have been unpredictable, producing public concern and demands for public action. Rolf Goetze has stated the issue as follows:

There is an increasing debate and confusion among urban policy makers about how to analyze neighborhood issues and how to respond to them. Equity issues are masked by ambiguous new terms, such as redlining, gentrification, displacement, and the most ambiguous of all, revitalization. These terms relate to changes that are not adequately explained by traditional housing market theories, such as filtration, where aging housing predictably trickles down to lower income residents. . . . The traditional filtration theory does not explain the new demand for blighted inner city row houses or predict the rapid conversion of disinvested apartments to condominiums. . . . Housing market fluctuations could be overlooked as minor in comparison with filtration until the 1960s, but since then the trickle down pattern has been irregular and unpredictable, particularly in larger cities. Neighborhoods no longer evolve in steady, straight-line trends as they mature.[88]

Changes in urban housing markets and urban neighborhoods have been subject to a number of "shock waves" since 1960, causing some communities to devise public policies and actions to address local markets that were either overheated or underheated.

Housing abandonment

The first major phenomenon affecting urban housing markets and neighborhoods was housing abandonment, which surfaced in the middle to late 1960s in some large cities in the East and Midwest, where both tenants and landlords began to abandon large numbers of residential structures. A 1971 study for HUD found general agreement that the causes of abandonment were multiple and deeply rooted. The study stated that it was primarily a "neighborhood phenomenon" but that remedial action would require a coordinated strategy and could well involve housing management and development assistance, tenant-management councils, real estate tax policy, code enforcement policy, property disposition, zoning, welfare family assistance, and public safety, among others.[89]

The National Urban League, in a survey released in 1971, cited the following likely causes: the changing economic function of the central city, racial change, decisions by mortgage lending institutions to disinvest in ghetto neighborhoods, and lack of a coherent and positive public policy for deterioration and abandonment.[90] George Sternlieb and Robert Burchell describe residential abandonment as "the end product of all the urban ills of our modern society," reflecting a "much deeper-seated and extensive phenomenon—the disinvestment of private capital in core cities."[91]

A second generation of rent controls

A second major housing market development to affect a significant number of cities, beginning in the late 1960s, was the rapid increase in rents due to escalating costs of housing operations, exacerbated in turn by national economic stabilization programs initiated in 1971. The response was the enactment of a second generation of state and local rent controls, the first time that such controls had ever been established for other than wartime emergency purposes. As of 1976, eight states (Alaska, Connecticut, Maine, Maryland, Massachusetts, New Jersey, Florida, New York) and the District of Columbia had enacted legislation, and two states (New Jersey and New York) had statewide rent control involving 97 local jurisdictions in New Jersey and 110 in New York.[92]

Displacement and gentrification

The third major housing market phenomenon to disrupt major urban centers, beginning in the mid-1970s, was a wave of displacement due to reinvestment in inner-city neighborhoods. In a process called "gentrification," middle- and upper-income families purchased housing occupied by lower-income families. The Department of Housing and Urban Development, in a 1979 study of displacement, found that "housing abandonment and disinvestment account for a significantly greater proportion of displacement than that occasioned by neighborhood reinvestment."[93] An analysis of the extent of displacement due to reinvestment conducted as part of the HUD study found that only 100 to 200 families a year had been displaced by reinvestment in several major cities.[94] If the number of cities and neighborhoods affected was small, however, the impact in those cities and neighborhoods was significant.

Conversions of rental housing to condominiums and cooperatives

The accelerating conversion of rental housing to condominiums and cooperatives was the fourth and final housing market phenomenon. A study done by HUD in 1980 found that widespread conversion to cooperatives and condominiums began about 1970; after that, 366,000 rental units had been converted. Of this number, only 18,000 were cooperatives. Seventy-one percent of the conversions during the 1970s (260,000 units) occurred during 1977–79—evidence of an increasing rate of conversion during the decade. Although most conversions are in large metropolitan areas, smaller areas were found to be increasingly affected. Furthermore, 49 percent of conversions in the large metropolitan areas were in suburbs.[95]

The HUD report also found that state and local governments had begun to react with regulatory laws and ordinances. Just about half the states had legislated protection for tenants in converted buildings and for purchasers of both new and converted condominium units. Although just over one-third of all local jurisdictions have had or still have conversion activity, fewer than one in five of those experiencing conversions had passed a regulatory ordinance.[96] In 1980 Congress also adopted national legislation on this issue.

Root causes and local responses

The causes for these massive disruptions of local housing markets over the past two decades are complex, often involving national economic and tax policies as well as local and regional shifts in economic and social structure. Consequently, the public reactions are also complex. The HUD study on abandoned housing concluded that none of the cities studied had an adequate, overall, citywide strategy for housing utilization; and none of them will come close to solving their housing problems until they formulate such a strategy.[97]

More recently, Rolf Goetze has commented: "The reaction of public policy precipitated by change often appears to exaggerate the effect. . . . Improved neighborhood data and analysis will help to detect trends earlier, to develop a more appropriate theory of neighborhood evolution, and to discover more constructive public interventions that will prevent disinvestment and deterioration on the one hand and speculation and displacement on the other."[98]

HOUSING AS A PUBLIC FUNCTION: EVOLUTION TO DATE
Reviewing the history of housing and local government since the early 1900s, it is clear that this linkage has dramatically exploded into a complex web of activities related to almost every aspect of local government planning and administration. It is also clear that these relationships are still evolving.

Analysis of the progressive involvement of local government in housing shows that in almost every activity—be it building codes, housing occupancy codes, property taxes, comprehensive planning, slum clearance, low-income housing, community development, economic development, local financing of housing, or responses to changes in the housing market— the state and federal governments have exerted tremendous influence on local policies and actions. While the relative roles of local, state, and federal governments in housing are changing, each depends on the others.

Three clusters of housing responsibility
From a local government perspective, three clusters of housing responsibilities and functions have emerged from the past decades:

Conserving and rehabilitating existing housing and neighborhoods: The evolution of housing occupancy codes, slum clearance, urban renewal, neighborhood improvement, and community development block grants, coupled with developments in local property taxes and shifting housing markets, have coalesced to produce a new cluster of activities— maintaining and managing the existing housing supply.

Developing and managing assisted housing: The evolving activities of public housing, low- and moderate-income housing assistance, leasing of private housing, locally financed housing development, local tax-exempt mortgage bonds, and the local housing assistance plan have coalesced to produce a second cluster of activities—providing and monitoring housing assistance for low- and moderate-income families.

Responding to the impact of housing dynamics: The major disruptions in local housing markets and neighborhoods since 1960 have added a new element to housing in the local community—the need to define public policies and programs to deal with both "poor" and "strong" local housing markets.

These three clusters make up the evolving local housing function for local government in the 1980s. They make up the prime chapters in this book. A separate chapter also deals with the growing relationships between state and local governments in the housing area. Managing housing activities through local organizational structures and administrative processes also is evolving, and the last chapter discusses how three different local jurisdictions are handling this responsibility. The last chapter also looks to the future in terms of trends and potential requirements.

Overall, the evolving role of local government in housing leads to the conclusion that the process is in midstream—it is just beginning to take shape.

1   Glenn H. Beyer, *Housing and Society* (New York: Macmillan, 1965), p. 3.

2   National Commission on Urban Problems, *Building the American City* (Washington, D.C.: Government Printing Office, [1968]), p. 56.

3   Richard P. Fishman, ed., *Housing for All under Law,* a report of the American Bar Association, Advisory Commission on Housing and Urban Growth (Cambridge, Mass.: Ballinger, 1978), pp. 411–12.

4   Charles A. Beard, "Political Parties in City Government," *National Municipal Review* 6 (March 1917): 202.

5   Arthur W. Bromage, *Introduction to Municipal Government and Administration* (New York: Appleton-Century-Crofts, 1957), pp. 151–52.

6   National Resources Committee, *Our Cities* (Washington, D.C.: Government Printing Office, 1937), p. 84.

7   Fishman, ed., *Housing for All under Law,* p. 487.

8   Ibid., p. 481.

9   *New York City Housing Authority* v. *Muller,* 270 N.Y. 33, 34, 41 N.E.2d 153, 155 (1936). Italics added.

10 For a comprehensive description of the zoning, land subdivision, and local use planning functions, see: Frank S. So et al., eds., *The Practice of Local Government Planning* (Washington, D.C.: International City Management Association, 1979), Chapters 14 and 15.

11 James G. Coke and John J. Gargan, *Fragmentation in Land-Use Planning and Con-* *trol,* prepared for the National Commission on Urban Problems, Research Report No. 18 (Washington, D.C.: Government Printing Office, 1969), p. 10.

12 American Society of Planning Officials, *Problems of Zoning and Land-Use Regulation,* prepared for the National Commission on Urban Problems, Research Report No. 2 (Washington, D.C.: Government Printing Office, 1968), p. 69.

13 Mary Brooks, *Exclusionary Zoning,* Planning Advisory Report No. 254 (Chicago: American Society of Planning Officials, 1970).

14 These are extensively discussed in: Fishman, ed., *Housing for All under Law.*

15 Ibid., pp. 36–38. The most influential of these plans, stimulating a whole series of areawide housing allocation strategies, was the one developed by the Miami Valley Regional Planning Commission in Dayton, Ohio, in 1970.

16 John Vranicar, Welford Sanders, and David Mosena, *Streamlining Land Use Regulation: A Guidebook for Local Governments,* prepared for the Department of Housing and Urban Development (Washing, D.C.: Government Printing Office, 1980), pp. 7, 69.

17 Frank Beal and Elizabeth Hollander, "City Development Plans," in *The Practice of Local Government Planning,* ed. Frank S. So et al., p. 163.

18 Ibid.

19 Mary K. Nenno, "The Evolving Relationship Between Housing, Comprehensive

Planning, and Community Development," in *Housing in Metropolitan Areas: Roles and Responsibilities of Five Key Actors* (Washington, D.C.: National Association of Housing and Redevelopment Officials, 1972), p. 50.

20 Ibid., p. 14.

21 In 1922, Herbert Hoover, then secretary of commerce, reported to Congress that conflicting and antiquated building codes were increasing building costs in the United States between 10 and 20 percent.

22 U.S., Advisory Commission on Intergovernmental Relations, *Building Codes: A Program for Intergovernmental Reform* (Washington, D.C.: Government Printing Office, 1966), pp. 87–88. The following discussion is based on this publication.

23 Ibid., p. 14.

24 Ibid., pp. 22–23, 32.

25 James C. McCollom, "Building Codes: A General Assessment of Their Status and Impact on Residential Building," unpublished report (Washington, D.C.: U.S. Department of Housing and Urban Development, June 2, 1973), p. 36.

26 U.S., Advisory Commission on Intergovernmental Relations, *Building Codes: A Program for Intergovermental Reform,* pp. 84–102; and National Commission on Urban Problems, *Building the American City,* pp. 266–70.

27 U.S., Department of Housing and Urban Development, *Housing in the Seventies* (Washington, D.C.: U.S. Department of Housing and Urban Development, 1973), p. 5–22.

28 Public Technology, Inc., *Inhibiting Effects of Codes on Low and Moderate Income Housing: An Information Bulletin of the Community and Economic Development Task Force of the Urban Consortium* (Washington, D.C.: U.S. Department of Housing and Urban Development, 1978), pp. 4–6.

29 Fishman, ed., *Housing for All under Law,* pp. 552–53.

30 Spencer Parratt, *Housing Code Administration and Enforcement,* prepared for the U.S. Department of Health, Education and Welfare, Public Health Service (Washington, D.C.: Government Printing Office, 1970), pp. vii–ix.

31 National Commission on Urban Problems, *Building the American City,* p. 282.

32 International City Managers' Association, *Housing Regulations—Their Administration and Enforcement,* Management Information Service Report No. 201 (Chicago: International City Managers' Association, October 1960), pp. 4, 10.

33 Joseph S. Slavet and Melvin R. Levin, *New Approaches to Housing Code Administration,* prepared for the National Commission on Urban Problems, Research Report No. 17 (Washington, D.C.: Government Printing Office, 1969), pp. 94–95.

34 Mary K. Nenno, "Community Development Block Grants: An Overview of the First Five Years," *Journal of Housing,* August–September 1980, pp. 436, 440.

35 Roger S. Ahlbrandt, Jr., *Flexible Code Enforcement: A Key Ingredient in Neighborhood Preservation Programming* (Washington, D.C.: National Association of Housing and Redevelopment Officials, 1976), p. 8.

36 U.S., Department of Commerce, Bureau of the Census, *Taxes and Intergovernmental Revenues of Counties, Municipalities and Townships,* Government Finance Report, GF79 (Washington, D.C.: Government Printing Office, 1980), pp. 1, 5.

37 Allen D. Manvel, "Land Use in 106 Large Cities," in *Three Land Research Studies,* prepared for the National Commission on Urban Problems, Research Report No. 12 (Washington, D.C.: Government Printing Office, 1968), p. 20.

38 U.S., Department of Commerce, Bureau of the Census, *Taxable Property Values and Assessment/Sales Price Ratios,* 1977 Census of Governments (Washington, D.C.: Government Printing Office, 1978), pp. 51–52.

39 Dick Netzer, *Impact of the Property Tax: Effect on Housing, Urban Land Use, Local Government Finance,* prepared for the National Commission on Urban Problems, Research Report No. 1 (Washington, D.C.: Government Printing Office, 1968), pp. 20, 21.

40 Harry J. Wexler and Richard Peck, *Housing and Local Government* (Lexington, Mass.: Lexington Books, 1975).

41 George E. Peterson, et al., *Property Taxes, Housing and the Cities* (Lexington, Mass.: Lexington Books, 1973), foreword by Edmund S. Muskie.

42 George E. Peterson, ed., *Property Tax Reform* (Washington, D.C.: The Urban Institute, 1973), pp. 111–12.

43 George A. Reigeluth, Ray M. Reinhard, and James Kleinbaum, *Property Tax Relief for Housing Rehabilitation* (Washington, D.C.: The Urban Institute, 1979), pp. 8–9.

44 Ibid., pp. 238–40.

45 Ibid., p. 242.

46 Robert W. Burchell and David Listokin, *The Fiscal Impact Handbook: Estimating Local Costs and Revenues of Land Development* (New Brunswick, N.J.: Rutgers University, Center for Urban Policy Research, 1978). See pp. 443–66 for an extensive bibliography of municipal cost literature.

47 George Sternlieb, et al., *Housing Development and Municipal Costs* (New Brunswick, N.J.: Rutgers University, Center for Urban Policy Research, 1973); and New Jersey County and Municipal Government Study Commission, *Housing and Suburbs: Fiscal and Social Impact of Multifamily Development* (Trenton, N.J.: New Jersey County and Municipal Government Study Commission, 1974).

48 Burchell and Listokin, *The Fiscal Impact Handbook*, p. 1.

49 Ibid., especially Chapter 13, "Demographic Multipliers for Standard and Specialized Housing Types," pp. 275–90; and Chapter 16, "Gross Income Multipliers for Residential and Commercial Properties," pp. 323–40.

50 Beal and Hollander, "City Development Plans," p. 145.

51 U.S., Department of Health, Education and Welfare, *The Role of Public Welfare in Housing: A Report to the House Committee on Ways and Means and the Senate Committee on Finance* (Washington, D.C.: U.S. Department of Health, Education and Welfare, 1969), pp. 11–13.

52 Elizabeth B. Rosenbaum and Rosemarie Noonan, "Welfare Housing," *Journal of Housing*, June 1979, p. 314.

53 Thomas Appleby and David L. Miller, "Welfare Shelter Payments Should Be Used to Stimulate Improvement in the Housing Stock," *Journal of Housing*, March 1979, pp. 137–38.

54 Rosenbaum and Noonan, "Welfare Housing"; and Westchester Department of Social Services, *A Proposal for a Comprehensive Welfare Housing Demonstration Program* (White Plains, N.Y.: Westchester Department of Social Services, November 1979).

55 Charles A. Beard, *American City Government—A Survey of Newer Tendencies* (New York: The Century Company, 1912), Chapter 11.

56 Rural housing mechanisms were substantially expanded under the Housing Act of 1949, administered by the Farmers Home Administration (FmHA), created in 1946.

57 Gertrude S. Fish, "Housing Policy During the Great Depression," in *The Story of Housing*, ed. Gertrude S. Fish (New York: Macmillan, 1979), pp. 198, 199.

58 United States Housing Act of 1937, Public Law No. 412, 1 September 1937, Declaration of Policy, Section 2.

59 Nathaniel S. Keith, *Politics and the Housing Crisis Since 1930* (New York: Universe Books, 1973).

60 Housing and Home Finance Agency, *Third Annual Report of the Housing and Home Finance Agency: Calendar Year 1949* (Washington, D.C.: Government Printing Office, 1950), p. 336.

61 U.S., Department of Housing and Urban Development, *1979 Statistical Yearbook* (Washington, D.C.: Government Printing Office, 1980), Table 62, p. 204.

62 U.S., Congress, House, Committee on Appropriations, Subcommittee on HUD—Independent Agencies, *Department of Housing and Urban Development—Independent Agencies Appropriations for 1982*, Hearings, Part 6, 97th Cong., 1st sess., 1981, p. 299.

63 Rural Housing Alliance and Housing Assistance Council, *Public Housing: Where It Is and Isn't* (Washington, D.C.: Rural Housing Alliance and Housing Assistance Council, 1972).

64 Raymond J. Struyk, *A New System for Public Housing: Salvaging a National Resource* (Washington, D.C.: The Urban Institute, 1980), pp. 5–6.

65 Ibid., pp. 11–13.

66 See: Frank de Leeuw, *Operating Costs in Public Housing: A Financial Crisis* (Washington, D.C.: The Urban Institute, 1970); and Edward White, Sally R. Merrill, and Terry Lane, *The History and Overview of the Performance Funding System* (Cambridge, Mass.: ABT Associates, 1979).

67 U.S., Department of Housing and Urban Development, Office of Community Planning and Development, *Sixth Annual Community Development Block Grant Report* (Washington, D.C.: Government Printing

Office, 1981), pp. 59–60 and Table A-III-1, p. A-107.

68 U.S., Department of Housing and Urban Development, *1979 Statistical Yearbook*, Table 72, p. 214.

69 United States Housing Act of 1949, Public Law 81-171, 15 July 1949.

70 See: James Q. Wilson, ed., *Urban Renewal: The Record and the Controversy* (Cambridge, Mass.: MIT Press, 1966); and "Myths/Realities of Urban Renewal," *Journal of Housing*, April 1973, pp. 170–78.

71 Robert P. Groberg, *Centralized Relocation: A New Municipal Service* (Washington, D.C.: National Association of Housing and Redevelopment Officials, April 1969).

72 National Association of Housing and Redevelopment Officials, *NAHRO 1976 Directory* (Washington, D.C.: National Association of Housing and Redevelopment Officials, 1976).

73 U.S., Congress, House, Committee on Banking, Finance and Urban Affairs, Subcommittee on the City, *Urban Economic Development: Past Lessons and Future Requirements: A National Urban Policy Roundtable*, 96th Congress, 1st session, 1979.

74 Charles H. Haar, *Between the Idea and the Reality: A Study in the Origin, Fate and Legacy of the Model Cities Program* (Boston, Mass.: Little, Brown, 1975), p. 215.

75 Mary K. Nenno, "Housing and Urban Development Act of 1968 Becomes Law," *Journal of Housing*, August 1968, p. 352.

76 "The Federal Role in Urban Affairs" was the title of a series of hearings conducted by the Subcommittee on Executive Reorganization of the Senate Government Operations Subcommittee (Senator Abraham Ribicoff, D–Connecticut, chairman) in 1966; and "Creative Federalism" was the title of a series of hearings conducted by the Subcommittee on Intergovernmental Relations of the same committee, in the same year (Senator Edmund S. Muskie, D–Maine, chairman).

77 For an explanation of this review process, see: Robert C. Alexander and Mary K. Nenno, *Required: A Local Housing Assistance Plan*, 3d ed. (Washington, D.C.: National Association of Housing and Redevelopment Officials, 1976), pp. 13–15.

78 U.S., Department of Housing and Urban Development, Office of Community Planning and Development, *Fifth Annual Community Development Block Grant Report* (Washington, D.C.: Government Printing Office, 1980), p. XIV–18.

79 Ibid., p. XIV–13.

80 Ibid., p. I–17.

81 William Witte, "Community Development's Third Year," *Journal of Housing*, February 1978, pp. 66–72.

82 Mary K. Nenno, "The Ten Year Housing Goals," *Journal of Housing*, July 1978, pp. 342–46; and U.S., Department of Housing and Urban Development, *The Tenth Annual Report on the National Housing Goal* (Washington, D.C.: Government Printing Office, 1979), pp. 26–27.

83 For descriptions of funding methods, see: Edwin C. Daniel, "Housing Innovations in Seven Localities: A Report on What Each Has Done in Response to the Housing Crisis," *Journal of Housing*, February 1976, pp. 90–92; Edwin C. Daniel, "Denver Housing Authority Takes Lead Role in Solving Communitywide Housing Problems," *Journal of Housing*, August–September 1977, p. 387; Nancy B. Nyman, *Locally Funded Low- and Moderate-Income Housing Programs*, Management Information Service Reports, Vol. 6, No. 4 (Washington, D.C.: International City Management Association, April 1974); and "Philly Pension Fund to Make Home Loans," *Washington Post*, 15 August 1981.

84 U.S., Congress, House, *Tax-Exempt Bonds for Single-Family Housing: A Study Prepared by the Congressional Budget Office for the Committee on Banking, Finance and Urban Affairs*, 96th Cong., 1st sess., 1979, p. 1.

85 National Association of Housing and Redevelopment Officials, Board of Governors, *Policy Statement on Local Tax Exempt Mortgage Bonds* (Washington, D.C.: National Association of Housing and Redevelopment Officials, 1979).

86 U.S., Department of Housing and Urban Development, Office of Community Planning and Development, *Urban Development Action Grant Program: Second Annual Report* (Washington, D.C.: U.S. Department of Housing and Urban Development, 1980), p. 53.

87 Ibid., p. 67.

88 Rolf Goetze, *Neighborhood Monitoring and Analysis: A New Way of Looking at Urban Neighborhoods and How They Change* (Washington, D.C.: U.S. Depart-

ment of Housing and Urban Development, 1980), pp. 1–2.

89 Linton, Mields & Coston, Inc., *A Study of the Problems of Abandoned Housing,* prepared for the U.S. Department of Housing and Urban Development (Washington, D.C.: Linton, Mields & Coston, Inc., 1971), pp. 8, 268–85.

90 National Urban League, Center for Community Change, *The National Survey of Housing Abandonment* ([New York:] National Urban League, 1971), p. 12.

91 George Sternlieb and Robert W. Burchell, *Residential Abandonment: The Tenement Landlord Revisited* (New Brunswick, N.J.: Rutgers University, Center for Urban Policy Research, 1973), p. xii.

92 Monica R. Lett, *Rent Control: Concepts, Realities, and Mechanisms* (New Brunswick, N.J.: Rutgers University, Center for Urban Policy Research, 1976), pp. 60–76.

93 U.S., Department of Housing and Urban Development, Office of Policy Development and Research, *Displacement Report* (Washington, D.C.: U.S. Department of Housing and Urban Development,1979), p. iii.

94 George Grier and Eunice Grier, *Urban Displacement: A Reconnaissance,* prepared for the U.S. Department of Housing and Urban Development (Bethesda, Md.: The Grier Partnership, 1978).

95 U.S., Department of Housing and Urban Development, Office of Policy Development and Research, *The Conversion of Rental Housing to Condominiums and Cooperatives: A National Study of Scope, Causes and Impacts* (Washington, D.C.: Government Printing Office, 1980), pp. i and ii.

96 Ibid., p. viii.

97 Linton, Mields & Coston, Inc., *A Study of the Problems of Abandoned Housing,* p. 245.

98 Goetze, *Neighborhood Monitoring and Analysis,* pp. 2–5.

Chapter 2

Conserving and rehabilitating existing housing and neighborhoods

In the 1970s and 1980s the local housing function in the United States has adopted as major goals the reversal of the decline in neighborhoods and the maintenance of housing and neighborhoods already in good health. Specific approaches to attain these goals have, historically, been in the form of special programs, usually federally funded or mandated, rather than integral parts of local government. Accordingly, such local efforts as concentrated code enforcement or publicly administered loan and grant programs have been grafted onto existing city administrative and policymaking machinery and very seldom have been fully integrated into local government operations.

This inability at the local level to tie together program-related activities more completely with other city functions very often has produced a fragmented and inconsistent local housing policy and neighborhood approach. As noted in Chapter 1, however, the bulk of city government activities directly affect the quality of housing and neighborhoods: building inspection, zoning, and code enforcement; tax policies; and such services as schools, police protection, and sanitation. Anthony Downs has pointed out that "It is unrealistic to expect city officials to coordinate all these policies so as to benefit neighborhoods,"[1] but cities and city officials can move toward a fuller understanding of how these seemingly unrelated activities define much of the local housing function.

This chapter explores approaches to the more direct and obvious housing functions and programs and discusses their effects on housing conditions and neighborhood health.

THE LOCAL CODES COMPONENT

As Chapter 1 outlined, housing and building codes were slow in coming to U.S. cities, but they are now widespread. With the spur of the federal "workable program" requirement, passed in 1954, local governments began to develop, legislate, and implement these codes.

Three immediate problems showed up as cities sought to develop their local codes: (1) which codes to use; (2) how to administer and enforce the codes; and (3) whether to use the same standards for old housing and new. These issues continue to face local governments as they seek a fully legitimate local housing function that encompasses not only safety and minimum occupancy standards but also maintenance of the housing stock and improvement of property and neighborhoods.

One key issue all local governments face is deciding on the kinds of codes to adopt and enforce. Much work has been completed in developing national and regional housing codes, but most cities have resolved these issues in a complex, hybrid fashion. The kinds of codes a local government may adopt include new construction codes, rehabilitation codes, minimum housing standards, and maintenance codes.

New construction codes

New construction codes typically apply to all new buildings—commercial, industrial, and residential—and represent the most advanced thinking on safety and new building techniques and materials. Often the adoption of a code using these standards on a citywide basis presents the difficult problem of how they should apply to existing buildings. Applying new codes to old buildings can have very serious economic consequences. Adrienne Levatino-Donoghue points out, for example, that in Chicago a rehabilitation effort requires the placement of electrical outlets every twelve feet, a provision of the code that may reflect needs of modern living, but that may exceed reasonable safety standards.[2]

Rehabilitation codes

In an effort to overcome the problem of fitting new codes to old buildings, some cities have adopted rehabilitation codes that seek to combine the key safety features of a new construction code with a more realistic view of the conditions of older housing stock, making it easier to rehabilitate older units by requiring that a less stringent test be met.[3]

Minimum housing standards

Minimum housing standards were developed in the early twentieth century in an effort to set minimum standards of decency for occupying housing. Dealing as much with sanitation and overcrowding as with safety, these codes often prescribe standards of cleanliness, space, and ventilation that must be met before a housing unit can be occupied, or standards it must meet if it is to remain occupied. The courts have accepted the philosophy of these housing codes to the point that an implied warrant of habitability is now seen to exist in a lease for a rental unit. Often the responsibility for enforcing housing codes is beyond the domain of the building code department and is the responsibility of a health department, creating serious issues of coordination between the inspection and enforcement agencies.

Maintenance codes

In addition to setting health and safety standards, some localities have developed codes requiring that certain levels of maintenance be achieved in an effort to provide a common standard for exterior conditions. These codes often cover such items as exterior paint and the condition of gardens and grounds. Since they have little to do with public safety, they are generally in place to protect the property values in a city or neighborhood and to prevent undermaintained properties from having a negative effect on nearby properties.

Federal code requirements

In many programs using federal funds or insurance, federally imposed standards must be met. The HUD minimum property standards for new construction, rehabilitation, or existing housing must be met whenever FHA insurance is used. In addition, to meet CDBG objectives, many cities have agreed to use a federal standard—in essence, a code—established in conjunction with the Section 8 existing housing program, which sets standards for decent housing that must be met if a unit funded with federal funds is to count as a standard unit.

Historic codes

Historic codes or standards require that any historic building, or any building in a historic district, be modified only in ways that recognize and protect the historical quality and value of the building. These codes are both national (the secretary of interior sets federal standards for historic properties) and local. The local codes vary widely, depending on the nature of the historic building or district.

ORGANIZATION FOR CODE INSPECTIONS AND ENFORCEMENT

The choice of codes to be adopted, interpreted, and enforced in a total housing improvement or maintenance program is broad and complicated. With the many choices made by local governments, the permutations have led to a fragmented code structure that is only now being mitigated by the adoption of "model codes" that help standardize codes throughout regions, or throughout the country.

The choice of which codes to enforce is easy compared with the complex issues involved in organizing for an effective housing and neighborhood conservation program. The issues to be addressed here include:

where in city government to place the codes and neighborhood improvement function; reporting lines; philosophy of administration, particularly toward code enforcement; size of staff; staff assignments and training; and, not least of all, quality control over the system.

In an insightful article comparing the efforts of three cities in organizing their minimum housing standards enforcement, Elizabeth Howe shows that code enforcement is a complex system requiring interaction among many administrative components. The inspection component, usually the responsibility of a city department, depends for its success in abating violations on the judicial branch, either a specialized housing court or a magistrate system. Poor coordination between these executive and judicial functions can bring ineffective code enforcement.[4]

Howe also describes a complete code enforcement system as one that includes a housing code, a regulatory agency charged with inspecting and enforcing the code, a special housing court to handle code enforcement cases, and a number of programs to help property owners bring their buildings into compliance with the code.[5]

The key variables in establishing a successful housing code enforcement system include the tractability of the code enforcement problem (measured by the number of deteriorated housing units) and the predominant single family–multifamily patterns of the housing stock. The better the housing conditions, and the more the stock is single family in nature, the easier will be the code enforcement process.

The salience of code enforcement in local politics is also a critical factor in how a city uses the tool. Housing code enforcement costs individual homeowners money, and it can be plagued with favoritism and inequities in administration. Local elected officials will back such a program only if it is viewed by the constituency—or at least a vocal minority of the constituency —as an important and useful program.

The importance of a city's political perception of code enforcement cannot be overstated. Political commitment is a prerequisite to development of an active code enforcement program, which, to be successful, must have all components working well together. For example, a city with a strong housing court, but with an inspection staff that is unskilled and politically appointed, is not very likely to develop an effective overall system. As Howe goes on to say, "There is no single answer to the code enforcement problem. . . . The system is a complex, interorganizational one whose pieces, including inspections, code enforcement and rehabilitation programs, must work together in a mutually reinforcing balance."[6]

Although each city's solution may be different, the housing maintenance and enforcement issues are the same. These issues fall into two major areas of code work: inspections and enforcement.

Inspections

TABLE OF ORGANIZATION   Code inspection is placed differently in cities. In some the function is part of a department of housing; in others, part of a department of licenses and inspections, a department of public safety, or a fire department. No one approach is necessarily better than another, but in all cases successful operation requires coordination with other parts of the city's housing machinery.

STAFF SIZE   Staff size is largely a budget issue, but obviously the size of the staff depends on the volume of inspections to be conducted and city officials' expectations about the frequency and quality of inspections. Staff size is also affected by the amount of time each inspector spends inspecting, compared with the time spent on the associated paperwork and processing of reports.

THE ROLE OF THE INSPECTOR AND JOB QUALIFICATIONS   Inspectors can be viewed as law enforcement agents or technical assistants to property owners, or a mix of both. The skills needed by code inspectors are both technical and interpersonal. A good inspector not only knows the technicalities of building systems and the code but also can work effectively with the public in a way that brings about improvement of property without leading to bad feelings from property owners toward city government.

The self-image of the inspector is critical in shaping the public response to code enforcement. A staff trained to be helpful to the property owner is much more likely to win public acceptance of the codes program than a staff that considers itself the strong arm of the law and imposes unpopular and perhaps unreasonable standards of compliance.[7]

INSPECTION SCHEDULES   Inspections can be scheduled on a routine basis, citywide, by complaint only, or on a neighborhood-by-neighborhood pattern. These choices are influenced by the local housing conditions and the ethic toward code enforcement. This decision can also be different for owner-occupied and landlord-owned properties.

These decisions have a dramatic effect on a city's ability to be effective in using code enforcement to improve the housing stock. For example, if a city chooses to use code enforcement in an effort to improve a neighborhood, it must be careful that the codes program and the neighborhood conditions are in harmony. Code enforcement in a neighborhood that has a very weak investment mentality can be a disaster. Code enforcement can cause abandonment if the cost of making repairs is well beyond the market value of the properties in the neighborhood.[8]

Enforcement

ORGANIZATIONAL ISSUES   Enforcement is generally a judicial function, handled in some jurisdictions by a separate, specialized housing court.

Without a strong enforcement arm, virtually all the decisions related to inspections are rendered moot. As one housing court magistrate put it, one of the most important features of a specialized housing court is that

> the inspection system itself . . . housing inspectors, policemen and prosecutors . . . soon sense the necessary support the court is lending to the cause. Rather than discouragement at seeing well-prepared, documented cases dismissed, the inspector watches a careful weighing of his evidence and, thus, feels his work is important and responsible.[9]

ENFORCEMENT STRATEGY   Should the inspectors be required to enforce all the code violations in a structure? Or should they be allowed to permit minor violations to go unabated, provided they pose no threat to the health and safety of the occupants? This level of common sense in the operation of any code enforcement system is necessary, but must be handled very cautiously so as not to permit common sense exceptions to become inconsistent administration, with enforcement varying among inspectors.

QUALITY CONTROL   Careful supervision will provide that the enforcement system is effective, fairly uniform, and, above all, honest. Avoiding graft, at either the inspection or the enforcement level, is an essential ingredient to a system if it is to have credibility with the public.

Putting inspections and enforcement together

The overall code enforcement machinery in any city is complex and must vary with particular circumstances. In any city, thoughtful decisions must be made about what the system is seeking to accomplish, whether it is meeting its objectives, and whether it is being administered as efficiently and as effectively as possible. The successful code enforcement system requires sophisticated administration. Larger cities have turned to computerized information systems to monitor inspection assignments, complaint processing, serving of notices, and so on. Adaptations and innovations in the codes themselves are ongoing responsibilities of well-trained code administrators.

The local code enforcement function has expanded well beyond the role of policing physical standards. It is now an integral tool in local housing programs and can be a key element in meeting housing rehabilitation and neighborhood improvement objectives.

THE LESSONS OF NEIGHBORHOOD AND HOUSING IMPROVEMENT PROGRAMS

Just as the 1954 federal requirement that cities have a "workable program" led to the proliferation of housing codes, the federal actions taken in the mid-1960s created incentives to tie these codes into comprehensive code enforcement programs, aimed at residential renewal rather than slum clearance. The laws passed in 1964 and 1965 created the federally assisted code enforcement (FACE) program. This program combined federal funds for staff, capital improvements (Section 117), demolition of structurally unsound or unfit units (Section 116), grants to low-income homeowners for property rehabilitation (Section 115), and low-interest loans to property owners to finance rehabilitation (Section 312).

These programs were important to the development of the local housing function for a number of reasons.

First, they were federally initiated. The federal government assembled a package of categorical programs and funds for which local governments could apply; it set the standards; and it funded applications in part on the basis of the local government's ability to conform to strict program application requirements and procedures. Further, the federal government was in charge of the program conceptually, with local governments choosing the areas in which to be involved and administering the programs to federal standards.

Second, program success was based in part on the ability of local governments to learn to operate administratively cumbersome loan and grant procedures established nationally. Eligibility for a Section 312 loan (nationally set at 3 percent, twenty-year terms, with a maximum allowable principal amount) was determined by HUD, with most procedures for loan approval and processing set by HUD. Thus what evolved was a very precise loan processing system that required work write-ups, formal bidding procedures, specified fund disbursement procedures, and so on. Each local government involved in the program developed its own cadre of experts in processing these loans and grants.

Third, the effort demonstrated that cities could physically improve a neighborhood through code enforcement, affordable financing, and public improvements, but that this physical improvement did not necessarily change the deeper-seated causes of neighborhood decay. Very little attention was paid to understanding the relationship between physical conditions in a neighborhood and the causes and processes of neighborhood decline.

The fourth and perhaps most important effect was that, despite their shortcomings, the programs had the dramatic effect of causing cities to focus on residential rehabilitation as an alternative to slum clearance. A corner was turned, and cities and the nation began the long process of learning how to promote neighborhood recovery.

As a result of these and other federal programs, but also as a reaction to the dissatisfaction with the level of federal decision making and control that they represented, the Nixon administration in the early seventies created a "New Federalism" approach that sought to transfer a great deal of decision making for housing and community development to local governments.[10]

The Housing and Community Development Act of 1974 revolutionized the philosophy and procedures for providing federal grants to cities for renewal functions. Gone were the lengthy applications for specific renewal areas; gone were the federal officials to make decisions on each application; and gone was the system that awarded federal dollars on the basis of city grantsmanship. Instead, the 1974 act established a formula based on need that entitled cities over 50,000 population to a specific amount in community development funds on an annual basis. In addition, the law and its subsequent HUD regulations laid out national objectives and broad categories of eligible and ineligible activities. Cities were encouraged to create programs of their own within these broad eligibility guidelines.

Generally, the 1974 legislation and the HUD regulations on community development block grants (CDBGs) permit cities to conduct housing programs that have one of two major objectives:

1. Activities are authorized that focus financial and other benefits on low- and moderate-income residents, as defined by HUD.
2. Programs are authorized that are aimed at the prevention or elimination of slums and blight.

The first major category includes activities such as the provision of grants to low- and moderate-income persons for housing rehabilitation (a followup on the Section 115 grant), rehabilitation financing (like Section 312), and rehabilitation services such as counseling, loan processing, and work write-ups (like Section 117).

The category of prevention and elimination of slums and blight includes acquisition, disposition, clearance, code enforcement, and related activities, all of which are direct extensions of the uses made of funds under the Title I renewal program. Under CDBG, a proportion of these activities are required to benefit low- and moderate-income persons.

These broad approaches enable local governments to create a set of programs that each considers necessary to meet its specific needs, given its own unique mix of population and neighborhood circumstances and problems. The degree of regulation from HUD has varied considerably based on the philosophy of the federal administration in power and the style of the particular area office of HUD. The Nixon and Ford points of view were generally freer of regulations than was the Carter administration philosophy. President Reagan, in keeping with his revised federalism, has eliminated many of the CDBG requirements.

Regardless of the varying levels of regulation, the CDBG program is less federally controlled than were the categorical programs. While city officials are required to formulate Housing Assistance Plans (HAPs) and Community Development Plans that permit strategies of change to be developed at the local level, they are not required to follow prescribed HUD procedures in developing and implementing eligible programs.

With this new approach, cities could choose to develop programs to assist low- to moderate-income people and could provide direct housing assistance to them, regardless of where in the city they lived. Cities could also choose to target their programs into areas of need (these came to be called neighborhood strategy areas [NSAs] under the Carter administration), in which case the goal of eliminating slums and blight permitted housing programs to benefit everyone in the area, regardless of the income of the beneficiaries.

Despite these new powers and flexibility at the local level, however, many cities developed programs from earlier experiences. For example, many cities that had been involved in the federally assisted code enforcement program invented local programs based on the same general assumptions and operating philosophy. In many instances cities merely replicated the federal system, choosing a neighborhood and establishing loan and grant programs and benefit deals identical to Sections 312 and 115.

While this approach was expedient in that it permitted a smooth transition from the categorical programs to the block grant system, and although it often used extant local capacities, it carried with it the cost of avoiding hard and thoughtful decisions about how the city should use its new-found regulatory freedom to match local needs more closely. Local officials were free to innovate but often did not recognize their freedom or were too constrained by local circumstances to act on it.

But change at the local level did occur. Cities reassessed the components of the FACE formula. For example, cities began to use their code enforcement machinery in different ways to deal with housing and neighborhood improvement demands. To most, code enforcement continued to be a critical part of a targeted program to force an investment decision from a property owner with the city standing ready, with CDBG funds, to make low-interest loans or grants.

Others, however, chose not to continue to use code enforcement as a stick but more simply to use their code as a standard against which they measured the success of their rehabilitation programs. A clear local code could provide the basis for knowing how much money to allocate for rehabilitating a property, but code enforcement did not have to be used to require action from an owner. Some city officials concluded that if the financial incentives were attractive enough, code enforcement would not be necessary.

Some cities developed very flexible approaches to code enforcement, using the tool in connection with a low-interest loan and grant program but adapting the code almost to meet the rehabilitation needs of the occupants of each property.[11]

Over time, code enforcement became a relatively small component of local CDBG programs. The much broader variations developed by local governments occurred in two other areas. First, cities varied widely in the choices they made about the kinds of neighborhoods they sought to recover and the comprehensive program elements needed to cause a neighborhood to improve. Second, cities developed a wide array of financial assistance programs aimed at providing affordable financing for needy property owners.

The ability to vary both the financial assistance package and the neighborhoods chosen for targeting led to the eventual conclusion that the really important conceptual issue at the local and national levels was not deciding on the correct neighborhood to work on or the best financial assistance package available, but developing the right fit between the two. Cities could vary financial assistance packages depending on the financing needs of the properties and the property owners in the selected neighborhood, and the neighborhood selected could vary in size, condition of housing, and socio-economic mix, based on the range of local financial assistance programs. For example, a particular program, such as the Neighborhood Housing Services (NHS) program, could be used in a city only in a limited number of areas because experience showed that neighborhoods had to be at a certain level of health in order for an NHS program to be effective. For other neighborhoods, cities were free to invent their own approaches, thereby operating different programs in different areas concurrently.[12]

This was a major conceptual breakthrough at the local level because the combinations of neighborhoods and financial assistance packages led to an extensive amount of trial-and-error analysis about what programs worked best, where, and why. If a program was not working, it could be varied by local officials, thereby permitting conceptual learning about the complex forces of neighborhood change and the effects of the intervention of the public sector on neighborhood dynamics.

LOCAL PUBLIC INTERVENTION

The increased flexibility available under CDBG places a heavy burden on local policymakers, who are confronted with all the critical issues associated with local decision making and control. They must resolve the difficult conceptual issues in allocating CDBG funds to meet their own assessment of needs; they must develop programs, implement them, monitor and evaluate them, and, ideally, modify the programs based on their own feedback—all this in an often heated political setting. As a HUD-funded report put it, community development funds

are highly "visible" and they have taken on a symbolic value which makes their distribution one of the more difficult tasks in City Hall today. Competing interests and expectations, conflicts of equity and efficiency, and local political considerations all inevitably come into play. And there exists no proven method of neighborhood diagnosis and treatment to show up the decisions that local officials make.[13]

Grappling with this new power continues to be a major theme in the emergence of the local housing function. Sometimes acting on instinct, sometimes on the basis of the newest theory of neighborhood change, cities have muddled their way into important and innovative approaches. The learning that is occurring at the local level involves a fuller understanding of the dynamics of neighborhood change and the role local government can play in effecting neighborhood improvement. Recognition of the importance of the private sector, especially lenders, and the involvement and support of neighborhood residents has become commonplace in most cities. Applying the concepts effectively in what appear to be unique environments, however, represents a continuing local challenge.

One of the most important conceptual breakthroughs of the 1970s was a recognition by some local officials that the objective in any neighborhood recovery program is not limited to the improvement of the physical condition of the housing stock but also includes altering the neighborhood's housing market in a directed way. The lesson of the earlier FACE programs is that such an approach is essential if physical improvements are to be sustained.

While in the past the goal of neighborhood recovery may have been measured by gauging the amount of physical improvement, such as the number of code violations abated, or the number of properties brought to code standards, the new measures of success—such as the change in property values or the ability to attract newcomers—were based on the actual market recovery of the neighborhood.

As cities began to adopt this broader approach to and definition of neighborhood recovery, major shifts in program development occurred. Cities began to intervene to change the overall dynamics of the housing market in a particular neighborhood. This required that cities learn a great deal about the way neighborhoods deteriorate and recover, the role local government can play in that recovery, and the role of the private sector—realtors, lenders, investors—in neighborhood recovery as well. In addition, other physical and nonphysical conditions in the neighborhood—quality of schools, location, neighborhood history, crime rate—all became recognized as important factors. In some instances, the goal of market recovery of the neighborhood was tempered by the goal of avoiding the displacement of existing residents to prevent displacement and gentrification.

On an even broader level, a goal of neighborhood recovery somehow had to fit into an overall local government strategy for dealing with the housing stock. The recovery of one neighborhood while others were deteriorating would do little more than keep city programs and efforts on a treadmill in which progress in one area would be offset by deterioration in another. In the early 1970s, urban theorists tried to provide guidance to local officials by postulating a classification of neighborhoods from those that were healthy and needed no help to those that were beyond help. These theorists suggested that city governments work on neighborhoods in which they could make a difference, those that could be saved or recovered.[14] Such an approach was labeled "triage" in the sense that it set up a system of priorities to concentrate city efforts in those neighborhoods where the efforts could be very effective and let the dying neighborhoods go without any city help. The selection of neighborhoods forced harsh political decisions on city officials, who recognized that they needed a better understanding of neighborhood change, and more data, to justify their decisions.

The key requirement in determining whether a public-sector-generated neighborhood recovery program fits well with neighborhood needs is to understand not only the physical condition of the housing stock but also the market conditions. The physical conditions are easily measured, but the more important market conditions are far less easily gauged. If the public objective is to recover the neighborhood—that is, to make it more attractive so that more buyers will be available for the market and for the neighborhood —then those factors that are deterring prospective buyers from purchasing housing in the neighborhood need to be identified and dealt with. Dealing only with housing issues, a city has at its disposal the carrot of cheap financing and the stick of applying codes to force investment decisions. The objective, however, need not be to have every below-standard house rehabilitated. The objective is more appropriately stated as changing market conditions so that the private sector will continue to finance housing purchase and rehabilitation in the neighborhood without subsidy dollars after the program has ended. As a measure of program success, this is considerably different from the percentage of substandard buildings brought up to code standards, as was often the measure in the earlier FACE programs.

UNDERSTANDING NEIGHBORHOOD CHANGE

A number of books and articles have appeared since the mid-1970s that seek to explain, via theoretical and documentary evidence, the process by which neighborhoods change.[15] Although the theories vary in content and sophistication, they have in common a focus on the neighborhood as a housing market. The variables that affect a neighborhood's housing market include housing conditions but are in no way limited to them. As Goetze and Colton have said, two neighborhoods in generally the same physical condition may have radically different housing market characteristics.[16]

The role of the local policymaker is to understand neighborhood housing market conditions in his or her city and develop programs that appropriately intervene in the market to effect the changes desired. "Policymakers must combine their traditional sensitivity to physical housing conditions with a new awareness of neighborhood market perceptions." This means public policy must become sensitive and countervailing to neighborhood dynamics, increasing demand where it is weak and areas are declining, and cooling it where markets are rising and causing dislocation and speculation.[17]

Local public officials must learn to read the signals in the marketplace. Declining neighborhoods do not inspire the confidence of potential home-buyers and investors relative to other neighborhoods. There may be an excess supply of houses for sale and apartments for rent, which usually leads to a decline in sales prices. Or buyers may be available, but their buying power may be less than sellers are asking, also leading to a decrease in prices.

In declining areas, property owners and investors are uncertain of future property values. Owners are reluctant to invest in their properties if they are not reasonably sure that the investment can be recovered through resale. Accordingly, lenders, who are also investors in neighborhoods, may be unwilling to issue mortgages on a long-term basis for fear that the fundamental protection for their loan, the value of the property itself, may not be sufficient to protect their loans. The neighborhood becomes redlined due to the lenders' perception about the future of the area. Government-insured mortgages or "creative financing" by sellers may be the only approaches available to finance purchases.

Conversely, a recovering neighborhood may be characterized by strong demand, price inflation well beyond the average for the city or the metropolitan area as a whole, and speculation by outside investors.

The appropriate public action in each of these housing markets is quite different. Declining areas need pump priming and demand stimulation, while recovering neighborhoods need protection from change and inflation of the housing market for existing residents.

The challenge at the local level is to understand neighborhood housing markets, to categorize and understand the housing market conditions in each of the city's neighborhoods, to develop intervention strategies based on a clear definition of the public purpose to be achieved by intervening, and to modify the program strategy based on changing neighborhood conditions.

In assessing neighborhood housing market conditions it is necessary to develop data that describe the operation of the housing market. These data go well beyond such standard measures as physical condition, vacancy rates, and the socioeconomic characteristics of neighborhood residents. New data are needed, both hard and soft.

Hard data indicators of neighborhood change include increases and decreases in the average value of real estate transactions, the percentage of mortgages financed through a lending institution, the volume of building permits, and the frequency of property tax delinquency.[18] "Soft" measures include the attitudes of lenders, realtors, and residents toward the area; the average time houses are listed for sale; and perceptions of the outlook for the neighborhood as a good investment.[19]

These market readings must be taken by local public officials to determine the kind of intervention needed in a neighborhood. The task of the local official is to develop and implement a strategy to counter the negative forces that the data indicate are present. And it is here that the public official is likely to feel political pressure, neighborhood pressure, and personal doubts about the theoretical underpinnings of the intervention strategy. Currently, the state of the art is primitive. Some local officials are only now learning about the appropriateness of various tools—and new tools are being created continuously at the local level to contend with changing circumstances. The state of the art is not scientific method, based on full knowledge and understanding of the effects of public intervention on the chemistry of the housing market, but an alchemy based on intuition and inventive experimentation.

THE NEED FOR A PARTNERSHIP
The new housing market indicators are measures of private actions taken in neighborhoods by a number of different actors: individual purchasers (homeowners and investors), specialists who handle real estate transactions (real estate agents), and persons who make decisions about the availability of private capital for purchase, rehabilitation, and new construction (appraisers, lenders, and insurance agents).

Local officials not only must understand the data about housing markets; they also must learn how the markets actually work and how local public action must connect with the neighborhood housing market. A local program has the potential for causing neighborhood change only when it ties in closely with other key actors in the housing market, solicits their points of view, and works from there. One key rule must be followed:

Local government can influence neighborhood housing markets only if public officials recognize that they are not the center of the housing market.

Local officials can be leaders in neighborhood change, but they can be effective only if they work in partnership with the other key actors. Local public officials must use the limited funds available to leverage and cause private investment. Perceptions about the neighborhood's future and what the private sector sees as possible and appropriate need to be built into public-sector decisions.

Neighborhood housing markets are no different from the stock market or the bond market. Prices are set and volume is generated by expectations about future prices and alternate investment choices. Markets rise and fall on the expectations of those able to invest. Therefore, a critical role of local public officials is to involve the key private-sector actors so that expectations and perceptions about neighborhood conditions and outlook are based on facts, not myths, prejudices, or stereotypes.

A PROTOTYPE OF THE WORKING RELATIONSHIP
In the 1970s the prototype Neighborhood Housing Services (NHS) program provided a great deal of insight and direction into making this local partnership work so that new capital would flow into deteriorated neighborhoods and perceptions held by lenders and appraisers would change.

Started in 1968 in a Pittsburgh neighborhood, NHS combines the efforts of neighborhood residents, local government, and financial institutions in a partnership that works toward the stabilization of a neighborhood. The program did not ask any of the three groups to compromise self-interest, such as community advocacy, sound underwriting practices, or reasonable city investment. Rather, it tackled problems of inner city neighborhoods by using the commitment and resources of these three groups to work together.[20]

This NHS model was replicated extensively in many cities through the work of the Urban Reinvestment Corporation, originally created by the Federal Home Loan Bank Board. The NHS program had a number of key features.

1. It was developed as a local program, with little or no federal government control.
2. The model is basically nongovernmental. City government plays an important role, but control is vested in a nonprofit corporation that is guided by neighborhood residents and participating lenders.
3. The programs are nonbureaucratic and can adapt to changing circumstances.
4. The program is basically a self-help effort in which neighborhood residents and lenders, committed to the future of a neighborhood, join with the city government to make creditworthy and high-risk mortgage and home improvement loans in a targeted area.

The intriguing lessons that the NHS model brought to the art of neighborhood revitalization were that neighborhoods could improve if the private capital could be tapped and that the perceptions of those involved could change more quickly than the perceptions of lenders and others not involved in the neighborhood recovery program.[21] To local public officials, the lesson was clear: involve the key actors in a neighborhood recovery effort both to gain access to private capital and to help base the perceptions of critical actors on facts about the neighborhood's strengths and weaknesses, rather than on misconceptions.

The key actors and their importance to the neighborhood change process are discussed in the following sections.

Lending institutions

Lenders—banks, savings and loan associations, and mortgage companies —are the institutional decision makers in control of the private capital needed for real estate purchases, rehabilitation, and new construction in all neighborhoods. No neighborhood recovery program can be successful unless this private capital is available to the area.

The availability of mortgages and home improvement loans for any neighborhood depends on overall money market conditions and lender perceptions of the security of investing in a neighborhood. When credit gets tight in the aggregate, mortgage and home improvement loans may be difficult to obtain or prohibitively expensive, slowing down the real estate market and lowering values. However, aggregate reductions of supply, if distributed uniformly, do not adversely affect one housing or neighborhood market compared with another.

The availability of private capital for real estate activities varies among neighborhoods based on the lenders' perceptions about the future of the area and on the credit standing of those desiring to buy properties in the neighborhood. Whether lenders illegally redline neighborhoods—that is, whether they actually cut off the flow of capital to a neighborhood because of negative expectations—is an issue that will continue to be discussed as evidence is gathered and analyzed.[22] Whether their actions are legal or not, lenders certainly make decisions based on the value of the real estate over time and their perception of that value. In any neighborhood in which market prices are perceived to be declining relative to other neighborhoods, lenders typically will be less willing to issue long-term fixed-rate mortgages, since the fundamental security for those mortgages—the property itself— may not be of sufficient value at some future date to pay off the mortgage if the lender must foreclose. Although this may be a prudent decision on the part of a lender, it also can become a self-fulfilling prophecy, since expectations that the neighborhood will decline can cut off capital, thus bringing about that decline. So dealing with lender expectations and working with lenders to provide a flow of capital is an essential part of any city government program to improve an area.

A key strategy for neighborhood recovery is to involve lenders so that they become increasingly comfortable making loans in the neighborhood. City officials should approach lenders in a businesslike manner, searching for the common self-interest between the lenders and the city government. While threats (such as calling on a lender to fulfill requirements to invest in inner city areas under the Community Reinvestment Act of 1975) can be helpful, such an approach should only be a last resort. A lending official who is participating in a program because he or she has been coerced will not be as active and committed as one who has agreed to participate because the benefits to the lending institution from a business standpoint are made obvious.

Lenders usually can be induced to participate in a neighborhood recovery program because it is profitable for the lender to do so. For example, many cities pay a fee to lenders to originate and service loans funded with community development block grant funds even though these loans are owned by the local government.[23] The fee is often attractive enough to permit the lender to derive some income for rendering the service. The secondary but more important effect is that the lender's perception about the bankability or creditworthiness of the neighborhood residents often improves, thereby making it more likely that the lender will make his or her own funds available when asked to do so.

Another important issue in "selling" a neighborhood to lending institutions is understanding the dynamics of demand for real estate in the neighborhood. Most neighborhoods decline not because they are redlined or because funds for investment are not available, but because the demand side of the equation is weak. Prospective homeowners and investors have stopped wanting to own housing in the neighborhood because they perceive that the neighborhood is a less desirable place to live than other available areas, or that property values will not keep pace with competing areas in the future. If demand is the problem, no solution that focuses on creating a supply of funds will be effective. Action must be taken to stimulate the demand for investment.

Stimulating the demand side requires a good understanding of why prospective investors are avoiding an area. For example, the problem may be that schools in the neighborhood are perceived to be inferior, or that the crime rate is too high. Many such neighborhood problems are beyond the scope of responsibility of local housing officials; but despite these problems, they can try to induce existing owners to reinvest and seek new investors and homeowners through marketing and financial incentives. For example, offering below-market-rate financing for home purchase or purchase and rehabilitation can be very effective in attracting new investment. Promoting neighborhoods through street fairs and advertising is another useful approach.

In addition, local officials must be thoughtful about the market for a particular neighborhood. An area with a reputation for poor schools, for example, could still be very attractive to singles and childless couples, both growing components of the housing market. Increasing demand is the strongest message to send to lenders about the future of an area.

Real estate agents

Perceptions about existing neighborhood conditions and the direction of change also affect the actions of real estate agents, which in turn can affect the future of an area. Real estate salespeople affect neighborhood change because their perceptions influence prospective buyers.

Real estate agents are paid on a commission basis by sellers at the time a sale occurs. Not surprisingly, agents often seek to sell houses as quickly as possible. The higher the sales price, the higher the fee. Therefore, in the aggregate, agents will work the hardest to sell houses in the best areas, those with highest prices, in order to maximize their commissions.

In addition to the problem that low-price areas are less attractive to agents, two other factors concerning real estate sales practices may be harmful to the future of an area.

First, real estate agents' actions may be based on their own conclusions that a neighborhood is declining. Acting on their decline expectations, or on expectations about racial or ethnic changes, agents may steer certain buyers to other areas, thereby inadvertently weakening demand and fulfilling their own expectation: the neighborhood declines. One pattern of this kind is racial steering. White buyers looking for housing in a general location in a city may be steered away from integrated neighborhoods or those experiencing some level of racial change. Obviously, if only nonwhite buyers are shown an area, the area will become predominantly nonwhite. While racial change does not equate with neighborhood decline, steering, by definition, reduces aggregate demand because important segments of the market are excluded.

Second, steering sometimes is a strategy used to enhance short-term sales and commissions. It may be profitable for real estate agents to have a neighborhood undergo a racial or ethnic change so that sales will increase. Existing residents are urged to leave the neighborhood before property values decline. Such blockbusting techniques can be extremely harmful and can cause serious disruption to the housing market in an area.[24]

Despite these instances of potentially damaging actions, real estate agents are an essential private-sector group to include in neighborhood improvement efforts. City officials should work with real estate agents to learn the agents' perceptions of demand for an area and their thoughts about the area's future. Equally important, city officials should communicate the city's plans and investment programs for an area so that agents can factor the city's contribution into their expectations. Over the long run, agents find it desirable to work with city government to help stabilize an area and to increase property values.

Neighborhood groups

City governments and neighborhood groups usually have, at best, an arms-length relationship and often a confrontational one. The first priority for organized neighborhood groups is to get all that they can from city government in the form of capital improvements, city services, or improved housing. At times this can produce cautious and noncommunicative local public officials, working hard to insulate themselves from competing demands by neighborhood groups.

While understanding and respecting the posture of neighborhood groups, local officials need to involve them in recovery strategies. Despite the difficulties sometimes associated with neighborhood involvement, it is essential for two reasons.

First, organized neighborhood groups—the leaders and the membership—are critically concerned with improving their neighborhoods. They personally are potential reinvestors in their areas, and they have the ability to influence other neighborhood residents to reinvest. Strong neighborhood groups can create a climate of reinvestment through self-help and cooperative efforts.

Second, good neighborhood leaders often have perceptions about the kind of program that is needed to stimulate reinvestment and can provide important grass-roots feedback to city officials as to whether a program aimed at neighborhood change is actually producing the desired results.

Specific roles that neighborhood groups can play vary greatly, depending on their organization and sophistication. In addition to general neighborhood advocacy, neighborhood groups can market and promote reinvestment to existing residents, including explaining the application and processing procedures for city-sponsored financing programs. They can attract and welcome newcomers to the area. They often can be more successful than city officials in persuading problematic property owners, lenders, or real estate agents to cooperate in the program. Neighborhood groups can be involved actively in marketing a neighborhood to potential residents and marketing a city's loan program to existing residents to urge their participation. They can provide peer pressure so other homeowners are encouraged to rehabilitate their properties. In addition, neighborhood groups can generate the neighborhood pride that helps stimulate reinvestment.

Neighborhood groups, often in the form of nonprofit or local development corporations, can play significant roles in neighborhood recovery by developing and implementing self-help efforts. The Neighborhood Housing Services (NHS) program is such an effort.

With the flexibility of CDBG funds, many cities also are working closely with local neighborhood development corporations that are conducting such programs.[25] One development in this area is the Local Initiatives Support Corporation (LISC), a national nonprofit enterprise that helps selected local organizations attract new private and public resources to revitalize communities. LISC's objective is to aid up to one hundred groups to work toward community improvement. To qualify for LISC aid, "a group should show a balanced strategy designed to attract stable, responsible, and credit-worthy new families while offering help to those that remain."[26] The LISC-funded neighborhood corporations are very sophisticated and able; they may be at the leading edge, enabling neighborhood groups to become more fully responsible for the neighborhood side of local housing.

City government

City government involvement in neighborhood recovery is essential in at least three critical roles:

1. Providing the leadership to bring together and change the attitudes and opinions of lenders, real estate agents, and neighborhood groups
2. Using public dollars—both capital improvement dollars and low-interest loan and grant dollars that go directly for housing—to stimulate reinvestment, and using public funds to leverage private dollars
3. Improving city services to enhance the livability of the neighborhood.

Neighborhood residents and the private sector typically look to local government to take the lead in developing the strategies to change neighborhoods and to improve housing and neighborhood conditions. Unfortunately, officials in some cities are not able to work effectively with the private sector because city officials have little understanding of the private sector or of neighborhood dynamics. All too often city officials see themselves as the center of the universe, automatically commanding the respect of the private sector. In addition, city officials often mistrust the profit motivation in the private sector. Only after these problems of communication are surmounted, and a common agenda found between city government and private sector, can all the pieces for neighborhood recovery be in place.

WHERE CITY GOVERNMENT FITS IN

As city officials grapple with neighborhood change and establish working relationships with lenders and neighborhood groups, they must also organize city government to operate, monitor, and evaluate programs. A local effort may be well thought out, but if it is operated poorly, it is unlikely to be effective.

City government must organize so that it can develop, implement, monitor, and evaluate a very difficult function conceptually, politically, and administratively. "Turning a neighborhood around" is more difficult to plan and carry out than repaving streets or providing clean water, simply because the state of the art has not evolved as fully as other municipal functions. It is difficult to know the level of resources needed to effect neighborhood change, to measure how much change is occurring, and to know when the program has succeeded to the point that the neighborhood no longer needs an improvement program.

Administratively, the function must be conducted so that local funds are delivered to the intended beneficiaries efficiently but without jeopardizing quality control or generating excess red tape. The last thing any local program needs is a scandal due to the misappropriation of public funds, but is it reasonable to conduct a program that costs as much in administrative funds to protect the public dollar as it makes available in loans or grants? How much is it worth in administrative costs and red tape to make a program 99 percent fraud free, rather than 90 percent fraud free? These are questions more often asked by quality control divisions of large corporations than by local governments, but they must be asked and answered by each local government.

City organization

The focus of control over housing rehabilitation and neighborhood improvement programs varies widely among cities. Often, city governments have a fragmented table of organization for housing programs that includes the general-purpose city government, a redevelopment authority, a housing authority, a community development department, a department of inspections, a department of relocation, and nonprofit corporations. Although no one structure is a priori preferable to another, the more diffused the roles and responsibilities, and the less clear the agency assignments, the more difficult it will be to administer a program effectively.

Unfortunately, many local programs have developed incrementally as federal programs have changed, and there often are many points of ambiguity and conflict. Some cities (e.g., Los Angeles) have divided responsibility geographically; others have created functional distinctions, with one agency responsible for policymaking, another for budget decisions and monitoring, and yet another for day-to-day program management. The desire to streamline operations, putting everything within one responsible agency, is often frustrated due to political or legal realities within a city. Nor is

Measuring neighborhood conditions During the seventies, cities discovered that they could move beyond simplistic projections of neighborhood change based on standard census data and windshield surveys. Other sources of data and means of analysis were developed not only to measure neighborhood condition at a given time but also to measure neighborhood changes that would affect housing markets. The best kinds of data for these purposes are those that can be gathered and analyzed on a regular basis to measure neighborhood trends—that is, how neighborhoods are changing relative to one another and to the city as a whole.

At least four measures are useful: market indicators, demographic information, attitudinal information, and physical change. (Social and health indicators also describe neighborhood conditions, but their effects are less well understood; therefore, they are less useful.) Neighborhoods are, fundamentally, housing markets, and measuring changes in economic health is the key.

Property values (real estate transaction prices): If sufficient demand exists for living in an area, the sales prices of housing should rise over time (assuming an inflationary economy), and prices in healthy neighborhoods typically increase faster than overall city averages. Sales price data, compiled annually, are an accurate measure of changes in values. Source: Usually available from real estate multiple listing or reporting service, or the city or county recorder of deeds.

Lending patterns: In normal markets, the patterns of lending by financial institutions can measure the effective demand for housing in the area—effective because the buyers of houses are able to afford the sales prices and are bankable. Lending patterns also indicate lenders' points of view about the future of the area. Source: Mortgage information is available from both the recorder of deeds and the Home Mortgage Disclosure Act (HMDA) reports prepared annually by lenders.

Building permits: The level of building permit activity is an indicator of reinvestment in the housing stock, and changes in dollar volume of rehabilitation reported through building permit applications is a useful monitoring device for changes in investment psychology. Source: Usually available in raw form from the city inspection department.

Property tax delinquency: Increases in property tax delinquency may indicate that an area is declining; that owners have cash flow problems in rental buildings and are disinvesting; or that property owners overall do not have enough disposable income to meet all housing costs. Skipping tax payments usually has less of an immediate penalty than nonpayment of the mortgage or utilities. Source: Usually available from city or county tax office.

Household income: Relative changes in median income among neighborhoods may indicate that those with more locational choices are moving to preferred locations, leaving less desirable locations to lower-income households. Assuming that, on balance, lower-income households have less disposable income for maintenance, this may indicate future physical deterioration. Source: Not readily available in time series except through R. L. Polk's Profiles of Change service.

Rent levels: Changes in the rent tenants pay is a good measure of change in housing market conditions. Source: Usually available by analysis of newspaper real estate rental ads.

Vacancy rates: Vacancy rates measure the overall level of demand for living in a neighborhood. Often an increase in vacancies indicates a relative decline in an area's attractiveness compared to other areas. Further, vacant units, if obviously vacant, can have a seriously negative effect on overall market psychology. Source: Available through R. L. Polk's Profiles of Change and from utility companies on shutoffs.

Other sources: Other "softer" but equally useful data about changes in neighborhood markets are available through surveys of real estate agents who can provide good information on the kinds of buyers they are finding for the area, the characteristics of sellers, and any important changes in the housing market.

The R. L. Polk Company provides a private service in over three hundred U.S. cities, measuring neighborhood change and conditions via Neighborhood Situation Ratings. These ratings are drawn from the annual collection of over a dozen key neighborhood measures, including residential units recently vacated, other vacant units, rates of household turnover, jobless heads of households, female heads of households with children, low-income households, and income by household.

Home Mortgage Disclosure Act (HMDA) reports are annual lending reports required of almost all federally regulated lending institutions. Institutions must list, by census tract, the number and principal amount of federally insured mortgages, conventional mortgages, home improvement loans, multifamily loans, and nonoccupant loans. Although such data are very difficult to manipulate, they can be an excellent source of information on mortgage lending practices by neighborhood.

centralizing all program responsibility always wise. The negotiations that occur among agencies partially responsible for program development and implementation are often a useful tempering device, distilling programs to their best common denominator.

Organizational decisions should be made in the context of program performance and administrative costs. First, a city should determine whether its program is accomplishing its goals. If it is not, then the organizational structure should be analyzed. Of course, cities also should routinely be asking whether the same performance could be achieved at a reduced public cost.

The CDBG program, and the increased local program flexibility, led to city organizational changes as well. Functions that had been carried out by separate redevelopment authorities were taken over by the general unit of local government in some cases. Departments of housing or community development were created. In Baltimore, all functions were under one department, the Department of Housing and Community Development, which handled renewal, CDBG, zoning, housing inspection, relocation, housing management, and economic development. With strong leadership and centralized management, Baltimore was able to move aggressively on its housing and neighborhood and downtown problems during the 1970s in a way that gave the city a national reputation for progress.

Program monitoring

Data on ongoing activities must be collected and analyzed on a routine basis. City government is, directly or indirectly, involved in housing rehabilitation, and its operations should be run in as businesslike a manner as possible. Program performance data must be reviewed and analyzed because the core problems may not be the same as the symptomatic problems. For example, a program manager may complain that his or her efforts are suffering because not enough owners in a neighborhood want to reinvest— the neighborhood investment mentality is poor. Even though this symptom may be present, the real problem for rehabilitation may be: (1) poor marketing (potential program participants may be unfamiliar with the program), (2) a shallow subsidy level (people who want to use the program cannot afford to do so), or (3) pessimistic perceptions (potential program participants are unwilling to invest in their properties because they fear that other owners in the neighborhood will not do so).

Evaluation and modification

Program success measures vary. If the objective is to change a neighborhood housing market, then the measures described earlier and in the accompanying sidebar are important indicators of success or failure. If the program is focused less on neighborhood change and more on assistance to low- and moderate-income owners to improve properties, then the number of properties improved for the intended beneficiaries is the more appropriate indicator.

The feedback from monitoring and evaluating data should result in program modifications and decisions to terminate some programs and begin others, based on their success or failure. As was pointed out earlier, two of the most difficult decisions that city government needs to make are the population it intends to serve with a program and the neighborhoods to target. These decisions are an intricate mix of professional and political judgments about public policy. Politically, it is difficult for city government to target all its resources into one neighborhood while ignoring others, especially if the city council is elected by district. Likewise, it is often difficult to continue a program long enough in one area to bring about a change before pressure mounts to move on to another area or another population group.

The monitoring and evaluation process can provide the information needed to modify programs so that, in fact, a program is as effective as possible in an area and provides indications about when it can be phased out. Phasing out a program in a targeted area requires careful analysis to make certain that the withdrawal of the program will not cause any market disruption in the area and thus reduce property values.

Program modifications should also be made periodically on the basis of changes in interest rates in the general money market. For example, a program that begins by providing an interest subsidy, reducing rates from market rates of 12 percent to 3 percent, perhaps should be modified if market rates jump to over 15 percent, since the program cannot provide financial assistance to the same number of units with the larger spread between rates.

As cities learn and share more among themselves, the state of the art will advance so that neighborhood programs can be more fully integrated into a comprehensive and permanent local housing function—one involving the full use of the city's development and taxing powers to achieve advanced and livable communities. This approach is more fully explored in Chapter 5.

1   Anthony Downs, *Neighborhoods and Urban Development* (Washington, D.C.: Brookings Institution, 1981), p. 10.

2   Adrienne Levatino-Donaghue, *The Rehabilitation Profession* (Washington, D.C.: National Association of Housing and Redevelopment Officials, 1979), p. 6.

3   Roger S. Ahlbrandt, Jr., *Flexible Code Enforcement: A Key Ingredient in Neighborhood Preservation Programming* (Washington, D.C.: National Association of Housing and Redevelopment Officials, 1976), pp. 13–16.

4   Elizabeth Howe, "Code Enforcement in Three Cities: An Organizational Analysis," *Urban Lawyer* 13 (winter 1981): 65–88.

5   Ibid., p. 87.

6   Ibid.

7   Ahlbrandt, *Flexible Code Enforcement,* pp. 28–34.

8   William G. Grigsby, "Economic Aspects of Housing Code Enforcement," *Urban Lawyer* 3 (fall 1971): 533–37.

9   Alan S. Penkower, "The Pittsburgh Housing Court: Catalyst for Effective, Comprehensive Code Enforcement," *Building Official and Code Administrator,* January 1978, p. 26.

10 The federal Neighborhood Development Program and the Model Cities Program both added to the federal controls and focus on neighborhood improvement efforts.

11 For case studies of such approaches, see: Ahlbrandt, *Flexible Code Enforcement.*

12 Urban Systems Research and Engineering Inc., *Creating Local Partnerships: The Role of the Urban Reinvestment Task Force in Developing Neighborhood Housing Services Organizations* (Washington, D.C.: U.S. Department of Housing and Urban Development, 1980), pp. 46–48.

13 John F. Weis et al., *Dividing the Pie: Resource Allocation to Urban Areas* (Boston, Mass.: City of Boston, 1980), p. 9.

14 For a recapitulation of this theory, see: Downs, *Neighborhoods and Urban Development,* pp. 61–71.

15 See, for example: Roger S. Ahlbrandt, Jr., and Paul C. Brophy, *Neighborhood Revitalization: Theory and Practice* (Boston: Lexington Books, 1976); P. Clay, *Neighborhood Revitalization: Issues, Trends, and Strategies* (Cambridge, Mass.: MIT Urban Studies Department, 1978); Rolf Goetze, *Building Neighborhood Confidence: A Humanistic Strategy for Urban Housing* (Cambridge, Mass.: Ballinger, 1976); Rolf Goetze, *Understanding Neighborhood Change: The Role of Expectations in Urban Revitalization* (Cambridge, Mass.: Ballinger, 1979); and C. Levin et al., *Neighborhood Change: Lessons in the Dynamics of Urban Decay* (New York: Praeger, 1976).

16 Rolf Goetze and Kent W. Colton, "The Dynamics of Neighborhoods: A Fresh Approach to Understanding Housing and Neighborhood Change," *Journal of the American Planning Association,* April 1980, pp. 184–94.

17 Goetze, *Understanding Neighborhood Change,* p. 34.

18 Ahlbrandt and Brophy, *Neighborhood Revitalization,* pp. 53–61.

19 See also: Rolf Goetze, *Neighborhood Monitoring and Analysis: A New Way of Looking at Urban Neighborhoods and How They Change* (Washington, D.C.: U.S. Department of Housing and Urban Development, 1980).

20 ACTION-Housing, Inc., *The Neighborhood Housing Services Model: A Progress Assessment of the Related Activities of the*

Urban Reinvestment Task Force (Washington, D.C.: U.S. Department of Housing and Urban Development, 1975), pp. 31–52.

21 Ibid.

22 John Tomer, "The Mounting Evidence on Mortgage Redlining," *Urban Affairs Quarterly* 15 (June 1980): 488–501.

23 For a fuller description of public-lender coordination, see: Michael M. Ehrman, *Making Local Rehabilitation Work: Public-Private Relationships* (Washington, D.C.: National Association of Housing and Redevelopment Officials, 1978).

24 "Blockbusting: A Novel Statutory Approach to an Increasingly Serious Problem," *Columbia Journal of Law and Social Problems* 7 (summer 1971): 538–78.

25 For a synopsis of some of these activities, see: U.S., Department of Housing and Urban Development, Office of Neighborhoods, Voluntary Associations, and Consumer Protection, *Neighborhood Self-Help Case Studies: Abstract of Report on Revitalization Project* (Washington, D.C.: U.S. Department of Housing and Urban Development, 1980).

26 *The Local Initiatives Support Corporation: A Private-Public Venture for Community and Neighborhood Revitalization* (New York: Ford Foundation, Office of Reports, 1980).

Local implementation: a case study of Pittsburgh's North Side

Among the many examples of successful neighborhood recovery programs conducted by local governments, Pittsburgh's North Side Revitalization Program provides a case study of a comprehensive effort that involved all the key actors in a multiyear program.[1]

In mid-1977, Pittsburgh's newly elected mayor, Richard S. Caliguiri, launched a comprehensive, neighborhood-oriented recovery program. The first and most important decision was that the housing and neighborhood improvement program had to be premised on private-sector investment rather than physical improvement of the housing stock.

Disinvestment in Pittsburgh was of concern because of a population paradox. Despite being the nation's third largest corporate headquarters city, with a strong, thriving downtown, the city lost 110,000 people from 1970 to 1980, reducing the population to 410,000 from a 1960 peak of 604,000. The city government therefore set as its primary goal the implementation of programs that would improve the quality and desirability of housing and neighborhoods for existing residents and potential newcomers.

The city's strategy was two-fold: first, the development of a set of programs to protect and improve the generally sound housing in the city, and second, the concentration of program funds and city efforts in neighborhoods that could be moved, with the public assistance, from a disinvestment to a reinvestment situation.

Pittsburgh's North Side, a major target area, consisted of six contiguous neighborhoods that originally formed the heart of the old city of Allegheny, annexed by the city of Pittsburgh in 1907. Each of the neighborhoods had major features in common: much of the housing was built in the late 1800s and early 1900s, with fine exterior and interior architectural detailing, and the areas were racially and economically integrated. The area had approximately 5,000 properties; 400 were vacant and vandalized at the start of the program, and another 2,000 needed moderate or substantial rehabilitation.

Median residential sales prices were considerably below the comparable city averages for 1974–1978. In 1978 the median residential sales price in the area was $15,800, compared with $31,900 citywide, and analysis showed the overall area to be in transition.

A consultant's report in 1978 indicated that "the time is ripe for a major initiative to physically and economically revitalize the City's North Side neighborhoods." The report stated that public intervention into the North Side housing market could assure that:

1. Revitalization proceeds at a fast enough pace to revise a pattern of decline and to assure substantial completion in the foreseeable future
2. Revitalization results in long-term economic and racial integration of the neighborhoods, encouraging middle- and upper-income families to move in while enabling lower- and moderate-income families to remain
3. Revitalization translates into economic opportunities for lower-income and minority persons
4. Revitalization occurs in a manner that is sensitive to the historic character of the area.

City officials were in agreement with the consultant. Parts of the neighborhood, the area called the Mexican War Streets, had begun a spontaneous recovery. With help from the nonprofit Pittsburgh History and Landmarks Foundation, historically sensitive restoration of older Victorian homes was under way. This recovery was far enough along that a neighborhood–city sponsored "great house sale" of vacant units at $100 each in the area immediately adjoining the Mexican War Streets in 1977 drew 1,100 prospective buyers for thirty-two houses. Demand seemed to be strong.

Other parts of the area, however, were not faring as well. Perry South, immediately to the north of the Mexican War Streets, had a declining housing market, caused by (1) the impact on the public school system of a large public housing community immediately adjoining the neighborhood, and (2) racial steering on the part of real estate agents who had largely stopped showing the neighborhood to prospective white buyers. The neighborhood had generally sound and very affordable housing, however.

City officials, then, saw a need for public intervention. Without it, two scenarios were possible. On the one hand, the decline in parts of the area would thwart the recovery of the Mexican War Streets and the immediately adjoining area. On the other, the area would gentrify, and long-time low- and moderate-income residents would be forced out. To resolve this dilemma, the city began to develop ideas for a housing reinvestment program that would facilitate recovery without displacement. Each of the six neighborhoods was represented by a neighborhood association, and the city conducted a series of meetings with these groups to develop a strategy for housing reinvestment and neighborhood improvement. Meetings were also held with lending institutions and real estate agents to exchange ideas about appropriate approaches. These discussions led in late 1978 to a comprehensive reinvestment program with the following components:

Below-market-rate first mortgage loans: The city's Urban Redevelopment Authority floated $28.3 million in tax-exempt mortgage revenue bonds to underwrite mortgages at 8.5 percent and 12 percent. These mortgages were based on the assumption that if the neighborhood had a supply of below-market-rate financing, two effects would be felt. First, the neighborhood would have a competitive advantage over other parts of the city and the suburbs, thereby making it more attractive for newcomers to buy and invest in the area. Second, the cheaper funds would make the neighborhood more affordable for persons who could not otherwise carry the costs of purchase and rehabilitation in the area. Although the program was designed to offer interest rates about 3 to 4 points below market, the actual spread under market was about 6 to 8 points, due to hefty increases in market interest rates during the 1979–1981 credit squeeze. Mortgages were provided throughout the area with no maximum income level established for eligibility. Both homeowners and investors were urged to participate.

Equity participation loans: Using a special allocation of urban development action grant and CDBG funds, the Urban Redevelopment Authority provided special second mortgages called equity participation loans. These were of two types. Deferred equity participation loans were used to reduce the amount of first mortgage principal to be borrowed by a low- or moderate-income participant. Twenty percent of the principal was lent to the borrower on a deferred payment basis in an effort to make housing purchase and rehabilitation more affordable. This special loan was due only when the property was resold and was subordinate to the first mortgage and the owner's down payment. The loan is payable, without interest, at the time the property is resold, provided sufficient proceeds are available from the sale to pay it. The second type, installment equity participation loans, were made available to any buyer at the same interest rate as the first mortgage in the event that the costs of property rehabilitation exceeded the after-rehabilitation appraised value.

Rent subsidies: To help prevent displacement of low- and moderate-income persons, the city targeted new, substantial rehabilitation and moderate rehabilitation Section 8 subsidies in the area. Overall, the city targeted three hundred units of this type to the neighborhood.

Other city rehabilitation programs: The city targeted citywide rehabilitation programs for moderate rehabilitation of owner-occupied and rental units so that existing low- and moderate-income persons could benefit. Over four hundred low- and moderate-income households used these programs during the revitalization effort.

Public improvements: Urban development action grant funds were allocated to make needed public improvements in the area to encourage property owners to invest.

Marketing: City officials understood that, as with any other product, the marketing of the neighborhood could increase the number of people who would "buy"—in this case in the form of investing in the neighborhood.

Relocation services: Although the city's intention was to avoid displacement, the high volume of purchase and rehabilitation meant that some residents would have to be either temporarily or permanently relocated elsewhere in the neighborhood. CDBG funds were allocated to cover the cost.

Neighborhood associations, lenders, and real estate agents were consulted frequently as the program was developed, and each had a role. The program was designed as a "private-sector" model—that is, the program procedures sought to tie into the normal real estate sale and mortgage process.

Lenders played a key role because they originated and serviced the first and second mortgage loans for the Urban Redevelopment Authority and were paid fees to do so. Twelve commercial banks, savings and loan associations, and mortgage bankers participated. Each first mortgage required a loan-to-value ratio of 75 percent or less, or required private or federal mortgage insurance. Lenders were asked to use their normal underwriting and commitment procedures, and they were free to promote their loan availability as they saw fit. The lenders were invited to participate in the program at a formal meeting attended by the mayor. Data on the recent history of mortgage lending and real estate prices were presented so that lenders unfamiliar with the area could have information that was based more on facts than on simplistic perceptions.

Real estate agents also were briefed on how to assemble packages for submission to the participating lenders. These agents were permitted to advertise the fact that properties in the area had special financing available, which they promptly did.

Neighborhood groups were involved fully. As the program began, six separate groups formed a federation, the North Side Development Alliance, which, through a memorandum of agreement with the city, took on two major responsibilities. First, the group monitored the program and provided advice to the city on overall program progress. Under the terms of the memorandum of agreement, city–neighborhood group meetings were held at least monthly. Second, the alliance supervised a neighborhood and program marketing effort to inform residents of the program, invite their participation, and market the program to potential newcomers. Offices with specially trained staff were established in each neighborhood.

The city was responsible for overall conduct of the program, for implementation of the public works component, and for administration of the rehabilitation component. All properties undergoing rehabilitation were inspected prior to loan closing to ensure that the proposed work included correcting any major code violations. Detailed work write-ups, however, were not performed, and program participants had wide discretion for the work to be done and the selection of the contractor.

Results achieved; lessons learned: The program was started in December 1979 as a two-year effort. By the end of 1980, virtually all of the mortgage funds had been committed; by the end of 1981, only a few special projects for which funds had been reserved remained.

The expenditure of the mortgage funds and the equity participation loans in such a short time showed that demand for living in the neighborhood was stronger than had been estimated and that private-sector operation could work effectively to process loans. The mortgage funds were sufficient to finance the purchase, or purchase and rehabilitation, of over seven hundred units, and many more property owners waited for another round of funding from the city.

The effects were dramatic. Visually, the quantity of rehabilitation was enough that neighborhood improvement became obvious; it was clear to the casual observer that the rate of improvement was accelerating. Real estate sales prices bore this out. The rate of change in sales prices from 1979 through 1981 was 17 percent, compared with 6.5 percent for the city overall. Appraisals went up, and the program met its first goal of causing recovery to occur.

At the same time, careful monitoring of displacement showed that the program was not forcing people out of the area. Of the ninety-one relocation cases handled, eighty-two were relocated within the targeted area—that is, moved from one residence to another but not displaced from the neighborhood.

However, the open operation of the system, the private-sector approach, was not without problems.

First, much to the dismay of neighborhood groups, people tended to buy in the stronger parts of the neighborhood, leaving some sectors without strong demand. While this may seem to follow normal recovery theory, it was disappointing to a neighborhood group to realize that some parts of the area would still need considerable help after the funds were gone.

Second, the most difficult properties—those that had been vacant and vandalized for years and were deterrents to neighborhood improvement—were the most difficult to sell, due to the availability of occupied properties that could be purchased and rehabilitated at lower cost and with less effort. At the end of the two-year program period, many vacant structures still existed.

Third, tension existed between the neighborhood groups and the city concerning the amount of public control over lending. The city had invited the lenders to participate based on a hands-off approach by the city government. Shortly after the program began, however, the neighborhood groups sought to modify the program to steer and allocate the flow of mortgage funds on other than a market basis. When some program changes were made to satisfy the neighborhood, some lenders reacted negatively.

Fourth, despite factual evidence to the contrary, some neighborhood leaders alleged that the program was causing displacement. Considerable time and effort were required to correct the impression.

One lesson of the North Side Revitalization Program concerns the potential deleterious effects of abandoned and vacant units. Although program designers hoped that the worst properties in the area would be financed and rehabilitated, this was slow to happen. Specific city intervention was necessary to steer some of the mortgage funds into the structures needing rehabilitation most. Perhaps city officials should have included specific incentives for buyers to rehabilitate vacant units, so as to steer program funds to the highest-priority units from the beginning.

A second lesson is that if one objective of neighborhood recovery is to increase property values across the board, then the levels of investment per property must be monitored. While it may be beneficial in some areas to permit an owner to invest more than the after-rehabilitation appraisal, in other instances the overinvestment may have no long-term effect on the market, suggesting that funds could have been used better elsewhere. Controlling the level of investment represents a significant trade-off, however, because it would require public-sector intervention in each deal.

Third, the role of neighborhood groups in the design and implementation of the program must be carefully considered. Neighborhood leadership can be extremely helpful in designing a program that meets neighborhood needs and in monitoring program performance. Responsibilities for implementing the program, however, must be carefully correlated to the neighborhood groups' skills and capacities.

Overall, the program was intended to bring together, under city government auspices, the key elements at a sufficient scale to make the recovery of a neighborhood possible over a two-year period. At the end of 1981, the program had accomplished much of what it had set out to do, and the city was continuing the cooperative working relationships with lenders, real estate agents, and neighborhood groups to develop the next phase.

1 For a fuller description of Pittsburgh's programs, see: Pittsburgh Department of Housing, *Housing: A Four Year Report* (Pittsburgh: Department of Housing, 1981); and Mary K. Reilly and Paul C. Brophy, *Reinvestment in Pittsburgh: Three Case Studies* (Washington, D.C.: U.S. Conference of Mayors, 1980).

Chapter 3

Developing and managing housing for unmet needs

The development and management of housing in the United States tradition-ally have been reserved for private enterprise. Governmental support for housing has been oriented toward helping the private home building indus-try procure development capital and helping families attain home ownership or rental housing through a government guarantee of individual or multi-family housing mortgages. Public involvement has been short-range, usu-ally initial development and financing, except in the case of default on mortgages. In addition, government housing assistance has been provided overwhelmingly by the federal government. Local government participation in housing development for years was largely limited to the regulatory area —the zoning and building permits required of private builders to locate and construct new housing.

The principle of government support for "unmet housing needs" in the form of "assisted housing" was launched in the 1930s with the initiation of the public housing program. A new concept was introduced into American housing—special assistance to low-income families who could not afford the housing provided by the private market.

The public housing program, including its financing mechanisms and relationships, dominated the assisted housing picture for over thirty years; the roles of major participants are summarized in Figure 3–1. The relation-ships of the public housing program both to the traditional private mortgage market and to general-purpose local governments (cities and counties) are limited. The fundamental financing instrument is a long-term bond issued by the local housing authority on the national bond market, with the assistance of private bond counsels and bond underwriters; there is no direct relation-ship to the local private financial community. The ties of the city or county government to the local housing authority are those of oversight and support-

Participant	Financing development	Site development and construction	Management and maintenance
Local public housing agency	30-year tax-exempt bonds issued by local public housing agency	Contracts with private developers and oversees construction	Manages development; pays in lieu taxes to local government
General-purpose local government	Provides exemption from local real estate tax	Approves project for federal assistance and site location under Housing Assistance Plan (HAP)	Provides municipal services spelled out in cooperation agreement with PHA; may contribute funds for project modernization
State government	. . .	. . .	. . .
Federal government	Provides exemption from federal income tax for bond purchasers; HUD guarantees annual contribution equal to debt service	Inspects development	HUD provides operating assistance to keep rents within reach of low-income families; oversees management; provides modernization funds
Private financial community (banks, developers, foundations, etc.)	Local PHA bonds issued on national bond market, through private entities	. . .	. . .
Private management community	. . .	. . .	Some local agencies contract with private entities for management or maintenance services

Figure 3–1 Major elements in federally assisted public housing, by major participants, 1982.

ing services; public housing is not typically a part of municipal operations, for either capital or operating budgets. Perhaps the most unusual feature of public housing, in contrast to earlier modes of government housing assistance, is the long-term public involvement: public housing is owned and managed by the local housing authority for a long period of time. Until the 1960s federal assistance for public housing was restricted to an annual contribution equal to debt service on the bonds. Until that time, the combination of tax-exempt financing and local tax abatement was sufficient to keep public housing rents within the reach of low-income families.

It is the thesis of this chapter that local government involvement in both the development and management of assisted housing is rapidly changing. A new and broader function is evolving, closely linked to local private financial institutions as well as private and nonprofit managers and directly tied to local physical and economic development objectives. While these new local initiatives do not replace a strong housing role by the federal government, or negate an increased housing role by state government, they do tell us that local government has a unique housing responsibility, which it is beginning to assume. This chapter describes the forces that generated this development and the new public activities that local governments are taking on.

FORCES BEHIND THE NEW LOCAL ROLE

Beginning in the early 1970s, a number of converging trends placed the traditional approaches to assisted housing under severe constraints. In addition, there was a growing body of experience demonstrating that "housing assistance" is an essential component in achieving priority community development goals. Basically, these trends include (1) the continuous changes in methods of federal housing assistance and frustrations with the uncertain levels of federal funding; (2) the collapse of the national tax-exempt bond market, as well as revolutionary changes in traditional housing finance markets; and (3) new experience in cities on the linkage between assisted housing and efforts to conserve neighborhoods and generate new economic activity.

Changes in federal housing assistance

Chapter 1 documents the erratic and changing nature of federal housing assistance: from 1954 through 1974, the basic housing assistance mechanisms for lower-income families (excluding public housing) were changed or substantially altered at least ten times. There was little opportunity to gain operating program experience or to foster a well-administered federal program of oversight. This led to some well-publicized examples of poor administration or misuse of funds and increased questioning of federal housing assistance, particularly in Congress. Funding for housing assistance programs, always a target, came under increasing pressure in the federal budget process. In January 1973, the Nixon administration imposed a moratorium on all new federal housing assistance. It was not lifted until the creation of the Section 8 housing assistance program in the 1974 Housing and Community Development Act.

The Section 8 program, building on experience in leasing and on interest in housing allowances for families, incorporated a new mechanism for federal assistance. Federal payments, while going directly to the housing provider, were calculated on the basis of family need—the difference between what a family could afford to pay for housing (at 15 to 25 percent of family income) and total housing cost (a "fair market rent" in the area). Unlike earlier mechanisms, the arrangement provided no federal support for financing the housing, other than the option of FHA mortgage insurance; there was no federal guarantee of bonds or subsidy to reduce interest rates. Housing developers were expected to arrange their own financing through private lending sources. The new program established a new set of financing methods and relationships between public and private entities, which are summarized in Figure 3–2 (Section 8 new construction and substantial rehabilitation) and Figure 3–3 (Section 8 existing housing).

As the Section 8 new construction and substantial rehabilitation program gained momentum, it soon became clear that the long-term budget authority committed by the federal government to meet the annual assistance payments was reaching levels of concern for federal budget makers.

The funding of assisted housing is distinguished from the budgetary treatment of nearly every other federal program in two important ways: (1) in funding lower-income housing assistance, Congress decides how much to add to a growing base rather than deciding what the ongoing level of assistance should be; and (2) assisted housing programs are funded on a multi-year basis—when new commitments are made, an amount of spending authority must be set aside that is assumed to be sufficient to pay the subsidy costs over the lives of these commitments.[1] The appropriations act for fiscal 1981 added $30 billion in new long-term budget authority in the federal budget, increasing the sum of all outstanding obligations to more than $220 billion. The former deputy director of the Congressional Budget Office summarized the net impact of this funding as follows: "As both the outlay increases resulting from earlier commitments and the volume of outstanding obligations become increasingly apparent, the budget pressures on assisted housing programs are likely to intensify."[2] This was an accurate harbinger of budget-cutting actions proposed by the Reagan administration beginning in fiscal 1982 and continuing into fiscal 1983. A program that is likely to be continued is the Section 202 loan program for elderly or

Participant	Financing development	Site development and construction	Management and maintenance
Local public housing agency	. . .	. . .	Local housing authority may be selected by private owner as manager
General-purpose local government	May provide abatement from local real estate taxes; provides local permits	Approves project for federal assistance and site location under HAP	. . .
State government	May provide abatement of property taxes	. . .	. . .
Federal government	May provide FHA mortgage insurance or GNMA tandem support; contracts with owner to provide housing assistance payments for lower-income families for 20 years; owner receives benefits under federal tax laws	Approves plan for financing and development; FHA inspects its insured projects	Approves management plan and choice of property manager; inspects property within six months after completion and annually thereafter
Private financial community (banks, developers, foundations, etc.)	Private owner/developer procures financing on the private market; may utilize FHA mortgage insurance or GNMA secondary mortgage support	Owner proceeds with construction and oversees completion	Owner prepares management plan and selects property manager subject to HUD approval
Private management community	. . .	. . .	Private or nonprofit management firm may be selected by private owner as manager

Figure 3–2 Major elements of federally assisted Section 8 new construction and substantial rehabilitation (private owners), by major participants, 1982.

Participant	Assistance method	Moderate rehabilitation (if applicable)	Management and maintenance
Local public housing agency	Contracts with federal government for assistance; administers local program	Facilitates rehab financing	Oversees condition of private housing leased before occupancy and annually thereafter
General-purpose local government	Approves Section 8 existing assistance as part of Housing Assistance Plan (HAP) or separately	May assist in financing moderate rehabilitation with CDBG funds or other ways	. . .
State government	May receive allocations of funds and perform functions similar to local PHAs	. . .	. . .
Federal government	Executes a contract with state or local agency to receive assistance funds and administer the program	Approves plan for moderate rehab; provides appropriate term of contract assistance	Monitors local compliance with federal assistance contract
Private financial community (banks, developers, foundations, etc.)	. . .	Local lending institutions may provide rehab loans to owners	. . .
Private management community	Private owner enters into housing assistance payments contract with state or local public agency and agrees to lease to lower-income households	Procures rehab loan and carries out rehab activity	Maintains unit in good condition and meets other occupancy requirements of contract

Figure 3–3 Major elements of federally assisted Section 8 existing housing (leasing private housing for lower-income households), by major participants, 1982.

handicapped persons. The financing mechanisms and public/private relationships for the Section 202 program as of 1982 are shown in Figure 3–4. In place of the other existing housing assistance programs (Section 8 and public housing) the administration in early 1982 proposed the substitution of a modified Section 8 housing certificate program to help families occupying existing private housing; this proposal was supported by the President's Commission on Housing.[3]

While the future directions of federal support for assisted housing are not yet clear, the changes and uncertainties of the 1970s and early 1980s indicate that almost exclusive reliance on federal assistance is at an end. State and local governments will have to assume added responsibilities if housing assistance is to continue at a significant level.

The revolution in housing finance

An informed professional in housing finance has stated that the 1980s will witness rapid change in housing finance that will be as significant, and perhaps as traumatic, as what occurred in the United States in the 1930s during the Great Depression. Signs of these changes have been evident since the mid-1960s.[4] The unique system of housing finance in the United States—composed of over 14,000 commercial banks, 4,000 savings and loan associations, almost 500 mutual savings banks, and over 21,000 credit unions—has been subjected to the shock of three costly housing cycles and is undergoing a fourth. The response to these events requires public and private cooperation similar to that in the 1930s, which produced new mortgage instruments and new federal institutions. Reform legislation on financial structure and regulation was passed by Congress in 1980, and further legislation is pending.[5]

The changes in housing markets in the 1970s have already left their toll on federally assisted housing programs. At the same time that the 1974 Housing and Community Development Act was requiring developers of new construction under the Section 8 program to seek their financing without federal support in the private market, forces were at work that severely limited financing possibilities, particularly escalating interest rates. The result was increasing difficulty in developing feasible financing packages. Government National Mortgage Association (GNMA) tandem funds made some Section 8 development possible through a combination of the secondary mortgage market and below-market (7.5 percent) interest rates. The supply of GNMA funds was, however, severely limited.

A major impact on the ability to finance newly constructed or substantially rehabilitated assisted housing was the virtual collapse of the tax-exempt bond market beginning in the mid-1970s.[6] Interest rates on tax-exempt bond offerings for housing soared up to 10 percent and above,

Participant	Financing development	Site development and construction	Management and maintenance
Local public housing agency	. . .	. . .	. . .
General-purpose local government	May provide exemption or abatement of local property taxes or low-cost land	Approves project for federal assistance under Housing Assistance Plan (HAP) or otherwise; provides local permits	. . .
State government	May provide exemption from or abatement of property taxes	. . .	. . .
Federal government	Provides below-market interest rate direct loan to eligible sponsor up to 40 years; may provide supplemental assistance to lower-income households; may involve FHA mortgage insurance	HUD approves development program and site	HUD oversees loan repayments and management
Private financial community (banks, developers, foundations, etc.)	Private consultants often assist nonprofit owners in preparing development package	. . .	Local social service agencies provide contract services
Private management community	Nonprofit private owner receives loan and initiates feasible development package	Nonprofit owner oversees development and construction	Nonprofit owner usually manages the development

Figure 3–4 Major elements of federally assisted Section 202 direct loan program for elderly or handicapped persons (nonprofit sponsor), by major participants, 1982.

precluding feasible financing. The issuance of permanent tax-exempt bonds for public housing development was suspended in 1974 because of high interest rates; developments under way were financed through the rollover of temporary notes. In 1980, HUD received congressional approval for permanent financing of backed-up public housing obligations through the Federal Financing Bank of the U.S. Department of the Treasury. A new financial mechanism—Section 11(b)—was developed for the issuance of tax-exempt bonds by local housing authorities on behalf of Section 8 developers; however, federal regulations on these instruments have constrained their use as a major vehicle for financing. Despite the uncertainties of the tax-exempt bond market, the first tax-exempt mortgage bonds for single-family housing were marketed by local governments and local public agencies in 1978; however, these bonds are also subject to erratic fluctuations in the tax-exempt bond market.

The prospect for additional federal support for housing in the nature of GNMA tandem funds or other federal credit resources is not bright. In fact, the Reagan administration has indicated its intent to severely curtail extensions of federal credit or loan guarantees for housing purposes. In late 1981 President Reagan announced a reduction in federal loan guarantee commitments for fiscal 1982 of $20.3 billion, of which $16 billion was in the GNMA program. In making this announcement, the president said that "this [GNMA reduction] and other administration policies will encourage and accelerate the development of a truly private secondary market for housing finance instruments."[7] This policy was carried forward in the administration's proposed 1983 HUD budget where GNMA tandem support is eliminated.

Conditions in the national mortgage market have had a particularly severe impact on financing new multifamily rental construction. Housing market analysts have pinpointed an "investment gap" reaching up to 23 percent in 1981 between the maximum new mortgage a rental housing developer could obtain, and the maximum cash down payment investors were willing to make in order to make the development feasible. In other words, the developers would be required to carry up to 23 percent of the total value of the project. In the opinion of these analysts, the "investment gap" can be eliminated only by a sharp reduction in the inflation rate or by higher rents— not an immediate prospect. Positive steps involving state and local government (as well as the federal government), however, could help sustain the drifting rental housing industry. These include tax abatement and access to sites not requiring extensive preparation.[8]

The keys to future assisted housing are (1) to identify the most viable financing mechanisms within the new, emerging system of private housing finance and (2) to develop innovative ways to fill the gaps left by private financing and limited federal housing assistance.

Assisted housing in community revitalization

As detailed in Chapter 1, federal housing assistance programs, initiated in the 1930s, were closely linked to the total physical and economic development of cities. Beginning with the "slum clearance" objective of the original public housing program; continuing with the efforts to relate housing to the urban renewal program; and culminating in the comprehensive approach to total community revitalization in the 1974 Housing and Community Development Act, the linking of housing assistance to total community improvement was a clear objective. It is no happenstance that the 1974 act required a local Housing Assistance Plan (HAP) in conjunction with the planning and programming required for the use of community development block grants (CDBGs).

Experience under the CDBG program since 1974 shows a growing use of these funds directly for housing purposes (largely housing rehabilitation). In the first three years of CDBG, the National Association of Housing and Redevelopment Officials (NAHRO) found that in a sample of entitlement communities, 26 percent used CDBG funds for acquisition of housing sites, housing site preparation, relocation of families, and similar activities; another 17 percent of these communities used CDBG funds for public housing repair and modernization.[9]

As the CDBG program has matured, expenditures for housing purposes have grown to complement those of the assisted housing programs. Under the three-year HAP goals established by entitlement communities in 1979, CDBG funds supplied 23 percent of all housing assistance, largely through rehabilitation of owner-occupied homes.[10] Thus, CDBG funds complement the use of other federally assisted housing programs, largely Section 8 and public housing, which go to assist low-income renter households.[11]

The most direct link between housing assistance and community development was launched by HUD in 1977 under the Section 8 neighborhood strategy areas (NSAs) program. This effort was designed to provide local governments with direct access to Section 8 assisted housing funds and to enable local governments to coordinate more closely the delivery of housing and community development services. Beginning with the first awards in 1978, 150 neighborhoods in 116 communities eventually participated, and 37,600 units of Section 8 substantial rehabilitation and 22,000 units of bonus new construction subsidy commitments were made.

In order to receive NSA designation, cities were required to (1) identify neighborhoods for concentrated improvement efforts; (2) develop comprehensive plans to identify housing rehabilitation and neighborhood improvement needs of proposed NSAs; (3) commit public resources to meet these needs over the five-year demonstration period; and (4) agree to provide resources and assistance to households displaced by Section 8 rehabilitation. In contrast to the regular Section 8 development process, NSA local governments are given responsibility for administering the Section 8 NSA housing program. That is, participating local governments are responsible for establishing Section 8 proposal selection criteria, soliciting proposals from owners and developers, selecting proposals, and assisting owners and developers in completing their proposals for approval by HUD. The NSA program assumes that cities have the knowledge of neighborhood conditions to select proposals that best meet neighborhood revitalization needs and can develop the expertise to assist owners, particularly owners of smaller rental properties, through the Section 8 development process.[12]

Another indication of the necessity for a direct link between assisted housing and the success of neighborhood revitalization was the allocation by HUD in August 1981 of 525 units of Section 8 moderate rehabilitation units and 475 units of Section 8 existing housing to the Neighborhood Reinvestment Corporation to support their neighborhood revitalization projects in selected cities.[13]

The push to coordinate and concentrate more resources in "targeted neighborhoods" comes from two sources. One is the concern of Congress and the administration that CDBG funds are disbursed in too random a fashion to achieve the national statutory objectives of revitalizing neighborhoods and communities. A report by the U.S. General Accounting Office in April 1981 called for still further efforts to target CDBG funds.[14] HUD's *Sixth Annual Community Development Block Grant Report* documents that "since 1979 the majority of CDBG Entitlement Cities have designated NSAs and have funded them with more than half of their CDBG grant funds."[15] This finding highlights the second force behind the move to coordinate and concentrate resources—particularly housing assistance and CDBG funds —that is, local communities themselves. The high priority given by most local communities to the conservation of existing housing and neighborhoods is now coupled with increasing recognition that assisted housing must be directly integrated into these efforts if they are to succeed.

An additional major component in the link between assisted housing and community revitalization is experience with the Urban Development Action Grant (UDAG) program. In terms of assisted housing, UDAG funds are not as constrained as CDBG funds; they can be utilized to support the direct financing and development of new assisted housing construction. As documented in Chapter 1, UDAG experience shows how a housing assistance component can be effectively linked to a wide variety of economic development initiatives. In the first two years, UDAG funds will be used to construct or rehabilitate 46,000 housing units; three-quarters of these are in neighborhood projects, about a fifth in commercial projects, and a small number in industrial projects. The form of housing assistance in UDAG varies, including interest subsidies for purchasers, loans and mortgages for developers, equity participation in the housing development, and defraying site development costs. As with neighborhood revitalization, economic development and revitalization is a high priority with most local governments.

THE LOCAL HOUSING DEVELOPMENT PROCESS

To take on a stronger role in assisted housing, local governments must learn about the private housing finance and development process as well as the sources and mechanisms of federal and state assistance. Above all, local governments must understand the character and resources of the local community itself and how all the available resources and participants can be brought together for housing development to the best advantage of the total community. These tasks require special knowledge and skills in local government staffing and strategic placement of this staffing in the local public structure.

The framework for finance and development

The key players in housing are landowners, developers, builders, mortgage lenders, permanent lenders, management agents, and facilitators. They represent local, state, and federal governments as well as local and national elements of the private sector. The way these players and resources are assembled makes up the basic elements of a *feasible* housing development. Figures 3–1 to 3–4 show how these elements are put together for public housing, Section 8 new construction, Section 8 existing housing, and Section 202 housing for the elderly or the handicapped. Figure 3–5 shows how the U.S. General Accounting Office has summarized the players, what they do, and their incentives within the context of the major federal housing assistance programs. A detailed GAO explanation, "Housing Production Incentives," appears in Appendix A.

Another way of looking at this process is shown in Figure 3–6, which is a matrix of financial strategies for multifamily housing—including both private finance and development mechanisms and public financial sources for community development, housing rehabilitation, neighborhood improvement, and economic revitalization. Figure 3–6 contains over forty different techniques.

Innovative local approaches

Increasingly, the key to putting together a feasible assisted housing development is to use local government resources to fill the gaps left by available private resources (particularly private lending) and available federal assistance. In November 1980 the Montgomery County (Maryland) Housing Opportunities Commission contracted for a report on "innovative program suggestions to preserve and expand the affordably-priced rental housing stock."[16] The subsequent report identified ideas for innovative programs that had been used or proposed in other localities and were particularly applicable to Montgomery County. Some of these programs are described in the following sections.

AIR RIGHTS HOUSING   High-rise, multi-unit rental structures are built above county-owned property in business districts (parking garages, police stations, fire and rescue stations, for example). Air rights are donated by the county to developers who agree: (1) to build rental units priced below certain limits; (2) to hold rent increases to a set level (perhaps indexed to the CPI); and (3) not to convert to condominiums for a minimum period (such as ninety-nine years).

CO-INVESTMENT   The county co-invests in development costs or purchase of existing property by providing up to some set proportion of the purchase price (such as 49 percent). The private owner is responsible for all property taxes, insurance, utilities, and maintenance. Upon resale, the county shares proportionately in the proceeds, and the funds are used for additional co-investment in properties. The balance of the financing can come from private lenders or other public sources.

CONVERSION RIGHTS   Owners acquire rights to convert existing rental units to condominiums on a unit-for-unit replacement basis. One conversion right is generated by each low- to moderate-income rental unit either newly constructed or added through conversion or rehabilitation (in projects of five or more units). Rights are transferable and may be sold.

FOUR-WAY PARTNERSHIPS   The county joins in broad-based partnerships with owners, tenants, and lenders to preserve selected multi-unit rental properties. Efforts are tailored to individual properties and may involve energy conservation improvements, improved security systems, restructuring of financing and taxes, and other measures to help keep units in affordable rental stock. The Neighborhood Reinvestment Corporation provides technical assistance and training and underwrites a substantial part of the initial program costs.

LIMITED EQUITY COOPERATIVES   The county assists tenants in forming cooperatives to purchase multi-unit buildings threatened by condominium conversion. Aided by low-interest loans supplied by the county, state, or federal government, tenants can purchase units with very low down payments ($100 to $500, for example, which can be paid in installments if necessary). Monthly payments are usually higher than before but can be largely offset by tax deductions. On resale, members of the cooperative are limited to recovering their initial down payment plus annual interest, thus minimizing future price increases.

MANUFACTURED HOME RENTALS ON IMPROVED PUBLIC LAND   Private developers install manufactured homes on vacant land donated or leased by the county at low cost. The county may also waive the developer's cost of infrastructure improvements or may extend the time for payment provided no change is made in the status of the units. Developers not only

Who they are and what they do	Incentives
Developer	
Conceives idea	10% BSPRA
Designs project	Can sell investment to profit motivated
Arranges financing	investor for about 20% of mortgage amount
Deals with owners	
Facilitates production	
Holds partial investment	
Builder	
Builds the project	Negotiated fee with developer usually 1% to 3% of mortgage amount
Profit motivated investors	
Provide money to developer; usually 15% to 20% of mortgage	Tax shelter: (1) accelerated depreciation, (2) construction period deductions, (3) rapid write-off if rehab
Supervise management agent	Opportunity for capital gain
	Some cash flow
Nonprofit sponsors	
Work with developer in conceiving idea	Provide housing for special groups such as needy families
Supervise management agent	Little equity required
Professional managers	
Screen applicants	Negotiated fee with owner
Manage daily operations	
Mortgage banker (FHA)	
Locates construction funds	Placement fee of 1.5% to 2.5% of mortgage
Locates permanent loans (usually GNMA)	amount
Sometimes services mortgage	Servicing fees
Evaluates project feasibility	
Applies for FHA insurance	
Monitors construction	
(MBS)	
Arranges "pass through certificates"	
State agency (SHFA)	
Evaluates project feasibility	Application fees
Lends construction funds by floating construction notes or other borrowings	0.5% to 1.5% of mortgage amount each month
Supervises construction	
Public bodies (11 (b))	
Distribute (sell) bonds	Usually public body is a "shell" entity created
Work with developer to achieve HAP needs	by the LHA and the developer to facilitate tax-exempt housing finance

Figure 3–5 Housing finance and development: the players and their incentives.

Who they are and what they do	Incentives
Bond underwriters (11 (b)) (SHFA)	
Distribute (sell) bonds	Underwriter's fee
Hire bond counsel for feasibility analysis and official statement	Gets spread between buying and selling prices
FNMA (FHA only)	
Borrows money to buy FHA insured mortgage	Interest earned on mortgage
Life insurance companies, banks, pension funds	
Purchase mortgage or mortgage-backed securities	Interest earned on mortgage
Life insurance companies, fire and casualty companies, banks, pension funds, individuals	
Purchase bonds, mortgages, or mortgage-backed securities	Interest earned on bonds, mortgages, or securities
GNMA	
Buys mortgages from mortgage bankers	Facilitate flow of funds to finance apartments for low- and moderate-income households
Resells mortgages to permanent lenders	
Guarantees timely payment of principal and interest (MBS)	
Syndicators	
Locate investors	Syndication fee
Bring developer and investors together	
Escrow funds	
Pay investors when due	
Bond counsel (11 (b)), (SHFA), (public housing)	
Prepares official statement	Bond counsel fee
Prepares bond resolution	
Renders legal advice	
May perform feasibility analysis for underwriter	
Trustee (11 (b)), (public housing)	
Ensures timely payment of bond principal and interest to bond holders	Initial fee of about $1,000 Yearly service fee of 0.5% of total obligations

Figure 3–5   (continued).

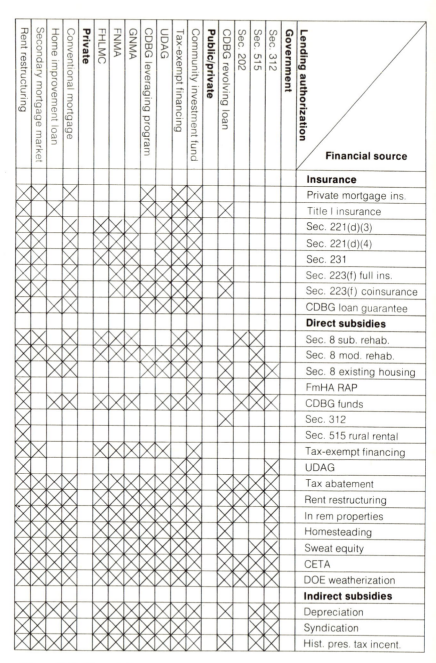

Figure 3–6 Financial sources for multifamily housing, by lending authorization, 1980.

must meet county standards for manufactured home construction and installation, but also must present acceptable site and landscaping plans. The deed requires that units be stationary and remain in rental status for a minimum of ten or twenty years. The county, using Section 8 or other funds, may subsidize a portion of the units for low-income occupancy. The remainder must be rented at agreed-upon maximum levels based on development costs (plus an annual increment, perhaps indexed to the CPI). Low-equity cooperative ownership is also a possibility.

TAX ABATEMENTS OR TAX DEFERRALS Developers are exempted from all property taxes for a certain period (such as ten to twenty years) on all new rental housing that meets county requirements as to number and size of units, rent levels, and so on. Units may not be converted to condominiums during the abatement period. Covenants in deeds maintain both controls and tax abatements in case of resale. An alternative to tax abatements is tax deferrals under similar conditions.

ADD-A-RENTAL UNIT IN SINGLE-FAMILY HOMES The county overrides existing zoning ordinances to allow inclusion of small rental units in single-family houses meeting minimum square footage requirements.

GRADUATED ASSISTANCE PROGRAM (GAP) The county provides graduated financial assistance to young moderate-income renters for six to ten years. Payments make up the gap between market rate rents and rents affordable by the families. As incomes rise, payments are decreased. After six to ten years, depending on incomes, the payments cease completely and repayment begins. GAP payments can be made for either rental or cooperative ownership; they go directly to the owner/developer or the cooperative association.

REDIRECTING INCREMENTAL TAX REVENUES The county determines the aggregate increment in local real estate taxes derived from increases in valuations due to condominium conversions. Thereafter, the total increment or a sizable proportion thereof (at least 50 percent) will be dedicated by the county to a special rental housing fund to pay for such purposes as below-market interest rate loans, property tax abatements, subsidies to rental developers, energy conservation grants and loans to owners of rental structures, rent supplements to individual low-income families, relocation services to elderly and other vulnerable households displaced by condo conversions, counseling and technical assistance to landlords to assist preservation of rental housing, and counseling and technical assistance to tenant cooperatives.

VARIABLE FEE PERMITS Charges for residential building permits vary with the degree to which units will serve existing needs. Permits for large developments of low- to moderate-priced rental units, for example, have a nominal cost. Fees for large luxury rentals or condominiums are much higher, and fees for small developments of either type, or intermediately priced developments, are somewhere in between.

OTHER INNOVATIONS Still further evidence of innovative local financing at the local level is documented by the Federal Home Loan Bank Board under its Community Investment Fund (CIF). A loose-leaf catalog of projects, entitled *Reaching Out,* contains condensed annotations of some seventy-three undertakings, including affirmative marketing, commercial revitalization, condominiums, cooperatives, counseling, energy, leveraging, multi-family units, new construction, partnerships, rehabilitation, rural lending, secondary markets, services corporations, and tax-exempt bonds. Many of these ventures involve public/private participation and demonstrate the new liaison between local government and the private financial community in the housing area.[17]

Profiles of innovative housing finance

Since the mid-1970s, there has been a remarkable emergence at the local level of innovative housing finance. This development has come not as a movement for a "public alternative" to the private mortgage system, but as a creative adaptation and extension of that private system. In fact, the success of these local programs has stemmed from their use of specific techniques that overcome barriers to private market operation.

Improvisation in individual city and state programs has now yielded an impressive (although not yet widely cataloged) array of "tools" that can focus the operation of any capital financing system. With the widespread future use of tax-exempt financing currently in doubt, these techniques and expertise in their use will assume even greater importance.

This emergence of local financing stands in contrast to the trends of the previous twenty years. During the 1960s and 1970s, federal policy supported "parallel" systems of financing for market rate and publicly assisted housing. Over time, these systems have moved apart and become rigid and insulated. Despite the fiscal capacity of both the private and FHA/GNMA systems to produce mortgages, increasing numbers of unserved subgroups have emerged. At the local level, the inability of these systems to work together to serve these groups—first-time buyers, buyers in target neighborhoods and historic preservation districts, buyers who plan substantial rehabilitation, and moderate-income renters and owners—has become a serious problem.

Innovation at the local level has involved a direct and specific "tinkering" with the larger system to attempt to bridge these gaps. Much as the UDAG program attempts to fill the 10 to 20 percent gap that would otherwise make a project unfeasible, local financing efforts have attempted to redirect the private mortgage financing system by that same 10 to 20 percent margin.

The program examples outlined at the end of this chapter were developed in the cities of St. Paul, Los Angeles, and Boston. They illustrate a further characteristic of the developing nature of such programs—they are directly tailored to the specific characteristics of the housing finance market in each locality. Thus, while affordability of housing is a national issue, many local characteristics and issues are unique. For example, the major issues in Los Angeles were basic affordability (especially critical given the extreme inflation of housing prices) and the open process by which the program was to be operated (use of multiple underwriters and lenders, lottery systems, price and speculation controls, and eligibility criteria). In contrast, while affordability remained a key issue in St. Paul, programs there emphasized neighborhood targeting, substantial rehabilitation, and the financing of projects that were already a part of the city's community development strategy. The Boston programs represent the link of housing to economic development packages.

These programs offer an additional contrast in alternative approaches to working with lenders and sources of capital—approaches based again on the local environment. The Los Angeles programs were developed in a state banking environment dominated by "superlenders" operating through a statewide branch banking system. St. Paul, however, utilized local lenders and underwriters combined with locally based private foundation capital. The relevant conclusion here is that many alternative financing solutions may be possible, but success is directly related to developing a program that recognizes and utilizes the local characteristics of the existing private financing environment.

Local capacity and management skills

The emerging blend of housing, land development, public and private financing, and local government revenues, expenditures, and services is forcing local government managers—and their private-sector colleagues—to redefine the skills needed to plan, finance, and develop housing. Specifically, the local government staffing for housing finance and development calls for persons with as much training and experience as possible in local government planning, community development, building design and construction, housing finance, "public housing" in the traditional sense of the term, and law. But that is not all. Overriding these professional and technical specialities is the need to put it all together—to facilitate, integrate, negotiate, compromise, and carry through—within a mélange of complementary and competing interests:

The city council or county board that is concerned about land
development, neighborhood reactions, and finding the money

Local facilitators and partners Understanding the historic and current practices of local financial institutions is necessary to facilitate working with the institutions that help deliver local housing finance. Local officials, because of many social and economic factors, are now facilitators and partners, rather than competitors, with local lending institutions.

Lending institutions, regardless of the source of funds, still underwrite projects at their standards of prudent lending practices. It is essential, therefore, to show that participation by the housing authority or local government benefits the financial institution. In addition to basic underwriting knowledge, local officials need the capacity, either in-house or under contract, to review and approve designs and specifications for any projects to be financed. Successful local programs depend on quality, not simply quantity.

Any successful local housing program needs staff facilitators who can manage the local review process thoroughly and efficiently. That process includes neighborhood approval; sign-offs by building, public works, police, fire, and zoning officials; and city council review, debate, and approval. Time is money, and to the extent that this is not a well-managed process, it results in either a more expensive product or one of inferior quality.

In essence, then, the local housing office has to be a one-stop operation where government officials, neighborhood representatives, private developers, investment bankers, and local lenders can find knowledgeable staff in underwriting, building, plan approval, construction, and planning and in local, state, and federal technical and legal restrictions.

Source: G. Terry McNellis, Deputy Director, Housing, St. Paul Department of Planning and Economic Development.

The local housing agency that is concerned about the elderly, the low-income families, the myriad of state and federal requirements, and the long-term quality of the development

The local bank or savings and loan that is concerned about the safety, liquidity, and equity of its entrusted funds

The local real estate community that is concerned about the housing market and the many neighborhood and area submarkets.

It is the art of management to bring these and other interests together. The focal point for these efforts may be the office of the mayor, the city or county manager, the local housing director, the community development director, or the planning director, but it takes an organizational point that is visible, unequivocal, and committed.

LOCAL GOVERNMENT AND HOUSING MANAGEMENT

As in the case of new housing construction, a direct role of local government in housing management was late in coming and limited in scope. The earliest, and by far the largest, involvement is the management by local public housing agencies of the 1.2 million federally assisted public housing units. These units, which are owned by local housing authorities, make up only

Skills for facilitators Six major skills are required to be a successful facilitator and packager of innovative financing programs.

Real estate economics: A working knowledge of real estate economics is necessary so that proposals can be analyzed to determine how various financing approaches will affect projects. It is not necessary to be a total expert, but a person must be familiar with analytical methods and general problems in this area.

Quantitative methods: The ability to deal with numbers comfortably is essential. While it is helpful to understand the quantitative aspects of bond programs—cash flows, discounting, and payment streams—the most important element is to "visualize" the way money flows as a system. Even those with considerable facility in the quantitative aspects tend to overconcentrate on specifics to the detriment of overall understanding.

Banking and lending: Familiarity with mortgage finance, underwriting, and various forms of debt (and their legal implications) is essential. It is not necessary to be an expert in mortgage finance, but to be conversant and comfortable with the field so that program options can be understood.

Accessing the experts: Packaging financial programs is creative work. The majority of persons one deals with in putting together financing programs are technicians. Therefore, it is necessary to combine the creative force that you bring to the program with the ability to work with the technical specialties of experts (lawyers, underwriters, mortgage bankers, developers, etc.) and their personalities, objectives, and professional values.

Detective skills: It helps to be a good investigator. The skills of persistence and research help in tracking down other programs and in locating key individuals.

Negotiations: Negotiating skills are extremely important. Whether you are dealing with the city attorney or a group of underwriters who are fighting over fees, the interests of the city (or county) and the program must be preserved.

Conclusion: Professionals who have some experience and training in a combination of areas do substantially better than those from a single area of expertise. Experience in community development, planning, real estate economics, finance, and law appear to be required in approximately equal measure. The "average" individual who is developing these programs generally has acquired some background in all these areas through a combination of education and job experience. The final characteristic is personal commitment and creativity to visualize, negotiate, manage, and implement.

Source: Douglas S. Ford, General Manager, Los Angeles Department of Community Development.

about 1.4 percent of the 80 million households in the United States. Nevertheless, the management of this housing, occupied by over 3 million persons, represents an important local housing function; this is particularly true in central cities, where 60 percent of these publicly owned units are concentrated. In addition, public housing management has developed areas of specialization—since 1960 in the management of housing for elderly persons, and since 1974 in the management of housing for handicapped and disabled persons. These types of housing require special management techniques and long-term support services from the local community.

Increasingly also, since the mid-1970s, local governments are involved in new relationships with all publicly assisted housing—whether owned by public, nonprofit, or profit-making entities. Local governments could not avoid involvement in the financially troubled federally assisted Section 221(d)(3) and Section 236 moderate-income projects in the mid-1970s. The physical condition and economic and social stability of this growing inventory of assisted units affected the total community. A related trend is the growing number of newly constructed assisted housing units in which the local government itself has participated in the financing and has a long-term stake in successful management.

Still other trends affecting the management of assisted housing for families at the local level are new forms of resident participation and ownership, new types of neighborhood-based housing management organizations, and new arrangements to contract assisted housing management services to private enterprise.

Finally, the rapid growth of the Section 8 existing housing program, reaching a total of over 800,000 units in 1982, has generated new methods and procedures for local public housing agencies to use in administering the leasing of private housing for lower-income families.

Understanding housing management

A systemic view of housing management would include *input characteristics* of housing stock, management, households, and environment; *organizational processes* of management behavior, occupant behavior, and operating income; and *outputs,* both current and future, of people with respect to assistance and participation, housing maintenance, financial return, and, ultimately, contributions to individual and household development.[18] The feedback in this model would be owner, management, and individual and household satisfaction.

The organizational process—the constellation of roles and behavior patterns of management, and tenants—serves to define how the given physical and human resources are employed. The ultimate products of this interaction are the contributions the project makes to the community, owner, and the personal development of its occupants.[19]

While this description of housing management applies to both unassisted and assisted housing, it has particular relevance to the management of the assisted housing stock for low- and moderate-income families. As the inventory of publicly owned and publicly assisted housing has increased, and as experience has been gained in its operation, there is increasing evidence of the complexity of its management and the specialization required to manage a particular housing site with a particular tenant body and a given package of financial resources. Two major requirements set assisted housing management apart from traditional private housing management operations:

1. The public requirements embodied in statutes and regulations that govern how the development will be operated, who it will serve, and what rents can be charged, with the accompanying reporting and accountability
2. The special requirements that flow from the fact that the residents are lower-income households: the housing relates not only to their shelter needs, but to other family needs as well.

The characteristics of the publicly assisted housing inventory are diverse, as are the characteristics of the occupants. The stock encompasses the 10-unit elderly development in a small community as well as the 1,000-family development in a large city. Each requires a different housing management approach.

Defining assisted housing management

In a report for HUD, the Urban Institute identified and defined nine major functional areas in a local public housing agency operation.[20] Many of these functions apply to any assisted housing development. The areas, defined in detail in Appendix B, are: maintenance and custodial functions; purchasing and inventory; management information, finance, and accounting; occupancy; general administration; personnel and training; project management; security; and social services.

In addition to defining the functional areas and their activities, the Urban Institute report catalogs the major, distinct approaches for carrying out the activities and identifies links to activities in other functional areas.[21]

As an example, the approaches to carrying out maintenance and custodial functions can involve a highly centralized or decentralized site approach or a mixture of both—the report describes five combinations that appear likely or typical, depending on the size of the operation and the type of housing stock. In the words of the report: "Small [public housing agencies] with small, scattered sites may use more central and zoned approaches. Medium sized [agencies] may mix and match. The really large PHAs are likely to have decentralized custodial and mixed maintenance."[22] In addition, the success of any maintenance/custodial system is highly dependent on its links with other functional areas, including purchasing and inventory, personnel and training, management information, and general administration. This detailed delineation of public housing management functions and operations not only reveals the potential complexity of larger operations, but also shows that there are no standardized organizational patterns or procedures for local public housing agencies. This same type of analysis relates to the other functional areas. An organizational chart of a local housing authority sets forth only the basic patterns for that operation. It does not illustrate or explain the basic management approaches, links among functions, or how the operation really works.

The Urban Institute analysis, however, reflects the increasing body of knowledge and experience in public housing management operations. Since 1970 many local public housing agencies have benefited from management improvement programs sponsored by HUD—the Housing Management Improvement Program of 1972–1975; the Target Projects Program of 1975–1978; and the Urban Initiatives Program of 1978. While these programs were important in developing new techniques, there is still no ongoing mechanism for sharing new knowledge among public housing agencies; nor are there adequate front-end resources to incorporate many of the new techniques into a total agency operation.[23]

Specialization in assisted housing

Beginning with the opening of the public housing program to elderly persons and the launching of the Section 202 federally assisted direct loan program for the elderly, both in 1959, a new era of specialization in assisted housing began—management of assisted housing for elderly persons. A deluge of studies and experiences followed, focusing on the techniques of managing housing for aging persons. In 1981, 46 percent of the public housing inventory was occupied by elderly persons, and the Section 202 program for elderly and handicapped persons had 97,000 units in management.

Managing housing for older adults requires not only skill in conducting a business operation but knowledge of the aging process, the characteristics of older persons, and the importance of environment and security; empathy with older persons; and above all, motivation toward human service.[24] The specialized functions of housing for an older clientele may include coping with varying degrees of functional disability on the part of residents, including possibly termination of tenancy if functioning declines, and establishing a "watch system" to assure the health and safety of occupants. Housing for older persons usually requires access to community services and may include meal services, housekeeping services, personal services, and appropriate recreation.[25]

The development of housing for another specialized group, handicapped persons, was stimulated by the National Conference on Housing and the Handicapped convened by Goodwill Industries in 1974 in Houston, Texas. A second major factor in this development was the deinstitutionalization of a great number of persons from state-administered institutions beginning in 1971. The chief vehicle for this growth has been the federally assisted Section 202 direct loan program, although a growing number of public housing developments also house handicapped persons. The International Center for Social Gerontology has pointed out that management of housing for handicapped persons is similar to that for the elderly in requiring "the shift of primary emphasis from business management to the social and human goals of the program, most particularly the services aspect."[26]

Management of housing for handicapped persons usually requires a package of community-based services designed to: compensate for functions individuals may not be able to perform or provide independently, meet any health-related needs (therapy, counseling), stimulate capacity for social interaction, strengthen community ties, promote normalization, provide new opportunities for a more fulfilling life, and offer training needed for self-management or for career or employment potentials.[27] Community-based services must be accompanied by an in-house supportive service package similar to that required for the elderly.

A factor that affects relationships to the local community is that much new housing for elderly or handicapped persons is not traditional apartment-type developments but small group homes or congregate living facilities.[28]

Troubled management in the 1970s

The difficulties experienced by public, for-profit, and nonprofit entities in managing federally assisted housing—particularly for families in inner cities in a period of rising operating costs—became a national issue in the early 1970s. These problems, and the resulting impacts on HUD, were a major factor in the moratorium imposed by HUD on all new federally assisted housing activity in January 1973.

Prime factors in these management difficulties were flaws in the federally assisted housing mechanisms themselves. The Section 236 multifamily rental program for moderate-income families was basically unworkable in that the limited level of the subsidy was not adequate to serve the eligible income groups. Ultimately, in 1974, Congress recognized this fact by authorizing (1) additional rental assistance payments for residents paying 25 percent or more of income for rent and (2) operating assistance for project owners to help cover tax and utility bill increases beyond their control. In the case of public housing, the ceiling on rent contributions by residents under the Brooke amendment of 1969 made the local operations unfeasible without additional federal operating assistance. In both cases, federal assistance was forthcoming—but too little and, in some cases, too late.

In the case of the FHA-insured Section 221(d)(3) and Section 236 developments, the result of these problems was an accumulation of a portfolio of troubled projects by HUD. By 1977 the FHA had responsibility for assigned mortgages covering 221,000 multifamily housing units and an additional inventory of foreclosed properties, owned by HUD, of 43,000 multifamily units.[29] By 1980 these portfolios had been reduced, but were still significant: 218,000 multifamily units in assigned mortgages and 34,000 multifamily units foreclosed and owned by HUD.[30] Inadequate federal assistance and inadequate federal oversight were two critical elements in the problem. However, other factors were also involved. In August 1977 the HUD Task Force on Multifamily Property Utilization came to this conclusion:

Following completion and initial rent-up, projects were found to be owned and/or managed by weak and often inexperienced administrators; half of the private sector interviewees especially mentioned that non-profit projects often have poor management. Specific management deficiencies frequently reported in the sample data were *rental activities* (including tenant screening and evictions), *maintenance practices* (repairing, cleaning and re-painting), and *fiscal and personnel practices*. Two other problems which have plagued projects after rent-up—vandalism of the project by tenants and neighborhood residents and rent deliquency—were also attributed, at least in part, to inadequate security and rental activities on the part of project management.[31]

The final report of this HUD task force made seven recommendations for "on-site management" of FHA-insured developments, including the requirement for a management plan to cover all aspects of the financial, administrative, physical, and social management functions.[32] These recommendations and the HUD oversight requirements to implement them were ultimately incorporated into HUD regulations for FHA-assisted housing management.

In the case of public housing, the Performance Funding System, initiated in 1975, conditioned federal operating assistance on a formula related to the performance of "well-managed" authorities; and a series of HUD-sponsored management improvement activities were initiated, beginning with the Housing Management Improvement Program of 1972–1975. But over the decade, public housing agencies struggled to maintain services while operating costs rose.

An additional perspective on management problems came to light during efforts to work out the problems of the most seriously troubled projects. This was a new recognition of the management approach—resources as well as management organization and style—required to successfully operate projects with very low-income families in difficult locations. More attention was focused on assessing all the elements involved—the characteristics of the housing stock, the management, and households as well as the physical setting—in devising a feasible management plan.

Whatever the reasons, local governments became increasingly aware in the 1970s that assisted housing developments in their localities were in management trouble, with consequent effects on the local community, including tenant and neighborhood unrest and demands for increased municipal services. Ultimately, successful management of these troubled projects involved the local community itself.

Local innovations in housing management

PUBLIC HOUSING INNOVATIONS   The most dramatic example of a new management structure growing out of a difficult assisted housing development was the Pruit-Igoe public housing development in St. Louis, Missouri. The name "Pruit-Igoe" in fact became a national synonym for problem housing. After a prolonged authority-wide rent strike, and complete reorganization of the St. Louis public housing agency, management of five large family developments was turned over to resident corporations, and all other developments owned by the local authority were contracted out to private management firms. The transformations took six years and substantially altered the functions and tasks performed by the public housing agency in St. Louis; the public part of the management operation has become oversight of management performance carried out by resident and private managers.

In the case of St. Louis this arrangement appears to be working in 1981—but project observers caution against viewing this model as a panacea, or a simple formula making troubled projects work out.[33] The idea of tenant management, however, was sufficiently promising to cause HUD and the Ford Foundation to jointly fund National Tenant Management demonstrations in six other locations beginning in 1979; the results of these demonstrations are still under evaluation by HUD.[34]

There was also an early effort to test private management of public housing developments from 1969–1976 in Washington, D.C., but with inconclusive results.[35] The idea of private management, or contracting out management services to private enterprise, has been revived by the Reagan administration and is being intensively explored.[36] The Lorain Metropolitan Housing Authority in Lorain, Ohio, is a local public agency that has contracted extensively for services with private entities. Public housing agencies also have explored the potential conversion of some public housing developments to cooperatives.[37] An earlier effort, the Turnkey III homeownership program, has developed some evidence of the potential for making public housing residents owners of their individual units.[38]

OTHER ASSISTED HOUSING INNOVATIONS   Since the mid-1970s, a variety of experiments have been conducted on a local level dealing with management of assisted housing; many of these relate to efforts to restore "troubled projects" financed under Section 236 or Section 221(d)(3). A report released by the National Housing Law Project in August 1981 contains ten case studies of alternative management organizations related primarily to successful experiences of community-based nonprofit or limited profit organizations.[39] These case studies also involve, in some cases, services or oversight by profit-oriented management or development organizations. Profiles of these case studies are included as Appendix C.

These local case studies show that no one management form is applicable to all assisted housing complexes and that each local community has a mix of housing management resources and skills to call on—private management companies, nonprofit organizations, and public agencies. The task is to analyze the housing management requirement of a particular development and tap the most effective resources for that particular situation.

In summary, the National Housing Law Project makes several observations: (1) the reason for the superior management performance in these instances seems to be the presence of a strong monitoring body and/or demanding executive; (2) it is the activities that go beyond "business management"—resident involvement and supplementary social services—that bring success; and (3) the successful management models tend to be small and centralized and do not depend for survival on continuous growth; in cases where ownership and management are separate, there is a community of purpose.[40]

As in the case of financing the construction of new assisted housing development, discussed earlier, new relationships among the local government, public agencies, and private and nonprofit organizations are emerging in the area of assisted housing management. Experience is bringing new management forms, and they could well be a trend for the future.

Leasing existing housing for lower-income families

A major new local housing function has emerged in the form of the administrative organization, procedures, and approaches to carry out the federally assisted Section 8 existing housing program. This program of leasing private housing for occupancy by lower-income persons reached a national level of over 800,000 leased units—two-thirds of the volume of the public housing inventory—only eight years after it was authorized under the Housing and Community Development Act of 1974.

The administration of this program differs from that of the traditional public housing program, as described by the staff of the Dakota County (Minnesota) Housing and Redevelopment Authority. In the Dakota County program, the staff is more directly associated with a greater variety of people —there is contact not only with the clients, but also with owners, managers, caretakers, public officials, and taxpayers. A strong public relations program, both internal and external, is vital to success. Many owners, without this approach, will refuse subsidized clients in their building, which defeats the purpose of the program.[41]

In addition to administering the specialized requirement for family eligibility and the record and control system of the entire operation, several unique functions related to this operation require (1) a day-to-day knowledge of the housing market in the local area to identify available units; (2) a negotiating role with private landlords; and (3) inspections to ensure sound physical standards for the housing to be occupied.

A structured system of federal government requirements surrounds the

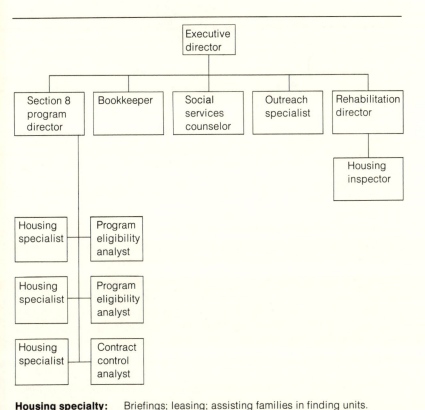

Housing specialty: Briefings; leasing; assisting families in finding units.
Program eligibility: Applications, verifications, determination of eligibility.
Contract control: Certificates, records, control systems, data compilation.
Social services: Mediating tenant/owner problems, providing direct coun-
seling and self-improvement opportunities.
Outreach: Distribution of program information to owners and poten-
tially eligible families.
Housing inspection: Inspections, damage claims, vacancy loss.

**Figure 3–7 Organization chart for
Section 8 existing housing, Dakota
County (Minnesota) Housing and
Redevelopment Authority.**

Section 8 existing housing program. It includes twenty steps and substeps from the original HUD allocation of contract authority to a field office to HUD monitoring of final contract compliance. The various steps include field office reviews, preparation and review of applications, formal certifications and notifications, family applications and selections, leases and contracts, and property inspections.[42] This process, largely laid out in laws and regulations, does not show the internal workings of a local public housing agency in moving through these steps. Figure 3–7 shows the program and organizational components for the Dakota County (Minnesota) Housing and Redevelopment Authority.

As widespread experience developed with the local operation of the Section 8 program, four areas received special attention in terms of developing effective procedures: housing quality standards, rent reasonableness, occupancy, and financial management. Based on field exploration, HUD issued an administrative practices handbook for the Section 8 existing housing program in November 1979.[43] It also contracted for the preparation of a procedural manual on housing quality standards and, using this manual, arranged for intensive training of public housing agency staff in inspection procedures in 1981.[44]

Local capacity and skills requirements
The changing forms and complexities of the job of administering and managing assisted housing programs for lower-income families requires a high degree of competence, skill, and dedication, incorporating business management techniques, communication skills to work cooperatively with low-income families, negotiating skills to reach agreements with labor unions and private landlords, and above all a commitment to the goal of improving housing opportunities in the local community.

In addition, the local housing administrator, particularly the executive director of a local public housing agency, must have a day-to-day knowledge of the dynamics of the local housing market and an understanding of and access to services or resources in private real estate management and nonprofit associations.

The personal qualifications for this top administrative job can probably best be met by the combination of special qualities set forth in previous discussions in this chapter—expertise and training in a combination of areas rather than a single one, the ability to deal with individuals from divergent backgrounds, and the creativity and persistence of a good detective.

The spectrum of functions and staffing involved in the administration of housing assistance programs at the local level is broad. Public agencies often are tied to civil service systems with standard position classifications and descriptions. Private management firms with large operations in housing management usually have skilled staff, although not usually in assisted housing. National professional organizations have begun certification of on-site housing managers. Nonprofit housing managers have not been as closely tied into a personnel system or a certification process.

All these housing management organizations—public agencies, for-profit management firms, and nonprofit groups—have suffered from the lack of a career ladder in the assisted housing operations, from its lack of recognition as a professional endeavor, and (in the public and nonprofit sectors) from the low level of compensation. All these things must be reversed if local assisted housing management is to address the complexity of its responsibilities successfully.

CONCLUSION

The growth of the assisted housing inventory in many local communities and its close relationship to the welfare of the total community—its lower-income families and its neighborhoods—has been increasingly recognized over the past decade. General-purpose local government has become involved by developing new assisted housing using innovative financing techniques and by assisting in difficult operating problems through local tax abatement and use of CDBG funds for public housing modernization and for other supporting services. As the federal government becomes less involved in assisted housing, there will likely be more local government responsibility. The traditional influence of local government over the location and character of new housing construction through zoning ordinances and building codes will not be sufficient to protect the community's interest in assisted housing, nor will a single action confirming that a new, assisted housing development is in conformance with its Housing Assistance Plan. New criteria to assess the design and environmental quality of proposed new assisted developments are likely. As the local government becomes involved in financing new development through tax-exempt mortgage bonds or UDAG projects, it concerns with the long-term stability of management operations will accelerate, and new techniques to monitor assisted housing management in the local community are likely to evolve.

1   Robert D. Reischauer, "Federal Budget Reveals Political, Economic Costs of Housing Assistance," *Journal of Housing,* March 1981, p. 145.
2   Ibid.
3   President's Commission on Housing, *Interim Report* (Washington, D.C.: Government Printing Office, 1981), pp. 6, 31–43.
4   Kent W. Colton, "Housing Finance in the 1980s: Economic Factors Indicate Future Directions," *Journal of Housing,* January 1981, p. 15.
5   Ibid.
6   During the 1970s there was a significant expansion in both the volume of tax-exempt state and local bonds and the purposes for which they were used. The volume rose from $30.7 billion in 1975 to $46.2 billion in 1981. Purposes were expanded to include not only tax-exempt mortgage bonds for housing, but other uses beyond traditional financing of local public facilities, including pollution control facilities at privately owned industrial

plants, privately owned hospitals, and industrial plants leased to private companies. All these demands on the tax-exempt municipal bond market, plus other credit demands, resulted in increases in interest rates. The yield on a thirty-five-year, A-rated, Section 8 new issue by state housing finance agencies rose from a low of 5.9 percent in 1977 to 10.75 percent in 1981; the high yield rose from 6.6 percent in 1977 to 14.5 percent in 1981 (Smith Barney housing indexes).

7   White House, Office of the Press Secretary, *Fact Sheet, Federal Credit/Loan Guarantee Reduction,* November 5, 1981.

8   Thomas J. Cain and Michael W. Scott, "New Rental Housing: Confronting the 'Investment Gap,'" *Urban Land,* May 1981, p. 7.

9   William Witte, "Community Development's Third Year," *Journal of Housing,* February 1978, p. 67.

10 U.S., Department of Housing and Urban Development, Office of Community Planning and Development, *Sixth Annual Community Development Block Grant Report* (Washington, D.C.: Government Printing Office, 1981), pp. 125–26.

11 Ibid., p. 127.

12 National Institute for Advanced Studies, *Neighborhood Strategy Areas: Neighborhoods and Programs 1979,* prepared for the U.S. Department of Housing and Urban Development (Washington, D.C.: Government Printing Office, 1981), pp. ii, 1.

13 U.S., Deparment of Housing and Urban Development, *News Release,* No. 81–218, Washington, D.C., August 18, 1981.

14 Comptroller General of the United States, *The Community Development Block Grant Program Can Be Made More Effective in Revitalizing the Nation's Cities,* Report to the Ranking Minority Member, Committee on Appropriations, United States Senate (Washington, D.C.: U.S. General Accounting Office, 1981), pp. 6–9.

15 U.S., Department of Housing and Urban Development, Office of Community Planning and Development, *Sixth Annual Community Development Block Grant Report,* p. 101.

16 Eunice Grier and George Grier, *After Rent Control, What? Innovative Program Suggestions to Preserve and Expand the Affordably-Priced Rental Housing Stock,* prepared for the Housing Opportunities Commission, Montgomery County, Maryland (Bethesda, Md.: The Grier Partnership, 1980).

17 Federal Home Loan Bank Board, *Reaching Out,* loose-leaf handbook of innovative financing under the Community Investment Fund (Washington, D.C.: Federal Home Loan Bank Board, [1981]).

18 Morton L. Isler, Margaret J. Drury, and Clay H. Wellborn, *Housing Management: A Progress Report* (Washington, D.C.: The Urban Institute, 1971), p. 9.

19 Ibid., pp. 9–10.

20 Raymond J. Struyk et al., *Case Studies of Public Housing Management: General Design Report,* Working Paper 1452-02 (Washington, D.C.: The Urban Institute, 1981).

21 Ibid., pp. 13–17.

22 Ibid., p. 15.

23 Robert Kolodny, *Exploring New Strategies for Improving Public Housing Management,* a study for the U.S. Department of Housing and Urban Development, Office of Policy Development and Research (Washington, D.C.: Government Printing Office, 1980), pp. 83–88, 106–109.

24 Marie McGuire Thompson, "Highlights of Managing Housing for Older Adults," *Technical Assistance Notes on Housing for Older People* (Washington, D.C.: International Center for Social Gerontology, n.d.).

25 Ibid.

26 Marie McGuire Thompson, *Housing for the Handicapped and Disabled: A Guide for Local Action* (Washington, D.C.: National Association of Housing and Redevelopment Officials, 1977), p. 66.

27 Ibid., p. 71.

28 For an understanding of this housing type, see: Marie McGuire Thompson and Wilma T. Donahue, *Planning and Implementing Congregate Housing for Older Adults* (Washington, D.C.: International Center for Social Gerontology, 1980).

29 U.S., Department of Housing and Urban Development, Office of the Budget, *Summary of the HUD Budget, Fiscal Year 1979* (Washington, D.C.: U.S. Department of Housing and Urban Development, 1978), pp. H-19 and H-20.

30 U.S., Department of Housing and Urban Development, *FY 1982 Budget, Revised*

(Washington, D.C.: U.S. Department of Housing and Urban Development, 1981), p. H-33.

31 U.S., Department of Housing and Urban Development, *Preliminary Findings from the Field Study: Report of the Task Force on Multifamily Property Utilization* (Washington, D.C.: U.S. Department of Housing and Urban Development, 1977), p. v.

32 U.S., Department of Housing and Urban Development, *Final Report of the Multifamily Property Utilization Task Force* (Washington, D.C.: Government Printing Office, 1978), p.8.

33 Kolodny, *Exploring New Strategies,* pp. 91–92.

34 Ibid., pp. 90–92.

35 Ibid., pp. 79–81.

36 U.S., Department of Housing and Urban Development, Conference on Private Sector Involvement with Public Housing, Washington, D.C., 10 December 1981.

37 Meeting of Local Public Housing Agencies and Others Interested in Public Housing Cooperatives, convened by the National Association of Housing and Redevelopment Officials, Washington, D.C., 13 April 1981. See also: Scott B. Franklin, "Housing Cooperatives: A Viable Means of Home Ownership for Low-Income Families," *Journal of Housing,* July 1981, pp. 392–98; and Carr Kunze, "Public Housing Cooperatives Reduce Dependence on Operating Subsidies, Modernization Funding," *Journal of Housing,* October 1981, pp. 489–93.

38 "Turnkey III Plus State Assistance Makes Early Home Ownership Possible for Low Income Families in Norfolk," *Journal of Housing,* May 1978, pp. 241–42; and "Turnkey III, Winston-Salem, North Carolina," in Federal Home Loan Bank Board, *Reaching Out.*

39 Margaret Weitkamp and Daniel D. Pearlman, *Alternative Approaches to the Management of Subsidized Housing* (Berkeley, Calif.: National Housing Law Project, Multifamily Demonstration Program, August 1981).

40 Ibid., pp. 85–86.

41 Dakota County (Minnesota) Housing and Redevelopment Authority, *Training Manual for Section 8 Existing Rent Assistance Program* (Hastings, Minn.: Dakota County Housing and Redevelopment Authority, 1977), pp. 1–3.

42 Thomas A. Duvall and Edward White, Jr., *Answers to Questions on Section 8 Lower Income Housing Assistance* (Washington, D.C.: National Association of Housing and Redevelopment Officials, 1975).

43 U.S., Department of Housing and Urban Development, *Public Housing Agency Administrative Practices Handbook for the Section 8 Existing Housing Program,* Handbook 7420.7 (Washington, D.C.: Government Printing Office, 1979).

44 U.S., Department of Housing and Urban Development, *Housing Inspection Manual: Section 8 Existing Housing Program,* prepared by Abt Associates, Cambridge, Massachusetts (Washington, D.C.: Government Printing Office, 1980).

Profiles of innovative housing finance

BELOW-MARKET HOME REHABILITATION, ST. PAUL, 1979

This was a tax-exempt mortgage program involving $47.9 million for substantial rehabilitation of 700 housing units with various income limits. The innovations included:

Substantial rehabilitation only (in excess of 50 percent of as-is value)

Nonresidential conversions to housing use

Mortgage insurance and underwriting of rehabilitation risk

Development of a marketable and rated rehabilitation bond issue.

The St. Paul below-market home rehabilitation (BMHR) program was the city's second major tax-exempt mortgage program. Earlier, the city had developed a tax-exempt (8.25 percent) single-family mortgage program aimed primarily at the city's existing housing stock, with 20 percent of those mortgage proceeds targeted specifically at ongoing redevelopment projects.

One of the major lessons from this earlier program was that neither the ongoing private lending market nor this initial public mortgage program was very effective in reaching units that required substantial rehabilitation (over $25,000 per unit). Due to the risk associated with first mortgage loans on a structure where substantial rehabilitation was yet to be undertaken, there was a general aversion on the part of lenders to such projects.

In addition, a normally structured bond issue to address this need would be unratable. Thus, simply because substantial rehabilitation was difficult, there had been no effective attempts to address the problem. The only assistance available had been city (CDBG) and state second mortgage programs. The inherent funding limitations of these programs were severely restricting the revitalization of a number of the city's older neighborhoods.

Participant	Financing development	Site development and construction	Management and maintenance
Local public housing agency	30-year tax-exempt bonds issued by local housing and redevelopment authority (HRA)	Several sites and structures sold to developers by HRA	. . .
General-purpose local government	. . .	Provides rehab technical assistance; issues priority permits for rehab work; contract between city/builder/lender allows drawdowns on first mortgage for construction	. . .
State government	Provides exemption from state income tax for bonds	. . .	. . .
Federal government	Provides exemption from federal income tax for bonds	. . .	. . .
Private financial community (banks, developers, foundations, etc.)	Provides underwriting of bond issue, bond insurance, mortgage origination and servicing	Contract between builder/lender/city allows drawdowns on first mortgage to fund construction	. . .
Private management community	. . .	. . .	All sales of units handled by developers/brokers; maintenance by homeowner association

Figure 3–8 Major elements of below-market home rehabilitation, by major participants, St. Paul, 1979.

The extent of housing rehabilitation needed for these structures generally exceeded the maximum loans available for the second mortgage programs. The BMHR program developed as an attempt to extend the extremely successful experience of the city's prior $50 million mortgage issue to finance and target substantial rehabilitation. The central breakthrough was in mortgage insurance.

The previous barrier was the risk associated with construction loans on substantial rehabilitation projects. The BMHR program was designed to avoid the need for a separate construction loan. The program's final takeout mortgages were structured to prepay and fund, in escrow, all principal and interest payments during the construction period. First mortgages were insurable with private mortgage insurance, thus yielding a marketable bond issue. In addition, a detailed builder/lender/city contract allowed drawdowns from the first mortgage to fund construction draws.

The St. Paul BMHR incorporated a second lesson learned from the earlier program. In the 20 percent new construction portion of the prior program, the city encountered difficulty in matching the targeted loan proceeds to the precise dollar and scheduling needs of the individual developments. Specifically, developers naturally relied solely on the available tax-exempt mortgages and sought to finance 100 percent of their mortgage needs through the bond programs. When buyers paid in excess of the minimum down payment (5 percent), "excess" mortgage proceeds began to accumulate in the program. Second, certain of the redevelopment projects ran into delays, which meant that the drawdown rate of bond program mortgages could be jeopardized. While this problem was not critical in the earlier program, it was seen as a potential liability in attempting a BMHR program made up primarily of these developer allocations.

Prior to final commitment and sizing of the mortgage program, the city was courted by would-be developers who wished to secure the lower-interest financing. However, with the finalization of the issue, the city suddenly was dependent on developer performance for timely and accurate drawdown of mortgage proceeds, maintenance of the bond rating, and assurance of full expenditure of the bond issue. Thus, considerable time and effort were put into devising a system of locating timely backup projects if additional mortgage funds became available. A rigid time line was established, and developers were held to it. At various checkpoints, funds could be withdrawn from individual developments and reallocated to backup projects. While in the past such an administrative system would have been seen as merely good business practice, new federal regulations have made perfecting these scheduling techniques absolutely essential. Under current law, the alternative for slow developer performance is a mandatory calling of bonds.

Such an experience will seriously damage a city's credibility in the financial community and jeopardize future bond issues.

The city realized in establishing the BMHR program that safeguards must be provided or the program could be misused and become a major source of accelerating conversion of existing rental housing to condominiums. For this reason, all such conversions were denied access to the program. In several St. Paul neighborhoods, numerous abandoned nonresidential structures had potential for housing reuse. The BMHR program provided the sole source of long-term mortgage financing for these projects and brought more than 10 percent of the bond proceeds in nonresidential conversions to housing.

When the 9.75 percent mortgages under BMHR were offered, market rate financing was generally available at 11 to 12 percent. Subsequent to this offering, conventional interest rates rose sharply. This change, coupled with market acceptance of rehabilitated units, created an unexpected participation in the BMHR program. Since the program was basically restricted to projects adding more than 50 percent to the as-is value of units, virtually all the 700 participating units resulted from previously substandard (many abandoned) housing units. The economic impact was remarkable, for both the neighborhoods and the city's tax base. The increased property tax flow from the BMHR program has been projected to exceed $1 million annually.

FAMILY HOUSING FUND, MINNEAPOLIS/ST. PAUL, 1981

This was a tax-exempt mortgage program, involving $120 million, combined with urban development action grants (UDAGs), foundation capital, and deferred equity. The fund provided for various income limits to a maximum of 110 percent of the median. The innovations included:

Equity participation

Multiple financing through tax-exempt bonds, UDAG, and a local foundation

Multiple buyer options with tiered equity participation

Applicability to rental housing.

The Minneapolis/St. Paul Family Housing Fund is an excellent example of the sophistication that has been achieved in the second generation of locally based financing. By early 1980 both Minneapolis and St. Paul had developed track records with local tax-exempt financing, but both cities were hit, as was the nation as a whole, by sharply increasing interest rates for tax-exempt securities. The Family Housing Fund sought to use both UDAG funds and the participation of the McKnight Foundation (through program-related investment in the form of additional equity) as a means of reducing the

Participant	Financing development	Site development and construction	Management and maintenance
Local public housing agency	30-year tax-exempt bonds issued by local housing and re-development authority (HRA)	Several sites and structures sold to developers by HRA	. . .
General-purpose local government	Equity participation through UDAG grant	Priority processing of permits	. . .
State government	Exemption from state income tax for bonds	. . .	. . .
Federal government	Exemption from federal income tax for bonds; UDAG from HUD used for equity loans	. . .	. . .
Private financial community (banks, developers, foundations, etc.)	Underwriting of bond issue; structuring program cash flow; bond insurance and bank letter of credit; mortgage origination and servicing; local foundation equity loans; construction loans	. . .	. . .
Private management community	. . .	. . .	All sales of units handled by developers/brokers; maintenance by homeowner association

Figure 3–9 Major elements of family housing fund, by major participants, Minneapolis/St. Paul, 1981.

effective monthly payments that buyers had to carry. In its final version, a portion of the mortgages issued under the $120 million dual city program (11.875 percent) was offered to buyers at a still lower effective interest rate by equity participation.

The program began when the McKnight Foundation expressed interest in providing both limited housing grant funds and program-related investment loan funds for about a ten-year term. The McKnight Foundation conditioned its participation on cooperation between Minneapolis and St. Paul. The two cities jointly issued $120 million of tax-exempt revenue bonds providing mortgages at 11.875 percent. The federal UDAG award of $2.9 million was then combined with McKnight Foundation funds of $5.9 million to provide equity assistance for approximately one-fourth of the mortgages.

The program contains a number of options for targeted individual buyers by combining limited equity grants (McKnight) of up to $3,000 with additional equity loans (both UDAG and McKnight) for a combined total per buyer of up to $18,000 in assistance. In the portion of the overall portfolio that is equity assisted, UDAG and McKnight funds stand in coequal second position with all interest deferred until point of future resale. Return on these equity contribution loans are generally the lesser of appraised value increases (appraisal at point of sale) or the statewide bank mortgage lending limit. In some selected cases, graduated payment loans (grant funds) were provided in addition to equity participation loans.

The complexity of grant and equity participation options was needed to meet the major objective of reducing monthly payments for individual buyers to approximately 28 percent of their monthly income. In total, the net interest rate reduction to eligible buyers brought the effective mortgage rate down to 8 to 9 percent. Further, these assisted buyers are able to buy with a down payment of only 5 percent of personal equity.

The McKnight Foundation assistance was conditioned on the guarantee that its funds would not remain outstanding for more than ten years. For this reason, UDAG repayments returning to the program are first used to retire the McKnight equity assistance; then all equity return and deferred interest accrue to the two cities for additional housing.

A final program element was a letter of credit provided by the Bank of America to allow structuring the program according to an assumed rate of mortgage prepayment. The certainty this agreement offered to bond holders resulted in a significant interest reduction to the program. The Minneapolis/St. Paul Family Housing Fund provides an excellent example of the type of sophistication that has been developed at the local level in an extremely short period of time. It results from a combination of experience, aggressive pursuit, and cooperation with the private sector, as well as capitalization on the particular strengths of the local financial community.

HOME MORTGAGE PROGRAM, LOS ANGELES, 1980

This was a tandem financing program of $50 million that combined tax-exempt mortgages for twelve years with guaranteed bank replacement mortgages for the thirteenth through thirtieth years. The income limit is 120 percent of the median. The innovations included:

Short-term (twelve-year) first mortgage bond issue for lower interest rate

Bank guarantee of conventional replacement mortgage

Developer buydown through interest subsidy of the mortgage rate for the early years

First-time home buyers only

Multiple public lottery.

In Los Angeles, the initial tax-exempt mortgage financings were done by the Community Redevelopment Agency (CRA). The CRA financing developed a number of innovative techniques but were targeted to individual redevelopment projects. The 1980 Los Angeles city home mortgage program was the first multiple-project, citywide housing finance effort to be undertaken. The 1980 program was developed as a large-scale citywide effort. There was great concern that any city mortgage program not foster speculation, displacement, or any abuse of open access. Previous tax-exempt mortgage issues in California had been criticized for a variety of reasons, including extreme sales prices and income limits, failure to target assistance, conversion of owner units to absentee rentals, multiple participation by individual applicants, and developer control of the buyer selection process. Early in 1980, it became clear that the city of Los Angeles would rather have no program at all than develop a mortgage program that was subject to local criticism and abuse. During this time, the state legislature placed severe restriction on participant income limits and unit sales prices. For Los Angeles, the mandated maximum unit sales price of $87,500 was substantially below the average price of newly constructed units being offered for sale in the city (approximately $120,000). Thus, while the $87,500 limit was an adequate and in many cases generous allowance for suburban and rural areas, it created considerable difficulties in Los Angeles's "superheated" housing market. In the lengthy discussions about how the city's mortgage program was to be conducted, these criteria were established:

1. The 1980 program should be restricted to first-time home buyers.
2. The 1980 program would require a substantial period of owner occupancy (in residence).

Participant	Financing development	Site development and construction	Management and maintenance
Local public housing agency	. . .	. . .	. . .
General-purpose local government	12-year tax-exempt bonds issued by local government (30-year amortization schedule)	Priority processing of permits	Public advertisement and lotteries for all projects
State government	Exemption from state income tax for bonds	. . .	. . .
Federal government	Exemption from federal income tax for bonds	. . .	. . .
Private financial community (banks, developers, foundations, etc.)	Letter of credit for takeout conventional mortgage for 12 years; underwriting and insuring of bond origination and servicing; construction loans	Monitoring of construction scheduling	. . .
Private management community	. . .	. . .	All sales of units by developers/ brokers; maintenance by homeowner association

Figure 3–10 Major elements of city home mortgage program, by major participants, Los Angeles, 1980.

3. Mortgage recipients must own no other homes.
4. All units within the program should be offered by citywide lottery with public advertising that would be regulated by the city.
5. The 1980 program should be limited to new construction.
6. The 1980 program should be made available to all lending institutions operating in the city (about sixty).
7. A multiple underwriting syndicate involving at least three lead underwriters would be used.

While these conditions were well intentioned, they placed an extreme administrative burden on the city. One of the major lessons of such innovative financing is that the best initial program is often the simplest. More complex, innovative, and comprehensive programs are best developed after initial experience and track records are established.

The large geographic area of Los Angeles also influenced the way in which the 1980 program emerged. Projects were to be scattered throughout the city's 500-square-mile area and were to be offered by public advertisement and open lottery to the city's three million residents. At this scale, many administrative issues usually encountered by state housing finance agencies appeared in a local program. The scheduling and marketing procedures developed for this program are, therefore, among the most comprehensive to be found anywhere.

The $50 million, 12.25 percent program was successfully launched in December 1980. It included twenty-six scattered-site new construction projects totaling 577 units. At this time the city faced extremely high interest rates and an unstable bond market. The bond underwriters said that they could not sell traditional thirty-year bonds at any interest rate that would provide acceptable mortgages.

The final 1980 program, therefore, involved a major innovation—tandem financing where the city issued twelve-year bonds that supported mortgages of a thirty-year amortization. A major lender, Security Pacific National Bank, provided a letter of credit to ensure that replacement mortgages (conventional) would be available at the end of the twelfth year (at the point of retirement of the tax-exempt bonds) to all holders of the mortgages. The replacement mortgages would be offered at the conventional, nontaxexempt market rate prevailing at that time. The program underwriters estimated that less than 20 percent of the original mortgages would still be in effect; thus the replacement mortgage option was not seen as applicable to the majority of the participants. Nevertheless, the ability of the city to finance its program with the interest rates applicable to a twelve-year term, as opposed to a thirty-year term, saved between 1 and 2 percent in the eventual mortgage rate.

Prior to this program, tandem financing had been considered highly risky, but the more sophisticated mortgage instruments evolving from the national track record of local programs showed what was possible. As the underwriting community became more comfortable with tandem financing, they began to propose adaptations to the more conventional programs. At the time of the 1980 program offering, several other cities were using floating-rate, tax-exempt bonds in a similar attempt to avoid the extreme instability and high interest rate of long-term bonds.

A further conclusion of the Los Angeles program is that it requires sophisticated, experienced, and innovative underwriters to assure accept-ance in the private financial community. It is doubtful that the Los Angeles program could have been marketed without participation by two of Califor-nia's "superlenders": Bank of America (underwriting) and Security Pacific National Bank. While the previously discussed programs in St. Paul were able to draw strength from the community-based lending structure in the state of Minnesota, the city of Los Angeles was able to draw on the central-ized financial power of California's banks. The Los Angeles program might not have been possible in Minnesota; nor could the short-term bond, tandem arrangement have been constructed in California using only neighborhood-based lending institutions.

In the 1980 Los Angeles program, the issue of matching mortgage funds to the specific needs of participating developments became especially criti-cal. A system was developed using a request for proposal (RFP) for selecting both projects and backup projects. The original 26 projects and 577 units were arrayed in four three-month quarters. As each subgroup of projects was constructed and became available, citywide public lotteries were held. The fund drawdown arrangement for the program was higly sensitive to any change in the scheduling of the original twenty-six projects as well as the possibility that original projects would drop out. Thus, separate series of RFPs were issued at quarterly points throughout the program year to solicit additional backup projects.

Although highly successful through 1981, there are certainly simpler ways to operate programs. The extreme complexity was necessary, how-ever, if the home mortgage program was to be an open and free-access one.

In the high-interest environment of 1981, developers began to introduce early year write-downs for marketing unsold units. The developer "interest rate buydown" was incorporated into the 1980 program after several months of operation. Developers could reduce the 12.25 percent mortgage rate during the first years of the mortgage by adding cash contributions as a means of accelerating the marketing of units. This device proved quite suc-cessful in marketing the units financed by the 1980 program.

CONVERSION OF A HISTORIC INDUSTRIAL BUILDING TO A MODERATE RENTAL PROJECT, BOSTON, 1982

In Boston's Dorchester neighborhood, a novel housing development pro-gram in a 110-year-old Bakers Chocolate mill building is getting under way in the spring of 1982. Located in the heart of the neighborhood's com-mercial district, this historic structure will be converted into 57 apartments —6 studios, 39 one-bedroom units, and 12 two-bedroom units, 6 of which will be duplexes.

Participant	Financing development	Site development and construction	Management and maintenance
Local public housing agency	. . .	. . .	. . .
General-purpose local government	UDAG award, invested in government-backed security	Provides a 12-month construction loan through CDBG funds	. . .
State government	Permanent financing for six years by Massachusetts Government Land Bank	. . .	. . .
Federal government	UDAG award from HUD; developer/owner/investor receives benefits under federal tax law	. . .	. . .
Private financial community (banks, developers, foundations, etc.)	Developer contributes investment loan funds	Construction loan by local savings and loan association	. . .
Private management community	. . .	. . .	Management of rental complex by developer or his management agent; at year 6, sales will be made to tenants who wish to purchase; units not sold will be rented to neighborhood residents

Figure 3–11   Major elements of the conversion of Lower Mills, by major participants, Boston, 1982.

More than a housing project, this development is a comprehensive revitalization strategy that will bring in more consumers, boost confidence in the commercial district as well as nearby residential streets, and begin industrial renewal in adjacent underutilized mills.

The development will provide moderate rental housing with an average rent of $450 (within a range of $300 to $600), not including heat and utilities. Rents will increase only on the basis of documented cost increases, not including management fees. Tenants will pay no more than 25 percent of household income on rent, and priority will be given to local residents.

The units will be offered for sale at the beginning of the sixth year of operation at a price determined by the sum of initial development costs, equity contributions, conversion costs (likely to be very small after so few years and with most tenants likely to purchase their units), and, finally, a 10 percent developer's fee.

Tenants will have up to a year to decide whether to purchase their units. Units not sold to tenants will go to moderate-income neighborhood residents. An antispeculation clause will be included in each deed.

The goal is low turnover. To further this objective, a second mortgage pool with an average of $15,000 per unit will be made available to tenants. Terms of second mortgages will be extremely flexible.

The project will receive no HUD mortgage insurance, financing, or Section 8 assistance. Nor will it receive any state housing finance agency assistance. This saves on many fees and provides greater flexibility in design. But this does not mean that no public subsidy is required to make this project feasible. On the contrary, this project requires a significant subsidy from the development partnership.

Development team

The development team consists of Frank Keefe of Frank Keefe Associates, a Boston consulting and development firm; and Robert Kuehn of Housing Economics, Inc., and Housinda Associates, a Cambridge-based consulting and development firm.

Financial structure

The total project cost will be $3.4 million. A construction loan will come from a Boston savings and loan, using the Community Investment Fund of the Federal Home Loan Bank. The loan will carry 15 percent interest for fifteen months.

Permanent financing for six years will come from the Massachusetts Government Land Bank, an independent state agency established to finance economic development projects in blighted areas with state-backed general obligation bonds. The land bank has given final approval to this takeout loan. The loan will carry an interest rate of 11 percent with a term of six years.

Even with these very favorable commitments in today's difficult public and private markets for rental housing finance, this project is not feasible. In fact, a revenue shortfall of $240,000 would exist, for two reasons. First, a condition of the land bank commitment is that rents average no more than $450, even though the market in the area could sustain this small number of units at $550 or higher in 1983. This accounts for about $80,000 of the shortfall. Second, the remaining $160,000 simply reflects the high cost of building new rental housing today. This shortfall represents a $238 premium that each unit would have to carry each month if some other source of subsidy were not found. And all this is after the attractive financing package the project has received.

Filling the revenue gap

The total revenue gap is $240,000 a year, or $350 per month, per unit. This has been filled as follows:

1. A $660,000 UDAG has been awarded to the city for investment in a government-backed security.
2. A contribution of $340,000 will be made to the city by the developer from funds raised from limited partners seeking a tax shelter.
3. The city will combine these funds, and an investment of $1 million will be made or an annuity will be purchased to maximize yield. The goal is to create a yield of at least $167,000 per year. To the extent that this yield cannot be achieved, principal can be withdrawn first down to $855,000 (or $15,000 per unit) and then down to $660,000 (or $11,000 per unit), the amount of the original UDAG. At the time of conversion, this fund will be reused for second mortgages to tenants. This leaves a revenue shortfall of $73,000.
4. The developer will lend $500,000 to the project, raised from the limited partners receiving tax benefits. This loan will be invested so as to fill this revenue gap entirely. Again, if this is not achieved in any year, then principal can be drawn down. At the end of conversion, the developer can take what is left of the $500,000.

The last problem to be solved before this project moves into construction is the extent to which construction contingencies are covered. Though the mortgage includes $120,000 to cover construction cost overruns (which are likely with rehabilitation), the land bank is concerned that this may not be sufficient; potential limited partners may be reluctant to invest in this project, since their payments must be committed to generating operating revenue, not to covering unforeseen construction contingencies.

To help alleviate these concerns, the developer has proposed that the city provide a twelve-month construction loan of $3.4 million with a "CDBG float" that would carry a 15 percent contingent interest payment. The CDBG float is basically an advance of CDBG funds already approved and authorized but not scheduled for expenditure for at least twelve months. The city can draw on the CDBG funds for other eligible activities with the necessary authorization. Since the 15 percent interest would be contingent, this frees up over $300,000 in the mortgage money that could potentially be used to cover additional cost overruns. This will satisfy the concerns of the permanent lender and the investors.

MIXED-INCOME, MIXED-HOUSEHOLD APARTMENT DEVELOPMENT, BOSTON, 1982

Westland Avenue Apartments is the first mixed-income, mixed-household development in Boston in many years and one of the few nationwide. Today, only 100 percent luxury or 100 percent subsidized residential developments are built. On Westland Avenue there will be 97 units—4 studios and 28 one-bedroom, 49 two-bedroom, 13 three-bedroom, and 3 four-bedroom units. Approximately one-third of the units will be offered at full market rent, one-third for moderate-income households, and one-third for low-income renters. By providing housing opportunities for people of different incomes and for families of different sizes, this development will serve as an effective response to the increased displacement pressures in the Fenway neighborhood.

Westland Avenue Association has overcome the numerous disincentives and risks inherent in various program regulations and tax requirements applying to mixed-income, mixed-household development. This achievement was made possible primarily by obtaining an urban development action grant for $2 million from HUD. The UDAG will be used creatively to provide a forty-year external income stream to the project by investing most of the $2 million in a government-backed security. This use of UDAG funds, too seldom used for neighborhood residential projects, was based on the simple fact that the UDAG could earn close to a 13 percent yield from government securities, while if used in place of debt, the savings would have been only 8.4 percent, the interest cost of the GNMA tandem takeout.

Almost 20 percent of the units will have a passive solar heating component, which can reduce tenant heating costs by 50 to 70 percent. If this experimental program is used by tenants consistently, it will provide them, in effect, with an inflation-proof rent break each month.

To guarantee the provision of a middle tier of moderate-rent units, the partners have made a commitment to put 15 percent of their earnings back into the project to reduce rents.

Participant	Financing development	Site development and construction	Management and maintenance
Local public housing agency	. . .	. . .	. . .
General-purpose local government	UDAG grant invested in government securities (40 years)	. . .	Provides 3-tier real estate tax; 12% for lower-income; 15% for moderate rental units; 18% for market rate units
State government	. . .	. . .	. . .
Federal government	UDAG grant from HUD; FHA mortgage insurance 221(d)(4); government loan through GNMA tandem; owner receives tax benefits	FHA carries out inspections	Section 8 rental assistance for lower-income occupants
Private financial community (banks, developers, foundations, etc.)	Development partners commit a share of earnings back to project to reduce rents	Construction loan for 17 months from local savings and loan association	. . .
Private management community	. . .	. . .	Project management by development team or designated agent

Figure 3–12 Major elements of Westland Avenue Apartments, by major participants, Boston, 1982.

To compensate the city for the UDAG and for a long-term tax agreement, the development team has made the city a partner in the financial benefits of the project. The city will have 30 percent of the net residual value of the project at sale or upon refinancing.

Development team

The development team for this project and the role each played is as follows: Harrington, Keefe & Schork, Inc. (Project Director, Frank Keefe), conceived the project and executed the strategy to make it feasible; Macomber Development Associates provided construction and cost control expertise and financial credibility; and Fenway Community Development Corporation obtained neighborhood support and promoted a passive solar heating experiment.

Financial structure

The financial structure of the project is as follows: Total project costs will be $6.3 million. Mortgage insurance will be under HUD Section 221(d)(4).

A construction loan of $6.3 million for 17 months has come from a Boston savings and loan (Homeowners Federal), using the regular advance program of the Federal Home Loan Bank. The bank interest for this advance was 11.1 percent, and the bank marked up the cost to the developer only 1 percent (to 12.1 percent) since the loan was insured and the purpose was a vital and visible neighborhood project.

A permanent loan has been obtained from the Government National Mortgage Association's tandem program—8.4 percent interest on $6.3 million.

Even with all this in place, the project was projected by HUD to run a $182,000 deficit annually.

To fill this revenue gap, an application for a UDAG was prepared by the developer, and the city sponsored it enthusiastically. In July 1980 a $2 million award was made to the city. Soon after construction started, $1,175,-000 of the UDAG was drawn down in total (a practice now discouraged vigorously by the UDAG office) and invested in a GNMA security with a yield of 12.75 percent for 40 years. The remainder of the UDAG was used to meet closing costs. The income, then, was more than sufficient ($226,000) to cover the revenue deficit of $182,000 and thus made the project financially feasible.

Social objectives

The community wanted mixed-income housing—one-third market, one-third moderate, and one-third low-income. The Fenway is an unusually mixed neighborhood—ethnically, racially, and financially—and the community wanted this project to reflect that. The inclusion of low-income households depended on the award of thirty Section 8 rent subsidies, which the HUD area office provided just before closing.

The market rate units were the responsibility of the developer. Could high rents ($500 for one bedroom, $605 for two bedrooms, $718 for three bedrooms, and $750 for four bedrooms) be obtained in the Fenway in what were burnt-out shells? The developer had to take this risk for twenty-seven units at a time when no developers were doing market rental housing except on prime in-town sites.

The moderate-rent segment proved to be the greatest challenge. Here again the UDAG proved to be of significant help, since $226,000 of income was generated while mortgage needs of $182,000 existed. Thus, the $44,000 surplus could be used for rent reductions for forty units.

But more was needed. Harrington, Keefe, & Schork, Inc., agreed to invest 25 percent of its share of syndication proceeds for fifteen years, the income from which would go to reduce rents. And the Fenway Community Development Corporation agreed to follow suit with 50 percent of its share of proceeds. Combined with income from the UDAG investment during construction, these contributions are estimated to yield an additional $29,000 in external income to reduce rents for the middle tier of units, bringing the total rent reduction fund in the first year up to $73,000, or an average of $152 per month per apartment.

Barriers to mixed-income housing

In HUD's Section 221(d)(4) processing and Section 8 programs:

For 100 percent elderly Section 8 projects, rents can be set as high as 126 percent of a community's fair market rents (FMRs).

For 100 percent family Section 8 projects, the rent can go up to only 120 percent of a community's fair market rents—a 6 percent penalty.

For mixed-income projects, two additional penalties apply. First, rents are based not on citywide FMRs, but on local neighborhood FMRs, usually lower in changing, mixed neighborhoods such as the Fenway. Second, only a 5 percent markup is permitted and only for the handicapped units receiving Section 8 assistance.

Thus, for developers who are willing to take risks by doing partially private projects and to provide the most appropriate mix of housing for inner-city neighborhoods, numerous hurdles stand in the way. In addition, the preferences in the tax code for 100 percent Section 8 projects make the tax shelter benefits (which are usually sold to raise funds to cover construction and operating contingencies and to provide a fee, often outrageously large) appear more attractive and, thus, are easily sold.

And, finally, local tax policy and HUD's requirements usually provide favorable breaks for no-risk subsidized projects. This causes municipal officials to look to private market projects for all the tax dollars they can get, a substantial disincentive to building new housing.

The city of Boston recognized the dilemma posed by Westland Avenue and agreed to a three-tier taxing policy for the three different kinds of units— 12 percent for Section 8, 15 percent for moderate-rent units, and 18 percent for market rate units.

Chapter 4

The impact of changing housing markets

Chapter 1 outlined the evolution of the local housing function with some discussion of the local government's ability or inability to intervene in private housing market dynamics to deal with such issues as housing abandonment, rent increases, gentrification, and the conversion of rental properties to condominiums and cooperatives. This chapter explores these issues in greater depth to put in some perspective the difficult choices—political and professional—that are faced in dealing with housing markets.

LOCAL GOVERNMENTS AS INTERVENORS

The evolution of the local housing function began with the passage of laws and codes to regulate the development, construction, and location of housing. This function, once narrowly defined, has expanded over the years to include not only the police or regulatory aspects of government but also the use of city-funded incentives to produce desired effects in the housing market. Urban renewal, for example, combined the local police power of property condemnation with the financial incentive of land sales to developers at prices below market value.

Neighborhood improvement programs, as described in Chapter 2, often combine city code enforcement with locally generated financial assistance to private owners to stimulate property improvements.

Reasons for intervention

Why do city governments take these actions? Perhaps the answer is obvious, but spelling it out can provide insights into the appropriate reactions of local governments to emerging issues.

Cities have intervened in local housing markets over the years for four reasons.

First, elected officials—mayors, city council members, and county board members—have a strong need to help solve human problems. People living in poor housing want something done about it, and advocates for the poorly housed make their views known and may vote on candidates with an eye toward improving housing and neighborhood conditions for those in need.

Second, the federal government has been a strong advocate for the disadvantaged and for improved housing since the New Deal and has even declared a national goal of "a decent home" for all Americans. The federal government has put pressure on local officials to improve housing and neighborhoods and has provided considerable funding for these purposes over the years.[1]

Third, deteriorated housing and neighborhoods are not in the best financial interests of a city because they translate into a decline in property and other local taxes. Cities try to be businesslike, to stimulate reinvestment in neighborhoods so that the municipal government income stream can be increased and stabilized.

Fourth, city officials have expanded the local housing function, as well as other municipal functions, to reduce social pathology and improve city livability. Improved housing and neighborhoods are part of a strategy to overcome human social problems.

The intersection of these attitudes, policies, and conditions sometimes produces difficult local government policy dilemmas. And, given the disappointment of professionals and the public with earlier local intervention, city initiatives are scrutinized to determine the full range of costs and benefits likely to be associated with any expansion of local housing. The issue can be stated succinctly for housing and for any other local function: What level of government intervention is appropriate, and how should it occur?

In a complex housing market the local housing function and the relationship of public actions to private decisions can be lumped into two broad categories. When the local housing market has gone cold in some areas, such as declining neighborhoods, local government tries to stimulate the market. When the market is overheated, disrupting some housing consumers, local government also has intervened to temper the market or, through regulation, to steer it in a particular direction.

The "cold" markets were discussed in Chapter 2 and generally are evidenced by declining areas and housing abandonment. Overheated markets are evidenced by displacement, escalating rents, and conversions of rental properties to condominiums. These overheated situations are all responses to changing housing market conditions.

Rolf Goetze in his 1979 book *Understanding Neighborhood Change* counsels that the policy aim for any neighborhood, regardless of condition, should be to steer between the market extremes. This means public policy

Rising (gentrifying)	Declining (disinvesting)
Symptoms and indicators	**Symptoms and indicators**
Excess demand	Excess supply
Price inflation	Uncertainty in property values
Speculation	"Redlining"
Strong press image	Negative press image
Immigration of higher class	Departure of the able
Investment purchases	Discretionary sales
Conversion of marginal space into more dwellings	Increase in low down payment and government insured lending
	Increase in absentee ownership
	Rising tax delinquencies
	Property abandonments
Corrective actions	**Corrective actions**
Dampen outside demand	Boost neighborhood image
Help disadvantaged to remain	Value insurance for resident property owners
Enforce codes	Improve jobs and income
Prevent illegal conversions	Support NHS if requested
Reassess only upon sale	Demolish excess housing (or mothball)
Control rents if necessary	Land bank vacant lots until stable
Build additional housing	

Figure 4–1 Steering between the extremes of rising and declining neighborhood housing markets. Stable neighborhoods fall between the extremes shown here and seldom have to rely on drastic corrective actions.

must become sensitive and countervailing to neighborhood dynamics.[2] Figure 4–1 graphically conveys this idea.

The dilemma for local officials in deciding whether or how to intervene in the housing market in either instance is to understand more fully the costs and benefits to the public and to understand whether the public actions will, in the long run, be productive or debilitating to the local economy and quality of life.

Constraints on local policies

Although the local government can do a lot to direct local housing markets, its role and the possibilities for intervention are quite limited and should be kept in context. Many factors are simply out of local government control.

The single most important influence over local housing markets is the condition of national credit markets. When credit is readily available at reasonable cost, local housing markets are relatively fluid and reflect more or less accurately the locational preferences of homeowners and tenants. Local government can do nothing to control the economy at that level, but local officials should be sensitive to the effects of credit markets on the local housing markets and local policies.

Second, national tax policies have broad effects on housing markets. The differential tax advantage of owning versus renting, for example, is an obvious spur to the conversion of rental units to condominiums—a form of tenure that carries with it the tax advantages of home ownership. Tax policies related to depreciation rules for rental properties, to rehabilitation, energy improvements, and tax credits for historic renovation all have the effect of providing differential advantages to various components of the housing market, and all are beyond the control of local government.[3]

Third, local governments have no control over broad changes in population composition, locational preferences, and housing tastes. The aggregate changes in population characteristics—smaller families, more single-person households, and so on—have important effects on the use of the existing supply of housing and the kind of housing constructed by the private sector. National immigration policies affect cities' abilities to house newcomers. These major trends are not fully understood, and gauging their implications for local housing policy in a particular city is extremely difficult.

In addition to these external determinants of local housing market conditions, local policy is shaped by the local ethic regarding the role government should play in the affairs of the population. Public opinion undergoes cycles in which reactions to previous public decisions form the basis for shaping current and future policies.

POOR MARKET CONDITIONS: LOCAL ATTEMPTS TO COUNTER DISINVESTMENT

The problem of poor market conditions and their effect on neighborhoods was discussed extensively in Chapter 2. In addition, of course, the problem of poor housing markets has important effects on the city overall and on the local government in particular.

At the risk of stating the obvious, perhaps some discussion of why local government should intervene to counter poor market conditions is in order. First, declining markets and property values have a direct effect on a city's ability to raise taxes for necessary public services, since property taxes, based on market values, are one of the major sources of general fund revenues for most local governments. As market values fall in central cities, governments are faced with a revenue loss, which means, other things being equal, that other taxes must be levied elsewhere or city services must be reduced.

Cities can fall into a downward spiral when disinvestment in property begins. As property values fall, cities increase the millage rate for property taxes, making the ownership of property in the city relatively less attractive compared with ownership of properties elsewhere or other investments, thereby further decreasing the value of property in the jurisdiction. Hence, measures by local governments to maintain or improve property values are critical to a healthy property tax base.

In addition, undesirable neighborhoods and the weakening markets that they represent are unable to attract middle- and upper-income residents, who bring with them not only wages and wage taxes to support local government operations, but also a presence and lifestyle that can enhance the community's livability.

Without question, then, it is appropriate for city government to develop a local housing function that seeks to stimulate poor housing markets by promoting investment where disinvestment and neglect seem to be occurring.

The economics of housing as an investment

In order to intervene appropriately in markets that are having difficulties (or in overheated markets), local officials need to understand housing as an investment, as distinct from housing as a place to live. Owner occupants decide on their housing location as both consumers and investors. As consumers, owner occupants are concerned with the style, size, and quality of the house, with the neighborhood, and with the quality of neighborhood services, such as schools, shopping facilities, and the location of and distance to employment centers. As investors, they are concerned with whether the house will appreciate in value relative to inflation and to houses in other neighborhoods—that is, whether their equity investment will yield an attractive rate of return over time.

Looking at rental properties specifically can help isolate the investment aspect of housing choice. An investor—that is, an absentee owner or landlord—invests in rental property in hopes of making a profit from one or more of three sources:

1. Cash flow. The investor may be able to structure the finances of a rental property so as to realize a net cash profit after rents are collected and all expenses paid.
2. Tax benefits. The investor may not realize a cash profit, but, when depreciation is factored in, may save sufficiently in federal income tax payments to produce a satisfactory return.
3. Appreciation. If the property is located in an area that has increasing property values, its value may rise over time, making a profit at resale an attractive incentive to an owner.

From an investment viewpoint, the problem in areas where markets are weak is quite straightforward. The rents that can be charged, given demand from tenants, are not sufficient to pay expenses and make the investment attractive, even with tax benefits.

One major public policy issue related to investor owned properties is the apparent unpopularity of using public funds to benefit "slum landlords." Contrary to long-established opinion, the owners of properties in declining or transitional areas in many cities are small-scale property owners who own less than twelve properties.[4] These owners have very little sophistication in property management, tax law, or accounting and often are faced with the prospect of selling or abandoning properties because of cash flow problems and their inability to generate the capital needed for maintenance and reinvestment.

Local government officials need to recognize the problems of declining markets for residential real estate as early in the decline process as possible. Often, owners neglect property taxes in an effort to spread scarce cash resources to other aspects of their buildings. Monitoring property tax delinquency rates can provide important information on the occurrence and location of disinvestment. Other indicators include sales data, utility shutoffs for nonpayment, and physical condition. Overall, it is beneficial for local governments to identify disinvestment in rental properties early and take steps to counter it.

Local government actions to counter disinvestment

Local government actions to counter disinvestment in rental properties have begun relatively recently.[5] A number of cities have used community development block grant (CDBG) funds to make the rehabilitation of rental properties more affordable and more attractive to investors. Although approaches vary considerably, CDBG funds are used to provide grants or deferred payment loans to cover part of the costs of rehabilitating rental units when the full cost of improvements cannot be borne by increased rental income. The public funds are often used with the stipulation that the units be rented to low- and moderate-income tenants or that they be in areas where the public investment could not result in a windfall to owners due to rapid rent increases.

For example, Pittsburgh's Rental Housing Improvement Program (RHIP) provides a grant of up to 50 percent of the cost of rehabilitation, provided that the property is in a deteriorated area or that the subsequent tenants are low- and moderate-income. St. Louis varies its public subsidy based on the willingness of investors to reinvest and awards subsidies to those most willing to invest their own funds.[6]

Some cities have combined two objectives—providing incentives to landlords and reducing energy costs and consumption—by creating programs that provide financial incentives to owners of rental property who make energy-saving improvements. These programs have the effect of lowering operating costs for the units for either the landlord or the tenants.

As another inducement to rental property owners to invest or reinvest, some cities have removed an important disincentive to reinvestment—increased property taxes based on the reassessment of the property after rehabilitation. Owners often face the dilemma of losing a substantial portion of new cash flow from rehabilitated buildings to property taxes, thereby reducing their willingness to reinvest in their properties. Cities have been able to exempt these improvements from additional property taxes for some period of time, thereby increasing the owner's incentive and ability to invest on the theory that, over the long run, the investment will result in additional tax revenues.

One of the most extensive programs of property tax abatements is the J-51 program in New York City. It has been credited with the creation or improvement of more than 800,000 apartments for middle-income people from 1955 to 1980, but it also has been criticized as too generous and unnecessary because many of the apartments would have been rehabilitated anyway, without the twenty-year tax abatement offered by the program.[7]

This program and others emphasize the importance of ensuring that the incentives provided by local government are not too generous and are used only where they are needed to make the difference in whether or not investment or reinvestment occurs.

The result of continuing disinvestment in areas of weak housing markets is housing abandonment. At this stage of property decline, cities are left with the unattractive alternatives of demolishing the buildings or finding new owners for them. Quite often, the nonpayment of property taxes on these buildings produces property tax delinquencies; such delinquencies eventually force the local government to assume ownership (technically "to take possession") of the properties. The local government then, after following exact legal steps, can attempt to recapture its money through a tax sale (usually an auction). The hope or expectation is that the real estate market is strong enough to restore these properties to the current and nondelinquent tax rolls. But this is not always possible. The property values (which combine *both* the building and land values) may be so low that an auction will not produce any bids.

At this stage, the local government is faced with a difficult situation. The building has been abandoned because the market is so weak that the existing owner has been unable to find a buyer for the property, and the cash flow condition of the property is so poor that operating expenses cannot be paid.

The problem of *in rem* property taking has increased greatly in recent years. New York City, for example, owned 2,500 buildings in 1976, but by

1979 the number had risen to 11,700 with a total of 166,000 units, almost 6 percent of the city's total housing stock.[8] New York and other cities have tried a number of approaches to saving these multifamily buildings, including permitting tenants as a group to manage the buildings, leasing the buildings through local nonprofit community groups, and using private-sector, profit-oriented managers.

Cities have attempted various other solutions to the problem of abandonment with little success. Urban homesteading, for example, has stimulated the rehabilitation of only a relatively small percentage of abandoned units.

Overall, recycling abandoned properties is extremely difficult. Anticipating steps that can be taken before abandonment occurs are much more effective and financially productive.

Cities can and are moving aggressively to recognize the problems of weak housing markets. Sometimes the weakness is perceived in neighborhood terms, and neighborhood recovery programs are initiated. In addition, the problem can be viewed as an investment problem, and cities can move to make investment in properties more attractive by decreasing the cost of reinvestment to the owner or by providing tax abatement incentives. In both cases, the approach must be weighed carefully so that public dollars produce the desired effect and are not used in situations where investment would have occurred on its own.

OVERHEATED MARKET CONDITIONS:
LOCAL ATTEMPTS TO TEMPER MARKET FORCES

Despite the fact that the emphasis in most cities since World War II has been on problems of neighborhood decay and blight and on economic development generally, the strength shown in some cities, and the apparent jump in market strength in some neighborhoods and some real estate sectors in the late 1970s and early 1980s, indicates that cities must learn to handle the problems associated with markets that are so strong that they have disruptive effects.

Just as national governmental leaders must grapple with an overheated national economy and its negative side effects, such as inflation, so too are local officials occasionally faced with housing markets or submarkets that are too strong. The Los Angeles area in the early 1980s is a dramatic example.

Market forces can cause neighborhoods to recover so quickly and so fully that low- and moderate-income residents are abruptly displaced. Developers may find markets for condominiums so attractive that widespread conversion of rental properties occurs, causing serious problems for those who would prefer to, or for financial reasons need to, remain tenants; or vacancy rates may be so low and the rental market so strong that owners of rental property can raise rents beyond the reach of incumbent tenants, causing turnover and displacement. These are not easy issues to handle, because problems of overheated local housing markets are a problem of success. The economic system is apparently working so well, and the city's housing stock is so desirable, that it becomes a highly valued commodity.

Confronted with runaway markets, the local government official has only a few available remedies. Local housing laws can be passed to regulate the market, and public funds can be used to protect those being squeezed out. But intervening to slow down a market is fraught with peril, because these measures can depress the market if they go too far. In addition, cities and counties are likely to encounter formidable legal restraints in state statutes, court decisions, and local charter provisions.

Neighborhood gentrification

Gentrification, a term used to describe the process by which inner-city neighborhoods are reclaimed and resettled by middle- to upper-income persons, is a relatively new word in American urban jargon. Gentrification was certainly not an important phenomenon before 1970, when racial disturbances left mayors wondering whether their cities had a future at all.

Most studies of the late 1970s and early 1980s have concluded that gentrification and the resulting displacement of households is not a national phenomenon but one occurring in selected communities and neighborhoods. HUD comes to this conclusion in its two reports on displacement (1979 and 1981).[9] In the 1981 report, HUD states that although displacement is not a widespread national phenomenon in terms of the number of persons and the percentage of recent movers who have been displaced, the data indicate that it remains a problem in some areas of major cities and can have a serious impact on the neighborhoods and households involved. In reviewing the 1979 HUD report, however, the Legal Services Anti-Displacement Project disputed the finding that displacement is not a national phenomenon; its study placed the national displacement figure in the range of 2.4 to 2.8 million persons per year.[10] The 1981 HUD report places the figure at 1.7 to 2.4 million, explaining that the higher figure is upwardly biased due to the inclusion of ambiguous cases that do not clearly represent displacement, and the lower figure would represent only 0.8 percent of all U.S. households.

However, there is general agreement that where it occurs gentrification can have serious disruptive effects. Writing about Washington, D.C., Goldfield has stated that ". . . private neighborhood redevelopment in Washington has generated a vicious side effect: the displacement of hundreds, perhaps thousands, of poor, black households by middle-income black and white newcomers."[11] HUD's 1981 report finds that displacement disproportionately affects minorities, low-income households, female-headed households, and renters, although not particularly elderly households or residents of long duration.[12]

Despite the fact that gentrification does not seem to be a major national problem, it is a major issue in some cities. In part, this is because federal policymakers, contending with the phenomenon of gentrification in their hometown of Washington, D.C., have been cautious about inadvertently causing the problem elsewhere. Second, the national media have often characterized the problem as rich against poor, and the organized poor in many cities have made it clear to local officials that neglecting the needs of low- and moderate-income neighborhoods is unacceptable, whether caused by the abandonment or the gentrification of areas.

A critical gauge of whether gentrification is occurring is the *rate* of neighborhood turnover and change. Neighborhood recovery that takes ten to twenty years may involve an eventual change in the socioeconomic characteristics of the residents, and property values may escalate. However, if the recovery is gradual, the change in population may result as much from normal turnover as from involuntary displacement.

Rapid neighborhood turnover, however, is difficult to stop or slow down. Washington, D.C., has attempted to deter speculative buying and selling of deteriorated structures by taxing profits on the sale of residential properties that are held for less than three years and that are below local code standards.[13] Enforcement of the law is difficult.

The 1981 HUD displacement report concludes that the most common goal of antidisplacement efforts is to help current rental residents remain in revitalized neighborhoods through such devices as rehabilitation subsidies, rent subsidies, antidiscrimination statutes, and housing counseling.[14] This is true although a number of localities have attempted to deal with family needs caused by displacement on a community-wide basis. Following this chapter are brief descriptions of the activities of twelve communities that received innovative grants under HUD's Community Development Block Grant (CDBG) program to deal with displacement needs.

Many approaches seek to soften the blow of escalating rents for existing tenants, who are most often the victims of displacement. The problem for homeowners is less severe, because escalating prices often mean that they benefit from the recovery when they sell. However, individuals on fixed incomes—particularly the elderly—may not be able to pay the increased property taxes that sometimes accompany recovery.

It has been suggested that reverse annuity mortgages be used in these cases. The public or private sector can provide monthly payments to owner occupants with the proviso that the grantor be deeded the property at the time of the death of the occupants. Such approaches have been tried only on a very limited basis but may show promise in the future.[15]

Overall, the local housing function is better equipped to handle the market problems caused by gentrification by cushioning the effects through subsidization rather than by attempting to regulate the market. However, the subsidization route is not easy. It is expensive to pay the increased costs of housing low- and moderate-income people in a neighborhood in which prices are escalating, and it is difficult to orchestrate the programs and subsidies in a way that is effective and benefits those most in need.

Rapidly increasing rents

One of the most difficult local housing policy issues is whether local government should become involved when market conditions permit rapid escalation of rents. For example, should a local housing effort include regulations that control the prices of rental housing via rent control?[16]

Rent control has not been widespread in U.S. cities, but shortages in the rental housing stock in the late 1970s and early 1980s have produced increased pressure for additional local controls. Sternlieb and Hughes go so far as to contend that rent control has caused fundamental changes in legal rights. "The classic elements of property rights have changed abruptly from a concentration on landlords privileges to the protection of the tenantry."[17]

The cry for rent control can be very persuasive, and local elected officials are often hard pressed to ignore the claims of tenants who can no longer afford increased rents. However, before local controls are imposed, officials must consider the long-range effects on the local housing market and local government revenues.

Considerable experience and literature argue that rent control damages the local housing stock and the local government balance sheet. As Joel F. Brenner and Herbert M. Franklin have concluded: (1) Rent control without subsidies has an adverse effect on the state of repair of privately owned rental housing; (2) it is difficult to design a rent control system that benefits only needy tenants or that allocates benefits according to need; (3) rent control contributes to the reduction in the supply of new rental housing, especially at the low end of the market; and (4) rent control provides an inducement to owners to take their units off the market or to convert them to other forms of tenure.[18]

Rent control can lead to disinvestment in rental properties and, in the extreme, to abandonment of rental housing. Once imposed, rent control is exceedingly difficult to repeal due to the disruptive effects on the tenants living in the rent-controlled units.

Sternlieb and Hughes have examined the effect of rent control on the tax base of Fort Lee, New Jersey, and they have found that rent control reduces taxes collected in the long run. As they put it, *". . . rent control represents more than a transfer of resources between landlords and tenants. It is not a two-party transaction, but rather a three-party concern, with the third party— all other property taxpayers within the community—having to bear the ultimate costs of the rent control subsidy."*[19]

Remedies to counter overheated rental markets through regulation at the local level are hard to find and harder still to implement. The real problem for the low-income renter is insufficient income; the appropriate solution may be federal minimum income support or a rent allowance to permit the person of low income to afford prevailing rents. Without question, however, such a subsidy is beyond the financial means of local governments.

Condominium conversions

Conversion of rental properties to condominiums represents a special local housing policy problem. Within the law, conversions of rental units to condominiums can cause serious disruptions for renters, who are often displaced by the conversion. In cities where condominium conversions are occurring at a rapid rate, public policy often focuses on measures to protect existing tenants from condominium developers and purchasers. Such local protections can come in the form of regulations or a limited-term moratorium on conversions. In either case, local public officials must be cautious not to ignore market demand for condominium ownership.

An extensive HUD study of conversion, completed in 1980, indicates that "the recent growth of condominium and cooperative conversions is a response to basic changes in the Nation's social and housing market conditions which, in its course, helps some and hurts others."[20]

On a national scale, by the end of 1979, 1.3 percent of the country's occupied rental housing stock had been converted, but with large variations among metropolitan areas. Six percent or more of the rental stock was converted in the Chicago, Denver, and Washington, D.C., areas, for example. Conversions have been numerous in metropolitan areas characterized by strong and growing market demand for home ownership, not in areas associated with distressed rental markets.[21]

For many rental property owners, the possibility of sale and conversion is extremely attractive, since, ". . . no projected amount of rental income, allowable tax depreciation, property appreciation, or tax sheltering can equal the return received on the sale of their properties for conversion."[22]

The attraction is there. Public attention is certainly focused on the issue, putting pressure on local housing officials to intervene. As the HUD report indicates, however, it is inappropriate to look at gross figures on conversions and assume that all converted units become owner occupied. Many purchasers of condominium units rent to a tenant. Taking all factors into account, for every one hundred rental units converted nationally, there is a net increase of five units for sale to owners and a net decrease of five available rental units.[23]

One of the key problems, of course, is the affordability of the converted units. About 42 percent of those studied by HUD who moved out of converted buildings had incomes that were too low to have permitted them to buy their units.[24]

What is responsible public action on this issue? When polled by HUD, 75 percent of local officials favored a policy of no intervention by the federal and state governments, and over 60 percent favored no local intervention into the market. Of the local officials who did see a need for public intervention, more than half preferred governmental actions that encouraged conversions while softening the negative effects for low- and moderate-income tenants.[25]

Many local officials have been caught off guard by the swiftness and volume of conversions and by community and public reaction to the phenomenon. Complaints from citizens focus on the displacement issue and the quality of the property after conversion. The frequency of conversion regulation is directly related to the amount of conversion activity among cities. Thirty percent of jurisdictions with high rates of conversion activity have enacted regulatory ordinances, compared with 11 percent of those with low volumes of activity.[26]

Local governments have enacted five types of regulatory ordinances: (1) temporary conversion moratoriums; (2) tenant protections; (3) buyer protections; (4) protection of rental stock; and (5) preservation of low- and moderate-income housing. Each of these approaches has been implemented with considerable variation depending on local conditions and public opinion.[27]

TEMPORARY MORATORIUMS   Temporary moratoriums are simply an effort by local officials to buy time on the conversion issue. Several local moratoriums have been struck down in the courts.

TENANT PROTECTIONS   Tenant protections imposed at the local level are widespread. Three-fourths of local regulatory ordinances require a minimum notice period. Some ordinances require that tenants be given right of first refusal to purchase their apartments. About one-fourth of local laws require that the converter provide relocation benefits or assistance to displaced tenants. Some municipalities have included special protection features for elderly and handicapped persons and families with children.[28]

BUYER PROTECTION   Municipalities have enacted buyer protections that tie into the building inspection process. These may require a property condition report to be prepared on the building and to be disclosed to prospective condominium purchasers.

PROTECTION OF RENTAL STOCK   Features to protect the rental stock have been enacted by a few municipalities. These provisions prohibit conversions if the vacancy rate for rental properties is below a certain minimum, usually from 3 to 6 percent. Some localities have set quotas on the total number of units that can be converted.

PRESERVATION OF LOW- AND MODERATE-INCOME HOUSING Laws enacted to preserve low- and moderate-income housing require either that converters set aside a percentage of the apartment units for low- and moderate-income tenants or that they replace low- and moderate-income housing. Los Angeles County, for example, requires that 1 percent of the purchase price of each unit be deposited with the county housing authority to be used to develop low-income housing.[29]

The effects and outcomes of these regulatory approaches must be carefully analyzed locally to ascertain the probable effect of the constraints on the housing market and on the city's overall economy.

Despite the problems associated with condominium conversion, as Sternlieb and Hughes have pointed out, *". . . from a strictly fiscal point of view, one can view the condominium conversion process as significantly upgrading the taxpaying capacity of middle and upper middle income housing, thus providing the wherewithal for financing the needs of less fortunate residents."*[30]

This point of view coincides with that of the local officials surveyed by HUD; but local government has traditionally protected the general public in the housing area, and some regulation, carefully thought through, can be an important and responsible part of the local housing function.

DEVELOPING A LOCAL STRATEGY

Local governments can play the legitimate role of stimulating depressed segments of the local housing market, or they can seek to constrain the market when it is overheated. Conceptualizing and implementing a local housing function that does both well is very difficult, in large part because of the inability to predict the dynamics of neighborhood change accurately. The 1981 HUD report on displacement documents that revitalization activity, for example, does not increase in an orderly or gradual manner but is subject to fluctuations and abrupt changes; there is no systematic pattern in which one set of changes precedes another. While such indicators as changes in sales volume, sales prices, and rehabilitation activity are extremely useful in monitoring revitalization, they cannot be used to predict it.[31] The indicators discussed in Chapter 2 for measuring neighborhood decline are a good starting point, but as noted, the state of the art is primitive. One thing that appears to be essential is that all indicators be based on an annual time series, rather than on detailed surveys at given points in time—the need is to measure trends.[32] Continual monitoring of the market effects of local policies and programs dealing with changing neighborhoods is also needed so that adjustments can be made in efforts to achieve the changes and stated objectives.

As suggested earlier in this chapter, national credit markets and national tax policies affect neighborhood changes in local communities. It may be, as Rolf Goetze suggests, that we are moving into a new dimension of housing policy in which it is recognized that these factors are as influential on local neighborhoods as direct subsidies.[33]

1   See: James Q. Wilson, "The Mayors Versus the Cities," *The Public Interest* 16 (summer 1969): 25–37.

2   Rolf Goetze, *Understanding Neighborhood Change: The Role of Expectations in Urban Revitalization* (Cambridge, Mass.: Ballinger, 1979), p. 34.

3   Rolf Goetze, "Federal Tax Expenditures Should be Restricted to Aid Urban Housing," *Journal of Housing,* October 1980, pp. 504–12.

4   George Sternlieb, *The Tenement Landlord* (Rutgers, N.J.: Rutgers University, Urban Studies Center, 1966), pp. 121–41.

5   For an overview of approaches to treating rental housing, see: Robert Kolodny, *Multi-Family Housing: Treating the Existing Stock* (Washington, D.C.: National Association of Housing and Redevelopment Officials, 1981).

6   For a brief description of an emerging federal viewpoint on rental rehabilitation, see: Robert I. Dodge, "Rental Properties Can be Rehabilitated Using Private Investment, Subsidy Techniques," *Journal of Housing,* October 1980, pp. 497–503.

7   Edward A. Gorgan, "Housing Program is Said to Commit City to $2 Billion in Tax Incentives," *New York Times,* 2 March 1981, p. 1.

8   Kolodny, *Multi-Family Housing,* p. 46.

9   U.S., Department of Housing and Urban Development, *Displacement Report to the U.S. Congress* (Washington, D.C.: U.S. Department of Housing and Urban Development, 1979); and U.S., Department of Housing and Urban Development, Office of Policy Development and Research, *Residential Displacement—An Update:*

Report to Congress (Washington, D.C.: Government Printing Office, 1981).

10   Richard T. LeGates and Chester Hartman, "Displacement," *Clearinghouse Review* 15, no. 3 (July 1981).

11   David R. Goldfield, "Private Neighborhood Redevelopment and Displacement: The Case of Washington, D.C.," *Urban Affairs Quarterly* 15 (June 1980): 457.

12   U.S., Department of Housing and Urban Development, *Residential Displacement —An Update,* pp. iii, iv.

13   Goldfield, "Private Neighborhood Redevelopment and Displacement," p. 463.

14   U.S., Department of Housing and Urban Development, *Residential Displacement —An Update,* p. 80.

15   An unfunded UDAG proposal in 1980 called for such an approach in San Francisco.

16   For an overview on rent control, see: Monica R. Lett, *Rent Control: Concepts, Realities, and Mechanisms* (New Brunswick, N.J.: Rutgers University, Center for Urban Policy Research, 1976).

17   George Sternlieb and James W. Hughes, "The Uncertain Future of Rental Housing," in *America's Housing: Prospects and Problems,* ed. George Sternlieb and James W. Hughes (New Brunswick, N.J.: Rutgers University, Center for Urban Policy Research, 1980), p. 263.

18   Joel F. Brenner and Herbert M. Franklin, *Rent Control in North America and Four European Countries* (Washington, D.C.: Council for International Urban Liaison, 1977), pp. 67–71.

19   George Sternlieb and James W. Hughes, "Rent Control's Impact on the Community

Tax Base," in *America's Housing,* ed. Sternlieb and Hughes, pp. 282–83.

20 U.S., Department of Housing and Urban Development, Office of Policy Development and Research, *The Conversion of Rental Housing to Condominiums and Cooperatives: A National Study of Scope, Causes and Impacts* (Washington, D.C.: Government Printing Office, 1980), p. i.

21 Ibid., p. ii.

22 Ibid., p. iii.

23 Ibid.

24 Ibid., p. vi.

25 Ibid., p. XII-32.

26 Ibid., p. XII-2.

27 For a brief compendium of local controls, see: U.S., Department of Housing and Urban Development, Office of Policy Development and Research, *Condominium Conversion Controls* (Washington, D.C.: U.S. Department of Housing and Urban Development, 1979), pp. 30–47.

28 U.S., Department of Housing and Urban Development, *The Conversion of Rental Housing to Condominiums and Cooperatives,* provides a detailed description of these approaches on pp. XII-8–XII-20.

29 Ibid., p. XII-31.

30 George Sternlieb and James W. Hughes, "Condominium Conversion Profiles: Governmental Policy," in *America's Housing,* ed. Sternlieb and Hughes, p. 307.

31 U.S., Department of Housing and Urban Development, *Residential Displacement —An Update,* pp. 19, 22.

32 Goetze, *Understanding Neighborhood Change,* p. 43.

33 Goetze, "Federal Tax Expenditures Should be Restricted to Aid Urban Housing."

CDBG innovative grants for antidisplacement activities in twelve communities

HOUSING ASSISTANCE CORPORATION, BALTIMORE, MARYLAND

The Housing Assistance Corporation (HAC) was established as a nonprofit corporation to provide home ownership opportunities in low-income neighborhoods where displacement pressures are building. Established as a nonprofit corporation, HAC has provided quick "intervention" buying in four neighborhoods. With a two-year goal in May 1980 of forty-four single-family structures and fifteen rental units, HAC had, by early 1982, acquired thirty-one single-family properties and was in the process of acquiring fifteen rental units.

EQUITY TRANSFER AND HOUSING COUNSELING PROGRAMS, BROOKLINE, MASSACHUSETTS

The city of Brookline has been awarded an innovative grant for a demonstration project aimed at mitigating or eliminating the effects of neighborhood displacement. The project has two components.

The first component is an equity transfer assistance program for low- and moderate-income households threatened with displacement due to condominium conversions. The program differs from other housing subsidy programs in that a permanent lien (second mortgage) in an amount equal to the equity assistance is placed on the dwelling unit. This second mortgage will be recapturable in full upon resale of the unit, thereby reverting to a permanent equity assistance fund assisting other low- and moderate-income households.

The second component addresses the human aspects of condominium conversions through a household counseling component that offers financial and rehabilitation counseling and referrals to help mitigate the trauma caused by the threat of condominium conversion and displacement.

HOUSING LOAN AND COUNSELING PROGRAMS, CHARLOTTESVILLE, VIRGINIA

The purpose of the Charlottesville innovative grant is to promote home ownership among low- and moderate-income families in the city's Tenth and Page neighborhood, an area whose stability is threatened by the influx of University of Virginia students seeking rental housing. This situation has led to rent increases, the construction of large apartment complexes, and the conversion of single-family homes into rental units. The grant will promote stability through three major components:

House Bank/Deferred Loan Program. Low- and moderate-income residents can buy rehabilitated homes at greatly reduced prices. The purchasing family will be able to apply for a deferred loan to finance all or part of the rehabilitation costs.

Short-Term Revolving Loan Fund. This fund would finance short-term low-interest loans to remove financial barriers to low- and moderate-income households becoming homeowners, and to finance repairs to eliminate city housing code violations.

Housing Counseling, Housing Code Enforcement, and Citizen Involvement. Funds will be used to enable citizens and nonprofit groups to develop and utilize their resources to stimulate housing rehabilitation and increase home ownership.

The city has purchased the first house bank property, and two additional houses are under option. The final regulations for the short-term revolving loan program have been approved by the city housing board.

Since February 1981, the city inspections division has inspected forty-eight dwellings under the innovative grant concentrated housing code enforcement program. The owners and occupants of the nineteen dwellings found to be in violation of the city housing code were given information on how to submit applications for the rental repair program.

HOME CONVERSION PROJECT, COLUMBIA, SOUTH CAROLINA

The city of Columbia's two-year program, which began in August 1980, helps low-income residents of rejuvenating neighborhoods to remain in the area by rehabilitating and converting their houses into duplex, triplex, or quadraplex housing. Eighteen houses will be converted into at least forty-two units through no-interest, deferred payment loans. HUD's Section 8 moderate rehabilitation program will be used to ensure that the newly created units remain affordable for low-income displacees. The city staff conducted neighborhood meetings in three of the city's neighborhood strategy areas, and promotional materials were distributed in the neighborhoods as part of the outreach efforts. Once potential applicants are identified, loan applications are prepared and processed; the specification writer drafts a preliminary specification and cost estimate for the house conversion; and the rehabilitation work is awarded to a contractor. After conversion, the management and maintenance of the units will be contracted to the Columbia Housing Authority.

RESIDENTIAL DISPLACEMENT STRATEGIES, DENVER, COLORADO

The program, as proposed, was to consist of six remedial and preventive measures to minimize displacement:

Interim financing for a nonprofit organization to buy and renovate a downtown residential hotel to protect and improve housing for low-income elderly persons

Mortgage payment assistance for low-income renters in neighborhoods undergoing revitalization

Referral services to provide one-step information and counseling to persons with housing problems

Education and technical assistance to encourage the formation of housing cooperatives, and the establishment of a fund to secure options on buildings where cooperative financing is sought

Section 8 set-aside for low-income persons displaced by private reinvestment activities (40 units)

Conversion of a surplus school to affordable housing for low-income elderly persons.

The Denver project has encountered a number of obstacles since its inception. Termination of the HUD Section 312 program, which would have paid for the proposed rehabilitation activities, has hampered renovation of the downtown Bart Hotel. The local school board's refusal to sell the schools has delayed conversion of a school to elderly housing. The referral services portion of the project, however, is in place and operating smoothly.

MOBILE HOME PARK RECONSTRUCTION, FAIRFAX COUNTY, VIRGINIA

The county proposed to improve the Woodley Hills–Nightingale Mobile Home Park. The privately owned park is overcrowded; the lot sizes are too small for modern mobile homes; the street system is poorly designed and has deteriorated; flooding and soil erosion are common; electrical service is a hazard; and the community lacks adequate fire protection, recreational facilities, and utilities. Despite these deficiencies, for many of its residents this is the only affordable housing they can find in Fairfax County. Through the use of innovative grant funds, the county will improve conditions in the park, provide opportunities for residents to own their mobile homes, and create cooperative resident ownership for the park itself.

CONDOMINIUM PURCHASE PROGRAM, KING COUNTY (SEATTLE), WASHINGTON

The King County Housing Authority bought twenty-five one-bedroom condominium units for resale to low- and moderate-income elderly residents who are affected by displacement pressures resulting from urban revitalization. The housing authority is now renting the units to qualified applicants.

SKID ROW TRANSITIONAL HOUSING, LOS ANGELES, CALIFORNIA

The city of Los Angeles started a three-year program in July 1980 to get displaced persons and homeless indigents into temporary dormitory housing, with the ultimate goal of placing them in conventional housing. This housing program is using innovative grant funds to buy a commercial/industrial building and convert it to accommodate 150 beds, group living quads, shower rooms, a kitchen and dining facility, offices for social service workers, a laundromat, and recreation and training areas. The Skid Row Development Corporation, a nonprofit group under contract to the city, has bought the building and will carry out the project.

The city of Los Angeles is engaged in a central business district redevelopment project, and the Skid Row revitalization effort is one component. The transitional housing project will include a number of social, health, and other services in addition to shelter. Continuing support will come from rental receipts, employment training programs, volunteer groups, church groups, interns from local universities, county department of public social services shelter vouchers, and fund-raising and economic development activities of the Skid Row Development Corporation.

RENTAL OWNERSHIP CONVERSION, MINNEAPOLIS, MINNESOTA

The primary objective of this project is to minimize the effects of displacement in the Phillips Neighborhood Strategy Area through the provision of affordable rental housing to the area's low- and moderate-income families and the conversion of these units into permanent home ownership through an option to buy.

The city plans to provide 104 rental units to low- and moderate-income persons. Other supportive activities will include housing counseling, career development, personal financing, home maintenance, family management, property ownership, and other social and economic services. During the rental period, the property will be owned and managed by a community-based nonprofit corporation. Program participants will receive assistance in the form of a decreasing rent subsidy through the Section 8 existing housing program.

COOPERATIVE HOUSING LENDING PROGRAM, SANTA BARBARA, CALIFORNIA

The city of Santa Barbara is undertaking a one-year program, which began in September 1980, to minimize the displacement of low- and moderate-income households caused by the very expensive and tight housing market in the city. The HUD innovative grant funds are being used to assist with the interim financing requirements of the acquisition and rehabilitation of a thirteen-unit complex that will be converted to a model limited equity housing cooperative. Twelve families were selected for the first cooperative effort. It is expected that the members will take occupancy as tenants and that the final financial closing for the project will occur in October 1981. The project will then be converted to a cooperative and the membership shares will be sold.

HOTEL REHABILITATION FOR SINGLE-ROOM OCCUPANCY, SEATTLE, WASHINGTON

The Atlas Hotel is being rehabilitated to provide forty-six housekeeping, studio, and one-bedroom units for lease to low-income permanent residents of the downtown Seattle area. The rehabilitation is to be financed through a development loan, of which $639,000 is innovative grant funds. Total loan costs should be approximately $1 million. Construction was scheduled to be completed in early 1982.

FIRST-RIGHT-TO-PURCHASE ASSISTANCE, WASHINGTON, D.C.

The District of Columbia was awarded funds to help tenants exercise their first right to purchase their present housing, as provided under the D.C. Rental Housing Act of 1977. The project is designed to facilitate direct ownership by lower-income tenants facing displacement in revitalizing neighborhoods.

The assistance will be provided to individual tenants in single-family and apartment units as well as to tenant associations. The assistance can include: earnest money loans; loans for purchase options; down payment assistance; subordinated trust mortgage loans, which provide "gap" financing for cooperative development costs; and management training for tenant associations in assisted multiunit buildings.

Source: Excerpted and abstracted from: U.S., Department of Housing and Urban Development, *Residential Displacement—An Update: Report to Congress* (Washington, D.C.: Government Printing Office, 1981).

Housing portfolio

Housing today is far more than zoning, subdivision regulations, mortgages, construction, and inspections. The photos on the following pages highlight neighborhood revitalization in Pittsburgh, below-market and in-fill housing in St. Paul and Minneapolis, adaptive reuse in Boston, and neighborhood involvement in Baltimore.

Photos 1, 2, and 3 show part of Pittsburgh's North Side revitalization where private-sector actions are helping spur investment and prevent disinvestment by involving all key actors in a multiyear program. Photo 4 dramatizes how responding to changes in the housing market can help ensure long-term improvement.

Substantial rehabilitation of institutional buildings is another approach to housing improvement. Photos 5 and 6 show housing converted from a former church and a former community center in St. Paul. Photos 7 and 8 show in-fill housing in existing neighborhoods in St. Paul. The equity assistance for home buyers included local government revenue bonds, an urban development action grant (UDAG), and foundation support.

The former Baker's Chocolate mill in Boston has been converted to 57 moderate rental apartments with a UDAG and reinvestment of syndication proceeds (Photo 9). Photo 10 shows a passive solar energy component in the atrium in Boston's Westland Avenue Apartments.

The extensive programs of the city of Baltimore and the Baltimore Department of Housing and Community Development emphasize neighborhood involvement (Photos 11 and 12). These and many other Baltimore activities are described in Appendix G.

Photo 1   Pittsburgh's North Side Revitalization (photo: Pittsburgh Urban Redevelopment Authority).

**Photo 2 Pittsburgh's North Side Re-
vitalization (photo: Pittsburgh Urban
Redevelopment Authority).**

**Photo 3   Pittsburgh's North Side Re-
vitalization (photo: Pittsburgh Urban
Redevelopment Authority).**

Photo 4   Pittsburgh's North Side Re-vitalization (photo: Pittsburgh Urban Redevelopment Authority).

Photo 5   St. Paul Below-Market Home Rehabilitation, former church (photo: St. Paul Department of Planning and Economic Development).

Photo 6   St. Paul Below-Market Home Rehabilitation, former community center (photo: St. Paul Department of Planning and Economic Development).

Photo 7 Minneapolis/St. Paul Family Housing Fund (photo: St. Paul Department of Planning and Economic Development).

Photo 8 Minneapolis/St. Paul Family Housing Fund (photo: St. Paul Department of Planning and Economic Development).

Photo 9   Boston's Lower Mills conversion (photo: Joseph Henefield).

Photo 10   Boston's Westland Avenue Apartments, passive solar component in interior atrium (photo: Herb Engelsberg).

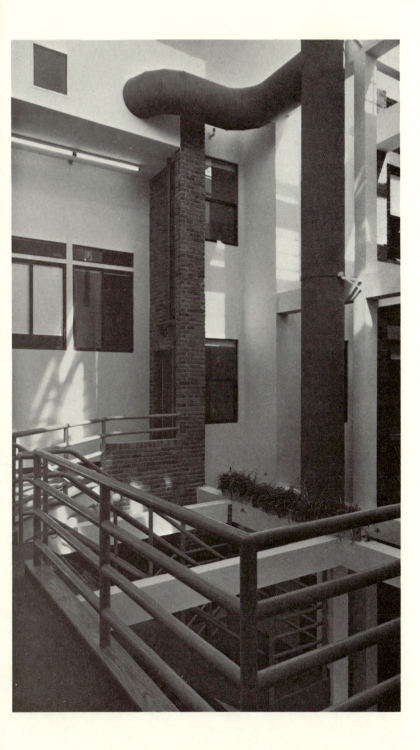

Photos 11 and 12   Neighborhood involvement in Baltimore housing activities (photo: Information Services Division, Baltimore Department of Housing and Community Development).

Chapter 5

Housing and
the states

By tradition and reputation, most states are viewed by those concerned with housing and urban revitalization at best as "sleeping giants" and at worst as potential barriers between local communities and federal government assistance.

This judgment is based on past experience; too often states have been removed from the increasing struggles of cities to survive fiscal and economic crises. In some cases this "noninvolvement" has had serious negative consequences for large urban communities:

State-approved industrial revenue bonds are often the chief means by which industries are able to leapfrog out of center cities into new industrial parks. Some states even permit these tax-exempt bonds to subsidize shopping centers and hamburger stands on outlying arterial highways.

States have literally paved the way for the job drain out of cities by upgrading peripheral roads and providing countless highway interchanges, curb cuts, and traffic signals for suburban industrial parks and shopping centers—all at public expense—while city streets are left in disrepair.

Instead of resisting the land-, energy-, and water-wasting practices of the Environmental Protection Agency's sewer construction program, some states continue to sewer cornfields and vacation lands while ignoring the pollution problems of central cities.

Many states have helped reinforce the exodus of jobs out of cities by relocating state offices and facilities—from community colleges to health clinics—out of central, in-town locations to peripheral areas not connected to public transportation.

Often decisions on major state-controlled construction programs are made without consideration of their potential for stimulating private investment where it is needed most—in the cities. The possibility of combining such programs to achieve economic revitalization in urban areas is often ignored or resisted by state agencies.

The absence of a clearly understood state role in the resolution of urban problems has bred suspicion and even hostility. The costs of this omission are great. For how can sound housing and community development be achieved in cities when the public facility investments, regulatory practices, and tax policies of state governments fuel random and haphazard development outside city boundaries?

Clearly, some state governments have contributed to local problems. For this reason alone, they should become part of the solution. As the National Commission on Urban Problems observed in 1968: "The states have tended to become forgotten members of the governmental family. By using powers they already possess, by assuming new authority when necessary, and in providing funds, they occupy a unique position to help bring urban areas out of confusion . . . and to restore a sense of community to our cities."[1]

SIGNS OF CHANGE

Beginning in the 1970s, there was evidence that states' perceptions of their roles relative to housing and community development were changing. One clear indication was the growth of state housing finance agencies; by 1981, they were established in forty-four states and had assisted in the financing of 305,000 single-family homes and 296,000 multifamily housing units (see Table 1–2). Another development was the growing number of states that were using their tax powers to grant tax abatements for assisted housing or tax benefits for housing rehabilitation. As of 1979, some twenty-five states had passed legislation to enable localities to establish property tax relief programs for housing rehabilitation.

Still a further sign of change was the initiatives taken in some states to revise building and housing codes and to develop new land use and growth strategies governing future development. A few states have developed "housing elements" as part of comprehensive planning requirements. These initiatives are summarized in Chapter 1.

The expansion and maturity of local housing functions in some communities is stimulating state action; this is particularly true where the traditional functions of zoning/land use control, building codes, and housing codes are being joined with later initiatives to provide lower-income housing, eliminate slums, and restore neighborhoods.

One of the most productive future relationships between states and localities in housing and community revitalization centers on state actions in traditional functional areas related to land use and growth strategies and in the regulatory functions of building and housing codes. In fact, the detailed recommendations for state actions in these areas proposed by the National Commission on Urban Problems in 1968 are still germane; they are included as Appendix D.

Another area for state action, particularly for smaller communities, is housing finance, which is clearly undergoing major adjustments. State activity can usefully take two forms: (1) state financing of locally initiated housing developments (particularly rental housing and housing for lower-income families), and (2) state technical assistance in housing finance to assist local public agencies in putting together public/private financing packages.

Beyond this, a potentially productive new area for state action to reduce the cost of housing is the so-called "affordable housing" initiatives. The U.S. Department of Housing and Urban Development (HUD) has launched a program called "Joint Venture for Affordable Housing," a collective effort of public/private-sector groups, including, as a key participant, the Council of State Community Affairs Agencies (COSCAA). Despite the growing interest in state-level policies to reduce the cost—or increase the availability—of housing, there is surprisingly little agreement concerning the kinds of policies that are likely to prove most effective. A recent study by COSCAA notes, with wry understatement, "the near total absence at the state level of any kind of rigorous analysis, evaluation or monitoring of the impact of state actions to promote affordable housing or to reduce the cost of housing."[2] Not only do state governments disagree on the relative importance of various housing programs, but they share few common assumptions concerning the criteria for judging such efforts. The three principal results are: (1) few state housing programs have been subjected to thorough and independent evaluation; (2) little research is done, either nationally or by the states, on the impact of the broad-scale tax, regulatory, and expenditure environment on the costs and pace of housing production; and (3) virtually no states have developed housing policy that is not at the mercy of changes in federal programming, tax policy, and mortgage market intervention. In many respects, the situation is comparable to that of economic development policy in the mid-seventies, when state-level efforts were largely a reflection of federal initiatives. Nevertheless, the potential for state action in these areas is a much greater opportunity than ever before. The basic issues for developing state housing policies are included in Appendix E.

PRIORITIES FOR STATE ACTION

One reason for the wide discrepancy among states in housing policy, and within states in the seemingly random inclusion of differing housing initiatives, is that little attention is paid to the overall objectives of housing policy. Apart from vague references to the preamble of the National Housing Act of 1949, surprisingly little attention is given to the underlying problems that housing policy should address. The result is piecemeal state programs that reflect general mandates and the powers and competencies of state housing finance agencies and departments of community affairs.

On the state level, five principal "problem areas" are susceptible to public policy:

1. Housing the homeless (most often, this refers to the provision of single-room occupancy units for transient welfare recipients)
2. Providing rental apartments for low-income households, including direct income assistance to families and individuals
3. Subsidizing new housing construction
4. Improving the affordability of owner-occupied housing
5. Reducing (or restraining the growth of) housing prices.

Each of these problem areas can be addressed through a combination of tools or "policy levers": direct grants, interest subsidies, regulatory changes, income assistance, tax changes, and new financing instruments. Some policies may, of course, address more than one objective. Standardized and aggressive code enforcement, for example, can not only prevent the deterioration of rental units to the point of inhabitability but also reduce the cost of code compliance by providing builders (and rehabilitators) with only one set of regulations to work with.

Of these five areas, two have been the subject of widespread attention by the states: improving overall housing affordability and subsidizing new housing construction (including the construction of new rental units).

In a survey by the Council of State Community Affairs Agencies, the responding states noted actions to improve overall housing affordability in four principal areas: (1) construction standards affecting the quantity, quality, and materials used in housing production; (2) land supply, development, and regulation; (3) labor costs; and (4) capital costs and availability.[3]

Construction standards

Although many construction regulations directly raise overall housing costs, the two types that are most frequently used by states are (1) standards for the materials and assembly of modular housing units and (2) building codes.

Although site standards are traditionally a local responsibility, states are rapidly moving to standardize component materials and assembly procedures for modular housing. As modular (or prefab) housing grows in importance, standardized regulations, reciprocity agreements among states, and adequate enforcement are likely to lower housing prices.

Building codes are also viewed as a major opportunity to reduce construction costs. The trend toward uniform statewide codes (rather than a patchwork of locally drawn codes) accelerated in the 1970s. Increasingly popular were "minimum/maximum codes," which set a minimal statewide standard that all construction must meet, and a maximum standard that local governments could add to their requirements.

There is also a growing interest in state-adopted rehabilitation codes that set standards less stringent than those required of new construction. Although only a few states have actually established separate rehabilitation codes (Massachusetts was the first), architects and industry groups are pressuring states to move in this direction. This is one clear way of reducing the cost of rental housing for low- and moderate-income people.

Land supply, development, and regulation

Although states have undertaken a variety of initiatives in land regulation in the past decade, it is still primarily a local function. Among the most significant state-level actions in recent years are (1) legislation prohibiting local governments from discriminating against the use of modular housing components and lower-income or higher-density housing; (2) state aid programs that penalize local governments for not meeting standards for the supply of affordable housing or the provision of wastewater treatment facilities and access roads; (3) legislation standardizing the issuance of permits for housing construction; and (4) actions that increase the supply of developable land, particularly near population centers. Among the most popular initiatives in this last area are the use of surplus property and air rights for housing development, grants or low-interest loans to communities for the purchase of land or the provision of community services to property used for low- and moderate-income housing, and permitting the use of tax increment financing for infrastructure investments in selected areas.

Labor costs

The only significant action in reducing labor costs in housing production is the repeal or weakening of state-level Davis-Bacon laws governing wage scales for construction workers in publicly assisted projects. These actions have taken place largely in southern states, where labor is under increasing attack from conservative business groups and others.

Capital

The states view those programs that directly provide housing finance as the most significant of all state-level policies affecting housing costs. One reason may be the tendency of governmental agencies to support most fervently those programs with outcomes the agencies themselves control. This would perhaps explain why, in the recent COSCAA survey, the states viewed programs that provide housing capital *directly* to be more important than programs that affect a much larger portion of private capital *indirectly*. In any case, direct intervention in the mortgage market is increasingly favored over the use of such indirect means as tax incentives.

Among the incentive programs offered, the most favored include (1) full or partial exemptions from property taxes for improvements made to both rental and owner-occupied housing (sometimes including a state reimbursement of local revenue losses), and (2) circuit breaker programs that reduce the property tax payments of either the elderly or the poor, with the reduction taking the form of either a direct rebate (for renters) or lower real estate taxes. Other incentive mechanisms employed by states include differential property tax assessments for residential property, abatements for the conversion of industrial or commercial structures to residential use or the conversion of temporary to permanent housing, exemptions from property taxation for housing owned and operated by not-for-profit organizations, metropolitan tax sharing, income tax credits for housing rehabilitation, increased state aid for communities reducing property tax levels, and allowing local governments to impose income or sales taxes to thus reduce reliance on local property taxes.

Although state governments have been engaged in direct financial intervention since the creation of the New York housing finance agency in 1960, it is only in the past decade that state housing finance agencies (HFAs) have moved beyond indirect subsidization of multifamily rental housing to more direct capital market intervention (for an overview of HFA activities, see Table 5–1). In 1974, for example, the state of Virginia issued tax-exempt bonds to raise capital for single-family mortgage lending, the first such effort in the nation. Within four short years, this form of financing accounted for 62 percent of all money raised by state HFAs. Unfortunately, as several recent studies have pointed out, much of this money has gone to finance housing that private institutions would have financed even in the absence of HFAs. Several agencies made little effort to distinguish between those borrowers who can qualify for private sector financing and those who are unreasonably denied access to mortgage loans.[4] The principal reason for this lies in the source of HFA financing—mortgage revenue bonds. These bonds are secured by the repayment of interest and principal and are most marketable when investors view the program participants as having credit characteristics that the private market would approve in its own banking activities. The widespread result has been the "displacement" of conventional private lending by public dollars. And as no accompanying change has occurred in private lending criteria, the overall volume of mortgage lending has failed to increase. (In fact, it has fallen, largely due to the virtually stagnant market for

Table 5–1   State housing finance agency activities.

Activity	No. of states[1]
Financial and lending services	
Single-family housing	
Direct construction loans	3 (21)
Direct permanent loans	7 (16)
Mortgage purchases	30 (5)
Loans to lenders	10 (18)
Multifamily housing	
Direct construction loans	23 (10)
Direct permanent loans	26 (8)
Mortgage purchases	9 (18)
Loans to lenders	3 (17)
General	
Seed money	11 (13)
Mortgage insurance program[2]	6 (11)
Rent supplement program[3]	7 (3)
Land acquisition[4]	6 (14)
Development activities	
Nonhousing[5]	7 (15)
Rehabilitation program	17 (23)
Administrative capabilities	
Technical assistance	29 (10)
Statewide housing needs evaluation	31 (6)

Source: Urban Institute Survey of Housing Finance Agencies, 1979.

[1] The number in parentheses refers to the number of states with authorization to perform this function but not currently doing so.

[2] Does not include reserve funds for uninsured loans.

[3] State funded.

[4] Through means other than eminent domain.

[5] Commercial and/or community facilities in conjunction with a housing project.

public bond issues, a continuing constraint on the growth of the money supply, extraordinarily high interest rates, and a generally flat economy.)

Although most of the activity in state housing finance has not been innovative, a few states have begun programs that do address genuine market failures. Among the most innovative is California's Homeownership

Coinvestment Program, a model effort for states seeking to help renters and mobile home dwellers move into permanent affordable housing of their own. Under the coinvestment program, the state provides financing so that eligible households and not-for-profit corporations can purchase property in exchange for a share in the equity of the property (and thus in subsequent appreciation in its value). Repayment to the state is made upon the future sale of the property, a factor which, assuming a continuing appreciation in property values, will allow the program ultimately to become self-financing. The state is able to reduce the monthly costs of housing—and thereby its affordability to low- and moderate-income people—by taking its "return" via an equity share in the dwelling rather than via the more traditional fixed payments over the life of the mortgage. The program permits funds to be used to purchase occupied rental units that are being converted to condominiums or cooperatives; to purchase mobile homes anchored on permanent foundations; and to purchase shares in a nonprofit cooperative that owns a mobile home park in which the borrower intends to reside.

Although not yet enacted, one other California program deserves close scrutiny by other states, particularly those interested in tapping the potential of public pension fund assets to spur housing construction and to provide alternative financial instruments to improve housing affordability. The California Housing Finance Agency has proposed legislation that would (1) insure mortgage loans made by public and private pension funds and (2) provide construction loans at below-market interest rates. The mortgage loans to be insured are of the "equity kicker" type frequently used in commercial real estate development. Through the use of similar techniques, the program will reduce monthly debt service expenses in order to produce a project with lower rental rates. Through the deferral of interest payments (due and payable on the sale of the project), these reduced rental rates are made feasible to the developer.

Both this program and the equity coinvestment program strike directly at some of the major impediments to home ownership and rental housing production in the structure of our financial markets (in this they differ from the more traditional mortgage revenue bond programs so popular with most housing finance agencies). Each in its own way works to complete the market for equity financing, which until recently was virtually nonexistent for owner-occupied shelter. Only for the purchase of existing rental units (or the development of new ones) was it possible to secure external coinvestors to provide funds for that portion of the cost that was not covered by the available mortgage.

Two additional areas where state-level innovation is beginning are (1) the development of alternatives to level amortization mortgages, which are increasingly unsuited to a market environment dominated by inflation, and

(2) the development of mortgage instruments that are tailored to an individual's likely income growth (and thus to his or her growing ability to manage relatively higher real payments over time). In the former case, the principal action required of the states is to allow graduated-payment mortgages. Many states currently do not; either they directly prohibit all but level-payment mortgages or they do so indirectly by prohibiting the collection of compound interest ("interest on interest"). Beyond this, certain tax changes may be required to permit lenders to defer interest without defining it as accrued income for tax purposes (and thereby raising the effective tax rate).

Interest rates, rent subsidies, and new financing instruments will not solve all the problems of the housing market. Poor and moderate-income people need housing that offers cost advantages without public subsidies. Perhaps the most interesting innovation proposed in this regard in recent years is the limited-equity housing cooperative. Essentially, this refers to a multifamily residential unit that is cooperatively owned, through shares, by the residents of the project. Rather than owning the unit in which he or she resides, each tenant owns a share in a not-for-profit corporation. This corporation, in turn, has taken out a "blanket" mortgage for all the units. In contrast to a market cooperative, the equity of the project resides in the corporation instead of the individual unit. Tenants are permitted to sell their shares only for the original purchase price plus some specified rate of interest, compounded annually. This ensures that, as tenants gradually turn over, the entry costs facing new occupants—the cost of purchasing a share in the corporation—are kept relatively low. Although this arrangement precludes owners from reaping a large capital gain, it does allow for the tax advantages associated with home ownership. Moreover, as the equity in the corporation builds up over time, tenants are able to borrow against it, should they so desire, to finance maintenance, improvements, and additions to the complex.

Limited-equity co-ops are growing, and the major role for state governments in spurring their wider use lies in the encouragement states can give to private lenders, many of whom are unfamiliar with cooperatives and thus reluctant to provide the blanket mortgages these projects require. (Bankers incur higher costs for lending in any nontraditional way; unfamiliarity imposes higher information and transaction costs, thus driving up the price of money and sometimes making such projects infeasible. Thrift institutions usually have a policy of not lending to co-ops of any kind.) More significantly, at least one state housing finance agency has begun to provide direct mortgage insurance for limited-equity co-ops. While this may mark a gradual trend, it is likely to have a smaller impact than could be achieved if the states were to indicate their willingness to purchase, via their public pension funds, permanent mortgages for such projects. In this way, mortgage originators could gradually become more familiar with this type of housing development and utimately be more willing to finance such developments with their own assets.

Income assistance

Although not cited as part of the COSCAA survey, an additional area for state initiatives is in "shelter allowances" under the welfare program. As noted in Chapter 1, states have decision-making authority as to whether shelter is included as part of a "flat grant" to assist welfare families. Experience in states with separate shelter allowances indicates that separate allowances present greater opportunities for ensuring housing quality for the individual housing unit as well as for the neighborhood in which the unit is located. The levels of "shelter allowance" are also subject to state discretion.

COMPREHENSIVE STATE STRATEGIES

"Comprehensive urban strategies," which have emerged in a few states, could be an additional element in state efforts to assume an independent leadership role in housing and community revitalization. In 1978 HUD defined "state urban strategy" as a coordinated and consistent set of plans, policies, programs, or activities aimed at *community conservation* (addressing existing conditions of distress or decline, including inefficient and disorderly growth) and *expansion of opportunities* (providing greater housing and employment opportunities and improving their accessibility to minorities and the poor).[5] In a 1980 analysis the National Academy of Public Administration expanded on this definition:

A state urban strategy can be defined as an explicit policy framework containing a set of articulated goals and policies with identified programs and activities which can address issues of growth, development or decline affecting the state's communities. A strategy should be comprehensive in its scope and address at least four major areas of state-local assistance: growth management, economic development and employment, community revitalization, and fiscal reform. A strategy should contain three basic elements:

Goals   A statement of the purposes and objectives of the strategy.
Programs   Identification of the programs or activities which will be used to reach the stated goals.
Processes   Identification of the methods and approaches to be used in program implementation, including the organizational and managerial methods by which individual programs will be coordinated with other programs and activities, and the methods of monitoring and evaluating progress in reaching strategy objectives.[6]

The development of these strategies was in part a response to the National Urban Policy announced by the Carter administration in March

1978 and its call for a federal-state partnership to respond to urban policies. But, more important, it was recognition of the need for state action to combat economic decline, obsolescence of physical plants, and poor housing, and to respond to problems of rapid growth.

As of 1980, ten states in five geographic regions had urban strategies (Connecticut, Massachusetts, New Jersey, Pennsylvania, Michigan, Ohio, Florida, North Carolina, Oregon, and California). These states represent both older areas and new growth areas. Nine of the state strategies put primary emphasis on economic development. Six give major attention to growth management. All the strategies address "urban revitalization" (special recognition of older, declining cities) and "community conservation" (which includes smaller or less urban communities). These strategies usually give special attention to housing, public facilities, and adequacy of public service. Some states include fiscal reforms to increase the equity of tax systems and the fiscal capacity of local government.[7]

A significant finding in these states was the linkage between urban revitalization, including housing, and growth/land use management. State housing initiatives typically included higher bonding authority for state housing finance agencies, better targeting for state housing programs, and promotion of tax policies to encourage housing rehabilitation.[8]

Two approaches to state urban strategies were identified among the ten states.

A horizontal strategy concentrates on the state government with respect to program coordination, regulatory approaches, financial aid, and tax incentives for local governments. The local government involvement is low with this strategy. The states using this approach are California, Connecticut, New Jersey, Pennsylvania, and Michigan.

A vertical strategy concentrates on housing policies and processes that change or guide the actions of local governments as well as state agencies. In three states, local government involvement in the process is high—Oregon, North Carolina, and Massachusetts; in one state it is low—Florida.[9]

One of the political dilemmas involved in developing and implementing a state urban strategy is the strong tendency of many communities to resist change. The desire to preserve and protect the distinctive character of communities and regions is best captured in the Massachusetts *Growth Policy Report of 1977:* "Villages don't want to be suburbs; suburbs don't want to be cities; and cities don't want to be wastelands."[10] States with urban strategies have found a way of reconciling the seemingly contradictory needs to grow while remaining the same. By emphasizing the revitalization of major regional centers and by facilitating the expansion of jobs and housing in central cities, states can help these communities preserve their character. Further, by encouraging the location of most of the increase in jobs and housing in suburban and rural towns in or adjacent to their centers, these communities can retain an identity separate and distinct from their neighbors, and the life of these communities can be enhanced.

Thus, most states have rooted their early development strategies in the goal of revitalizing city and town centers. Even more important than simply preserving character, this strategy serves other valuable objectives. The revitalization of centers is a direct response to the loss of farmland, the deterioration of the environment, exorbitant state and local taxes, the waste of limited energy resources, the anticipated demand for decent housing by an unprecedented number of new households, and the nagging problem of chronic unemployment.

States that have taken the lead in urban strategies have also made impressive strides toward translating these policies into concrete action. They have channeled public facility funds for roads, sewers, and parks into areas of greatest need. Schools, government offices, and post offices are kept in urban places. New tax incentives and financing mechanisms have been targeted to in-town locations. Urban neighborhoods have received greater protection against arson, tax delinquency, and redlining. More money is spent to reuse and improve the urban housing stock. Because of the importance of these state strategies, an executive summary of this ten-state experience is included as Appendix F.

These strategies have been developed without major financial incentives from Washington. They are due largely to the leadership and commitment of the governors in these states.

Housing is a central component of all these strategies, but its relationship to the other facets of the development strategy is not as clear as it might be. Reasons include the loss of momentum of many housing programs assisted by the federal government and the pressing need for a variety of housing in every community.

REQUIRED STATE ACTIONS

States can alleviate housing problems by: (1) discouraging the abandonment and destruction of urban housing stock; (2) halting disinvestment in urban neighborhoods; (3) rejecting projects that destroy housing or displace residents; (4) integrating the state housing strategy with other development policies; (5) providing technical assistance; (6) providing investment funds to stimulate housing production; and (7) reviewing housing standards and regulations.

Discouraging abandonment or loss of housing stock

Perhaps the most important way to solve housing problems is to discourage the wholesale abandonment and destruction of the urban housing stock. Governors and state legislatures are in a unique position to respond to these problems without expense. The states could put more severe penalties on, and require more aggressive pursuit of, tax-delinquent owners of multifamily rental housing. The states could take the profit out of arson by putting an end to overinsurance, by requiring insurance companies to train investigators and to conduct investigations, and by forcing purchasers of fire insurance to pay all taxes owned on the property first. Further, the state could increase the detection of, and penalties for, redlining.

Halting disinvestment in urban neighborhoods

In deciding where to invest in highway, park, and sewer improvements, many states follow the path of least resistance out of the cities and into the corn-fields. This pattern of disinvestment in the public facilities of urban areas is most striking in urban neighborhoods, especially neighborhood shopping districts. A state government can add substantially to neighborhood stability simply by shifting its development priorities; it does not need to spend more money. Repairing neighborhood infrastructure, upgrading neighborhood parks, and repairing neighborhood access roads and transportation systems can stimulate a positive belief in the future, so critical to a neighborhood's survival.

Rejecting projects

Because of the numerous difficulties in producing new housing, it is particularly important for states to turn their backs on new highways, community colleges, airports, and other projects that require the demolition of tens or hundreds of housing units, displacing people from their homes and neighborhoods, unless there is a firm commitment to affordable replacement housing.

Integrating housing and other development policies

The various state government agencies pursuing and promoting transportation, environmental, and economic improvements must be made to reinforce and support the state's housing strategy, and vice versa. This will lead to the placement of housing in locations most able to accommodate it.

An example from Massachusetts illustrates the point. Prior to 1977, industrial revenue bonds (IRBs) could be used only for manufacturing expansions. But, consistent with the emerging emphasis on the revitalization of distressed city and neighborhood centers, the IRB program was expanded to lend assistance to commercial projects in those centers, called commercial area revitalization districts. Thus, restaurants, offices, supermarkets, and retail stores could all obtain lower-cost financing in the existing centers that needed them most, but *not* outside them. In addition, since these centers frequently have many existing buildings with empty upper stories, a provision was passed to make this form of lower-cost financing available to developers willing to convert the upper stories of these buildings to housing. This program has met with great success; almost $150 million in new commercial investment occurred in the state's existing centers from 1978 through 1981. However, the housing provision was recently stymied by Congress when it restricted the availability of this financing to projects that could provide 20 percent of the units to Section 8 eligible tenants for twenty years. Instead of reusing vacant buildings in depressed commercial centers for lower-cost housing, developers have been forced to become dependent on a secondary subsidy source, a source that is rapidly disappearing.

The development strategies of state governments must not only be internally consistent and reinforcing, but must be firmly grounded in local development needs, which vary from community to community. Thus, in planning their development strategies, states must communicate with and be responsive to local officials and agencies.

Providing technical assistance

With the withdrawal of federal leadership in solving housing problems, housing initiatives will have to come from state and local governments. Local officials especially—those most directly exposed to the problems in need of remedy—must meet the housing challenges of the 1980s. In this context, states can provide significant help by offering technical assistance to local agencies and nonprofit sponsors. Many states pay lip service to technical assistance, and some provide genuine support, but what local governments require is a systematic, independent capacity to transform the commitment and enthusiasm to solve housing problems through progressive action.

Another case from Massachusetts offers a good example. In 1977 the Community Economic Development Assistance Corporation (CEDAC) was established to provide the technical expertise needed by community development corporations to embark on housing and commercial and industrial ventures. With an appropriation of $2 million, CEDAC is able to pay for expert consultants, offer seed money, and build coalitions of community residents, bankers, lawyers, developers, and builders.

Local agencies and corporations need this kind of nonbureaucratic direct assistance if they are to confront the housing problems of their communities. As the states assume direct responsibility for administering HUD's Small Cities CDBG program, the existence of a source of technical assistance funds for local governments and nonprofits to tap should help to bring about substantial improvement in the quality of projects funded by CDBG.

Providing investment funds

Perhaps the single most noticeable effect of the current housing crisis is that little or no new rental housing is being built. The states can assume several roles here. Already mentioned are initiatives to encourage pension funds to place mortgages on new or rehabilitated private rental housing by providing guarantees. States could also place these guarantees on their own housing finance issues to attract buyers and to lower interest rates. More bold would be the provision of direct assistance in the wake of reduced federal assistance. States with public housing programs of their own could explore ways of using those funds indirectly to trigger private housing production, with interest rate write-downs, revenue subsidies, or see-saw loans against operating deficits in the early years.

Massachusetts has created two independent agencies with the capacity to engage in experimental housing efforts. CEDAC was funded with $10 million, which in turn could be loaned to or invested as equity in private housing or job-generating initiatives in distressed communities through a community development corporation serving as an intermediary. With this flexibility, local community development corporations can work creatively with private enterprise to get the most intractable small housing projects off the ground. To date, few success stories exist to provide much support for this assertion, but the framework is in place.

The Government Land Bank was begun in 1975 to create jobs and housing on abandoned military bases. Funded by a $40 million general obligation bond (fully backed by the state), the land bank supports projects proposed by local governments on behalf of private developers. One drawback is that the land bank is interested in relatively short investments of no more than three to six years in order to stimulate the maximum number of projects.

Two housing developments recently obtained final approval. One involves the takeover by a nonprofit corporation of twenty or so abandoned two- to three-family structures that were in relatively good repair. The land bank would provide the money to upgrade these units for resale at $20,000 to $30,000 to local moderate-income residents. The other project is described in Chapter 3—the Bakers Chocolate mill conversion in Boston. The land bank's funds would be used as a permanent six-year mortgage at a low interest rate for 1982 (11 percent based on a thirty-year amortization term). At the end of six years the units will be sold at a small markup in price (10 percent) to tenants.

Similar kinds of direct state financial assistance to local housing initiatives must be made an integral part of any overall state development program, and such a program must expand its housing elements at least to meet the needs no longer provided for by the federal government.

Reviewing housing standards and regulations

As mentioned earlier, many states have reviewed their development-related rules and regulations to determine whether they unintentionally constrain housing production while doing little or no service to another policy objective, such as environmental quality. Exempting certain kinds of projects from environmental reviews (the rehabilitation of existing buildings with fewer than one hundred to two hundred units, for example), and adapting state building codes to encourage, rather than impede, the rehabilitation of buildings are just two examples of regulatory reforms that promote local housing objectives.

A more interesting and intricate pursuit is the creation of financial incentives to induce new housing production for needy families. Granting a sales tax exemption to building materials used in the renovation and upgrading of existing housing for moderate-income tenants in older, poorer communities is one small gesture. Providing direct tax credits to small owners and builders to increase the number of dwellings in large, older structures may be another. An idea being refined by the Massachusetts legislature's Special Commission on Growth is especially significant—the allocation of bonuses in additional state aid to communities with the necessary capacity to accept housing growth, especially subsidized housing growth.

THE STATE-FEDERAL RELATIONSHIP

In the late 1970s, an objective of the federal government was to encourage states through incentives to assume their fair share of responsibility to distressed local communities under a new partnership with the federal government. It is now clear that there will be far fewer incentives from Washington.

The challenge of the 1980s, therefore, will be to elicit from governors and state legislatures a willingness to assume a larger share of responsibility. As the momentum of federal housing assistance decreases, at least in the immediate future, local pressures for the states to do more will increase dramatically. Recent initiatives provide hope that state governments will respond; perhaps in turn their actions can stimulate a new response at the national level, directly related to both local and state leadership.

STATE-LOCAL RELATIONSHIP

In summarizing the conditions that are the most likely to encourage or facilitate state actions to promote affordable housing, the COSCAA report states that "the most significant test" may be in future changes in basic state-local relationships:

Declining federal aid to localities, increased local government program responsibilities, and on-going local revenue constraints may continue to make housing less affordable to communities. The future allocation of roles and responsibilities between state and local governments in program delivery and program financing, especially in infrastructure, and the availability of revenue and capital financing sources to local governments may be central to solving the affordability dilemma in the long run.[11]

It is clear that the expanding housing involvement of local governments and the increasingly pressing demands for them to respond to local housing needs will have a great impact on the states.

1   National Commission on Urban Problems, *Building the American City* (Washington, D.C.: Government Printing Office, [1968]), p. 30.

2   Council of State Community Affairs Agencies, *State Actions to Promote Affordable Housing* (Washington, D.C.: Council of State Community Affairs Agencies, 1982), Appendix C.

3   Ibid., pp. 12–16.

4   This is partially explained by two factors: legislative resistance to targeting such programs to families that are unable to obtain private financing under conventional terms, and inadequate staff resources. This problem may be abating somewhat on the state level since the congressional efforts in 1979 to curtail abuses in the mortgage revenue bond program.

5   U.S., Department of Housing and Urban Development, "Comprehensive Planning Assistance (701) Program, Incentive Funding for State and Regional Strategies," *Federal Register,* 21 July 1978, p. 31796.

6   Charles R. Warren, *The States and Urban Strategies: A Comparative Analysis,* prepared for the U.S. Department of Housing and Urban Development (Washington, D.C.: Government Printing Office, 1980), p. 3.

7   Ibid., pp. 26–32.

8   Ibid., pp. 30–31.

9   Ibid., p. 21.

10   State of Massachusetts, *Growth Policy Report of 1977.*

11   Council of State Community Affairs Agencies, *State Actions to Promote Affordable Housing,* p. 12.

Chapter 6

Housing and
local government

The public role in housing is expanding and maturing. At the same time, the relative roles of federal, state, and local governments are changing. The once dominant federal government role as almost the sole public source of funding for housing credit and housing assistance is being reduced. State governments are increasingly active, not only in housing finance but also in state development programs and state support for local housing initiatives.

At the local level, a major reason for the assumption of new housing responsibilities is the changing attitudes of local elected officials. Prior to 1974, most mayors and council members viewed housing as an issue best left to private developers or, in a public sense, as within the purview only of redevelopment agencies and housing authorities. With passage of the Housing and Community Development Act of 1974, however, mayors were given statutory responsibility for allocating large sums of federal money under the Community Development Block Grant (CDBG) program and for tying the use of those monies to a Housing Assistance Plan (HAP). At the same time, the country was in the throes of possibly its greatest housing recession since World War II. The inability of the private housing industry to deliver new housing also helped raise the issue of housing to a new level of political importance in city halls. Both the structure of federal assistance programs and an uncertain economy have reinforced an increased role for mayors and councils since 1974. The U.S. Department of Housing and Urban Development (HUD) made special efforts, particularly after 1977, to involve mayors to a greater degree in federal housing assistance decisions and in program implementation as well. This reflected both an increased awareness of the housing issue in city halls and an effort to increase the political constituency for housing programs. The Section 8 neighborhood strategy area (NSA) program, created in 1978, in which set-asides of Section 8 substantial rehabilitation funds were offered to larger cities for direct allocation to developers, is the best example of this change. Several other dynamics, notably the deteriorating condition of the public housing stock in many large cities and demographic and life-style shifts that led to "gentrification" and displacement of lower-income residents, also contributed to the awareness of housing as a local government issue. Finally, the initiation in 1978 of tax-exempt mortgage revenue bonds provided mayors with a direct financing tool to address the politically attractive home ownership issue.

The two historical strands of local public involvement in housing are increasingly interwoven: (1) regulations governing land use, building construction, and housing occupancy dating back to the early 1900s and (2) slum clearance and housing assistance for unmet needs initiated in the 1930s under federal government programs. Three mature "clusters" of local housing responsibility resulting from this interweaving—conserving and rehabilitating neighborhoods, developing and managing housing for unmet needs, and responding to changes in local housing markets—have been defined and explored in the preceding chapters.

But the tide of evolution has not abated. There is an increasing trend for local governments to coordinate management of *all* functions affecting housing and to link direct housing initiatives with the entire municipal structure: taxes, capital budgets, operating budgets, and municipal services. While this trend is still in an early stage, there are clear signs that the decade of the 1980s will see some major developments in this direction. Housing is becoming, in fact, a true municipal function.

The emergence of this *local public role* in housing places additional burdens on local governments to develop new relationships with the private institutions, nonprofit organizations, and citizen groups that perform important housing tasks; to advance the professional capability of public employees; and to develop more sophisticated systems to monitor and evaluate housing progress.

PROFILES OF LOCAL HOUSING ADMINISTRATION
The characteristics of local housing institutions in the United States, both public and private, are varied and complex. So are local governmental structures. An assessment of the particular strengths and weaknesses of these local institutions and structures forms the basis for successful housing administration. These attributes change over time; there is no one organizational mode that can be laid on all local governments; every local structure must adapt as conditions change.

The four profiles that follow this chapter (describing the housing functions in the city and county of San Francisco; Montgomery County, Maryland; the city of Baltimore; and the city of Pittsburgh) represent the efforts of four different local governments to manage their housing responsibilities within the particular demands and resources of their areas. Although they are different, each represents a new awareness of the linkages between public and private housing activities and the mechanisms to tie direct public interventions in housing to the total municipal or county government structure.

AREAS FOR LOCAL ATTENTION

An analysis of the evolution of local involvement in housing and a review of current experience bring to light some key areas for special attention if local communities are to respond to the changing housing circumstances of the 1980s. These areas require new techniques for local public management.

Assessing neighborhood and community change

Chapter 2 highlighted in some detail the importance of viewing neighborhood conservation and rehabilitation from the perspective of changes in the dynamics of local housing markets. Chapter 4 described some of the impacts of these changing housing markets on local communities. In short, local officials must be able to read better the signals in the marketplace as well as understand how markets work. The source data and techniques to monitor market changes are still rudimentary, but, as shown in Chapter 2, increasing attention is being focused on this need.

Achieving involvement and communication

The evolution of local housing interventions, as well as current experience, dramatically demonstrates the need to establish strong, ongoing relationships among all the interests concerned with housing actions. These include particularly the private business sector and neighborhood residents. Involvement on a "single project" basis is not sufficient to cope with the scope and complexity of today's housing activities. In addition to traditional institutions, rapid growth is taking place in a variety of special-purpose housing institutions, including housing and community development corporations and (as shown in Chapter 3) new housing management agencies. Involvement and communication are built into the political process; in localities with strong mayor governments, a natural initiator is the mayor; in other jurisdictions, different techniques are required—an example is a housing policy document adopted by the county council/county executive of Montgomery County, Maryland. Sometimes a well-respected local institution, such as a private foundation or a university, can initiate the process. Beyond citywide and neighborhood involvement, each housing entity is increasingly required to establish internal communication mechanisms; a particular case in point is the growing involvement of low-income residents in housing management.

Integrating housing with community/economic development

The traditional concept of linking housing with community development and economic development initiatives, inherent in all national housing legislation dating back to the slum clearance/public housing requirements of the Housing Act of 1937, is still valid. Recent experience with neighborhood restoration under the CDBG program and with economic revitalization under the UDAG program demonstrates again the validity and importance of the housing linkage. Local instruments and organizational mechanisms to achieve this linkage will vary from community to community, but the essential concept has been tested and proven by experience.

Utilizing the tools of governance

The growing integration of housing into the total municipal structure is well demonstrated by both evolution and current experience. The traditional local regulatory functions involving building, housing, and zoning codes are being joined increasingly with the slum clearance/assisted housing/community improvement activities that began in the 1930s. Increasingly, also, housing activities are being integrated or coordinated with local community capital budgets and, in some instances, operating budgets. This integration provides new opportunities for communities to utilize all their tools of governance, including their tax structures, to advance housing objectives. From the viewpoint of evolution, it is not uncommon in 1982 to have all assisted housing development activity, including major housing rehabilitation or modernization, reflected in the city's comprehensive capital budget. However, a major area that has not yet been effectively joined with housing is the municipal service structure, including such important functions as police and fire protection, municipal refuse collection, and education. Yet the importance of these ongoing municipal services to the success, and particularly the staying power, of housing improvements is without question. One major reason for reluctance to interrelate municipal services with housing initiatives is the tightness of municipal service budgets. However, such linkages could prove to be cost-effective and might well be a next stage in the continuing evolution of local housing relationships.

Adopting new management mechanisms

The housing function is unusually complex, interrelating and intersecting with almost every other public function in the community structure. The achievement of housing objectives, even in the internal operations of an individual housing agency, requires special management techniques.

Recent experience points to efforts to utilize new management forms. At the community level, almost all larger communities now utilize interagency coordinating groups, usually convened by the office of the mayor; these groups usually concentrate on coordinating capital development. An increasing area of management innovation is the use of "teams" assembled to carry through special projects, drawing staff from across operational divisions. A few institutions, such as the Montgomery County Housing Opportunities Commission, incorporate "standing" teams to implement agency objectives identified in the annual budget planning process. It is likely that this cross cutting mode of management will be increasingly utilized in implementing local housing policies.

Financing and managing assisted housing

The growth of innovative mechanisms to finance local housing rehabilitation and development has been documented in Chapters 2 and 3. The range of local innovation is likely to grow as major adjustments and new housing finance instruments are generated by private financial institutions. The challenge to local government will be to fill the gap in housing finance left by private financing and limited federal housing assistance. Packaging feasible housing endeavors at the local level will require new personnel in local government, knowledgeable about private financing as well as about available federal and state assistance, and with the skill to bring resources and participants together to the advantage of the local community.

Local governments are just beginning to recognize their responsibilities not only in guiding initial development but also in monitoring the ongoing stability of all housing in the community that is supported in any way by public resources. The quality of design and construction, as well as that of management/maintenance, is of critical concern to the health and well-being of the community. The track record of communities in carrying out these responsibilities will directly affect the community's access to private markets for housing finance, as well as the confidence of potential partners in the private business community.

It may be that the current Housing Assistance Plan needs to be regenerated, not solely as an instrument to procure federal housing assistance and guide its location but as an instrument that sets guidelines for the design, construction, and management of all assisted housing and for monitoring mechanisms to assure that such guidelines are carried forward.

Evaluating local housing efforts

Local housing efforts come under scrutiny from a number of directions. Funding sources, such as HUD, look to see whether programs are being operated consistently with regulations. Local elected officials often consider the success of programs on the basis of whether constituents seem pleased with them. Program administrators, community groups, and local public interest groups often evaluate efforts on the basis of whether particular objectives are being accomplished.

Evaluation should be an important part of any local housing effort, and the best approach is to measure local activities based on the goals and objectives of those who design and implement the programs or activities. Sometimes such measures are quite straightforward. For example, to evaluate whether low- and moderate-income persons are benefiting from local efforts, an enumeration of beneficiaries is all that is necessary.

However, if the objective is neighborhood recovery, as outlined in Chapter 2, or intervention to counter certain market effects, as described in Chapter 4, evaluation is, of necessity, much more complex. The subtleties of changing market conditions in the area need to be tracked, and attitudes and practices of lenders need to be identified.

If the overall objective is to renew and sustain housing as part of long-term community revitalization and stability, then evaluation beyond enumeration of activities is required. The concepts and processes for such evaluation are not yet in place.

Some ongoing evaluation of the local housing effort should be built into the table of organization, so that evaluative feedback can be part of policymaking. If the evaluation process is structured well, periodic evaluations can be performed in ways that are not threatening to elected officials responsible for overseeing local housing efforts. Evaluations in a local political climate can be very difficult and can make local officials act defensive. A well-structured evaluation process can identify gaps in program effectiveness and provide the experience to improve overall local performance.

Such evaluation often requires sophisticated systems and analysis and may be beyond the capability of local government. In that case, creative and useful relationships can be fostered with local corporations or universities, which may have the capacity to provide the needed evaluation service.

Increasing the capacities of local housing professionals

As any student of public administration or business administration knows, good systems cannot work without qualified people carrying out their responsibilities. Local governments find themselves with increasing responsibilities related to housing, but without easily identifiable local talent to handle the various complex aspects of the local housing function.

Although national professional certification programs exist for some of the key responsibilities now found at the local level, identifying professionals for newer housing functions is still sometimes hit-or-miss. Senior-level housing officials come from diverse backgrounds: city planning, law, public administration, real estate, and business administration, for example.

Accordingly, the newness of much local housing responsibility requires local officials to be conscious of the need for staff training and professional development. In-house training on changes in federal assistance programs, on innovative financing techniques, and on successful approaches to housing management is especially important. The requirements for housing finance specialists are spelled out in Chapter 3.

National groups such as NAHRO, the HUD-sponsored community rehabilitation training center, and others can provide very useful information and professional development opportunities for local professional staff. Public housing managers, for example, are certified by NAHRO, the Center for Housing Management, and the Institute for Real Estate Management. Building code inspectors are often certified for particular national codes. NAHRO has announced a certification program for housing rehabilitation specialists.

As responsibilities for housing have shifted from the federal to the local level, local housing officials have shown enormous initiative and creativity in handling added local responsibilities.

Sharing ideas among housing professionals in different cities—peer exchange—continues to be the single most important method of professional capacity development. A structured method of information exchange among cities, national training programs and conferences, and in-house training are the best approaches to developing skilled local professionals capable of responding to new local housing responsibilities.

The basic approach to ensure professionalism for housing responsibilities at the local level, however, should include two key ingredients—a recognition of housing as an important local public function that has long-term stability and prestige, and competitive schedules of compensation based on the skills and training required to carry out the tasks.

THE STATES AND HOUSING

As documented in Chapter 5, with or without the adoption of a national policy of "New Federalism," new involvements of state government in an expanded and maturing role in housing appear likely. The maturing of the housing function at the local level (in particular, the joining of the traditional local housing regulatory functions with the housing and improvement initiatives of the 1930s) into more cohesive efforts provides new opportunities for state governments to use their traditional powers and resources. Updating building and housing codes through state initiatives is one potential area. Another is integrating statewide development planning more closely with local housing and development.

With state government assumption of federally assisted community development block grants in nonmetropolitan areas, there are new possibilities for linking rural and small community housing with community development.

In the area of assisted housing finance, state government is taking an increasingly large role in financing both single-family and multifamily housing that needs to be coordinated with local housing activities. The financing expertise of many state housing finance agencies could well be made available to local governments, particularly smaller municipalities.

In the area of assisted housing management, a few states now manage or closely monitor the management of the housing they have assisted. Guidelines to govern the quality of design, construction, and management have been developed, and staff has been trained to implement them. These resources should be made available on a broader scale to local communities.

There is a wide range of state operating functions where action could well be taken to support an expanded local housing role. One area of particular significance is shelter allowances for families receiving public assistance. States have the responsibility for setting public assistance budget levels, including the option of including a shelter allowance in a "flat rent" covering all family needs or as a separate shelter allocation. Significant opportunities exist to raise the quality of housing occupied by families receiving public assistance as well as to enhance local efforts to restore neighborhoods. States could make "shelter allowances" a separate item in the family welfare budget and provide incentives for using these shelter allowances in conjunction with housing rehabilitation and neighborhood improvements.

THE FEDERAL RESPONSIBILITY

As demonstrated in Chapter 1, the federal government was a predominant influence in the assumption of direct housing responsibilities by local governments beginning with the slum clearance/public housing assistance of the 1930s. What is becoming increasingly clear, however, is that the federal influence on local housing markets and neighborhoods is not solely from direct housing assistance, but from far more extensive federal credit allocations and tax policies. A recap of this activity, compared to direct housing assistance, indicates that federal government outlays under credit allocations and tax policy are five times the outlays under the assisted housing programs.

In the area of credit allocations, in fiscal 1982, the federal government estimated that direct outlays for mortgage credit and direct housing loans totaled $2.8 billion: $1.0 billion for mortgage activities of the Government National Mortgage Association (GNMA); $711.0 million for direct loans for Section 202 housing for elderly or handicapped persons; and $1.1 billion for the rural housing programs of the Farmers Home Administration. This is exclusive of $3.2 billion in outlays for the rural housing insurance program under the Federal Financing Bank. The Reagan administration has undertaken an initiative to cut back and constrain these credit allocations for all domestic programs, including housing.

In the area of the indirect subsidies under the income tax, in fiscal 1982, the write-off of mortgage interest/property taxes by homeowners is estimated at $35.2 billion; other deductions by homeowners and housing investors are estimated at $4.8 billion. In contrast, the 1982 direct outlays of the federal assistance programs for lower-income families are $8.2 billion, covering both HUD and the Farmers Home Administration.

Additional perspectives on federal housing interventions are that they are not centered in any one federal agency and are not linked together in any way in support of national housing objectives. There has not been, nor is there currently, an explicit national housing policy that seeks to relate federal housing interventions in a cohesive strategy. The one formal attempt to link housing goals to national economic policy—a requirement under the ten-year housing goals adopted by Congress in 1968—was never implemented.

In addition to the overriding issues of federal credit and tax policies are the critical issues of federal housing assistance to lower-income families. Two major streams of activity influence the future direction of this assistance. One is the traditional concept, taking on new momentum, of linking housing assistance directly to economic revitalization and community development.[1] The second is the movement since the early 1970s of viewing housing assistance as one of "income support" for individual families using housing "vouchers" or housing "certificates" in the private housing market.[2] The essence of the debate between the two policies has been expressed in two terms—assisting "people" and assisting "place." In reality, assistance to both "people" and "place" is required. The need is to sort out the appropriate policies and responsibilities, particularly among federal agencies, in order to achieve affordable housing for all families as well as sound neighborhood environments and local communities.

Looking ahead in the 1980s, it is clear that there is a need for "sorting out" the policies and responsibilities of the federal government in areas affecting housing, including:

The federal policy of credit allocation for the entire housing sector, at a time of intense competition for investment capital

The federal policy for providing special financing to assist the construction of new housing for lower-income families in areas with tight housing markets

The federal policy governing the use of the income tax structure to support housing, including the relative benefits for both owner- and renter-occupied housing, and for all income groups

The federal policy relative to "income support" for families at the poverty level, including their ability to pay for housing

The federal policy governing the relationship of housing to economic and community development, designed to achieve sound neighborhoods and local communities, as well as a balanced development strategy for the nation as a whole.

HOUSING AND A NEW FEDERALISM

The issues in national housing policy listed above will be debated over the next few years in the context of national priorities and the many changes affecting American institutions, public and private. One of the important new influences on future national housing policies will be the expanding and maturing housing function now emerging in local and state governments. In an ironic turnabout, this *local* influence on *federal* housing may be as strong as the *federal* influence on *local* housing of an earlier period. The depth of this local influence may well depend on the speed and momentum of local action—on how quickly and effectively local governments can gear themselves to manage their growing housing responsibilities. Housing could well become one of the pivotal issues in the upcoming debate over a "new American federalism," a new alignment of federal, state, and local governments that is geared to tackle the priority domestic problems facing the United States in the 1980s.

1   See: Karl E. Case, *The Role of Housing in Urban Development Strategies*, prepared for the U.S. Department of Housing and Urban Development (Cambridge, Mass.: Urban Systems Research and Engineering, Inc., 1980).

2   See: Raymond J. Struyk and Marc Benedict, Jr., eds., *Housing Vouchers for the Poor: Lessons from a National Experiment* (Washington, D.C.: The Urban Institute, 1981). In terms of relationship to community development, note especialy Chapter 11, "Policy Implications: Moving from Research to Programs."

Profiles of innovative local housing administration

CITY AND COUNTY OF SAN FRANCISCO

The leadership and coordination for local housing in San Francisco are in the mayor's office, which also handles some direct housing functions. Full coordination is difficult, since responsibilities for real estate and building inspections, by provisions of the city charter, are assigned to the chief administrative officer. Nevertheless, San Francisco is a good example of a city hall that has taken an increasingly active role in housing. Next to crime, housing has become the biggest issue facing elected officials in San Francisco—a city of slightly under 700,000 people squeezed into forty-nine square miles, a city with market dynamics that have produced the highest housing prices in the country. Partly due to its charter, the city has never formally consolidated its many offices—Bureau of Building Inspections, Real Estate Department, Redevelopment Agency, Housing Authority, City Planning Department, and Mayor's Office of Community Development—which have some responsibility for housing. Rather, a deputy director for housing in the Office of Community Development has assumed for the mayor a role that is part administrator, part housing finance expert, part coordinator, and part troubleshooter. Under this scenario, the mayor's housing staff acts not as a developer but more as a lender and packager of resources: it serves as a below-market-rate financing window for any developer—private for-profit, nonprofit, or redevelopment agency—seeking to finance low-, moderate-, or middle-income housing. The staff oversees and coordinates the distribution of CDBG funds used for housing, Section 8 new construction, substantial and moderate rehabilitation funds, state funds, and private funds the city has begun to raise through an unprecedented policy of requiring office developers to build or contribute to housing in the city. In addition, the city (as well as its redevelopment agency) can issue mortgage revenue bonds; it has developed a program of bond-financed, shared-appreciation mortgages on the ownership side; and it is working on a multifamily rental production program.

Problems and prospects

The San Francisco experience sheds light on a number of advantages and disadvantages of a housing coordinator in the mayor's office. The most important issues involve technical capacity and authority for program implementation.

A recurring problem in San Francisco, as well as in other cities, has been that the technical expertise and experience in housing among the mayor's office staff has not always kept pace with the responsibilities that have accrued. This has been particularly true in financing and has often necessitated reliance on outside consultants. In San Francisco, the Office of Community Development has doubled the size of its housing staff in an effort to recognize these increasing technical responsibilities.

The issue of authority and diffusion of responsibility for program implementation is more subtle. The mayor's office in Pittsburgh has managed to coordinate and ultimately consummate one of the more successful housing programs in the country, despite a diffusion of program responsibility among the mayor's office, the redevelopment agency, the housing authority, and the city planning department. In San Francisco, as in many western cities, this diffusion of responsibility in housing not only exists but is compounded by a city charter that places certain responsibilities—real estate and building inspection—under a chief administrative officer rather than under the mayor. San Francisco has begun to deal with this by utilizing the mayor's staff to coordinate a weekly meeting involving all city agencies that have a role in housing.

It is important to emphasize that in most instances, including San Francisco, the mayor's office has not chosen to act as an actual developer of housing. The role remains one of program development and packaging, coordinating, and expediting. San Francisco utilizes a combination of private developers, neighborhood-based nonprofit development corporations (there are eight), and its redevelopment agency (acting only in designated redevelopment areas) to do the actual development or rehabilitation. In most cases, these entities also provide all technical services such as work write-ups and specifications.

Thus there is the potential disadvantage of extra layers of bureaucracy, but this problem can be offset by the ability of the mayor and the mayor's office to serve not only as a central reference point for housing developers but also as an advocate for housing in the political process. In San Francisco the latter role is particularly important. Indeed, it has been the mayor who has been the prime mover in pushing for and achieving management improvements and modernization in the housing authority and its projects and in initiating the rezoning for housing of several key parcels in the city.

The future role

Just as an increasing flow of federal housing funds through mayors' offices helped increase the involvement of city hall in housing, the looming cutbacks in and elimination of those funds might be expected to diminish that involvement. A combination of demographic changes, continuing high interest rates, and political visibility will likely offset the impact of a loss in public funds, however, and keep housing high on the city hall agenda.

Mayors' offices in San Francisco and many other cities have developed both an abiding interest in housing and some technical capacity to address it on an ongoing basis. This role encompasses policy in local issues with great political visibility: first, rent control and condominium conversions, and second, the development of financing mechanisms, in conjunction with private lenders or through tax-exempt securities, to address the dual concerns of home ownership and the production of rental housing.

MONTGOMERY COUNTY, MARYLAND

In Montgomery County, Maryland, the county executive, the county council, and the local law on "affordable housing" represent a unique effort to define and implement a specific housing policy, embodied in local law, with assignments of responsibility to a range of county agencies under the coordination of the Montgomery County Department of Housing and Community Development.

Montgomery County, a diverse county of both urbanized and new growth areas in metropolitan Washington, D.C., is a rare example of a local government that has carefully assessed the full scope of its housing responsibilities, developed a housing policy for the 1980s, and incorporated the major elements to meet these responsibilities into local law. Many local jurisdictions have housing policy and housing plans; few have sorted out all the responsibilities among local public agencies and charged these agencies with implementation.

Key documents in the Montgomery County system are: *Housing Policy for Montgomery County in the 1980's* (hereafter referred to as *Housing Policy*), adopted by the county executive and the county council in October 1981,[1] and Chapter 25B, title "Affordable Housing" of the Montgomery County Code 1972, adopted in March 1982.

The scope of the county's housing efforts can be seen in the statements of its responsibilities in relation to private builders (outlined in the accompanying sidebar) and in the definition of the local government's role (see

---

The county and the private sector
The private sector has the primary role for producing housing in the County. The County Government's principal role in housing is to assist the private sector by assuring the provision of:

Available financing programs for housing to achieve moderate monthly payments for both sale and rental units.

Adequate water and sewer service.

Adequate transportation system.

Adequate supply of zoned land in each density to meet the needs of the next decade.

Improved building codes and regulations.

Efficient development approval process.

Taxation policies that discourage land speculation.

Adequate schools, parks, libraries and other community amenities.

When the private sector fails to provide a range of housing choices in certain categories resulting in economic hardship to certain segments of the community, the County Government shall determine how those deficiencies can be ameliorated, either through legislation, incentives, financial assistance or direct participation.

Source: Montgomery County (Maryland), Department of Housing and Community Development, *Housing Policy for Montgomery County in the 1980's* (Rockville, Md.: Montgomery County Department of Housing and Community Development, 1981), p. 4.

Figure 6–1). The following narrative statement summarizes the county's understanding of its housing mission:

Local governments play a large and vital role in the provision of housing by creating the proper environment for housing activities to exist. The local government's activities that affect housing tend to fall into six categories. Under each of the categories are a number of specific activities, programs and responsibilities that, taken together, will stimulate or retard housing production, increase or decrease the availability of certain types of housing, improve or diminish housing opportunities for certain groups within the community, and generally influence the standards and living conditions of most of the citizens. Many of the responsibilities and activities enumerated are traditional to the role of local governments; however, it is clear that the scope of local government's involvement in the financing and production of housing through a variety of programs has grown in recent years as more and more families have become strained by the changing economic and housing conditions. Therefore, it is essential that the activities of the many local agencies having a role in housing be coordinated by a lead agency in order to avoid program duplication, overlap and function. In order to secure the best efforts of the various agencies, the County Executive shall recommend legislation to the County Council clarifying the mandate of the Department of Housing and Community Development and fixing responsibility for assessing, directing, coordinating, and monitoring the programs which provide housing assistance, grants, loans, services, and information for housing in Montgomery County.[2]

Under the "affordable housing" amendment to the Montgomery County Code, the county executive is charged with a broad range of responsibilities

Land use planning and implementation
Comprehensive and functional planning
Zoning ordinance
Development staging
Adequate public facilities regulations
Subdivision regulations
Urban design approvals

Regulations and administration
Construction codes administration (regulations, permits and inspections)
Subdivision road code
Moderate priced dwelling units requirement
Housing code—single- and multifamily
Landlord–tenant relations/rental facilities licensing
Fair housing legislation
Condominium legislation

Public facilities and services
Transportation systems and services
Water and sewer systems and services
Public safety services
Educational/cultural services
Solid waste services

Financing and production
Housing Opportunities Act
    1. Financing
    2. Development and operations
Housing site acquisition
Development feasibility fund
County urban renewal program
Rehabilitation loan fund
Revenue authority development and operations
Homeowners construction loan fund
Public facility area development funding
Condominium conversion emergency aid fund

Taxation and fees
Real estate taxes
Real estate transfer taxes
Sewer and water capital facilities charge and connection fees
Condominium transfer tax

Intergovernmental relations
Lobbying of federal government in areas of fiscal policy, tax incentives, etc.
Assisting in development of programs at the state and federal agency levels

**Figure 6–1 Major county
government activities that affect
housing in Montgomery County,
Maryland.**

in the implementation of housing policy. Some of these responsibilities include: targeting county-owned land, public facilities, and services to implement housing objectives; exploring county funding sources to finance site acquisition and construction of affordable housing; encouraging tenant cooperatives or other forms of tenant ownership; developing incentives to encourage the private sector to provide affordable housing; and investigating the "new creative financing plans available in the private sector" to help increase the supply of affordable housing. The county executive is charged with preparing a consolidated annual housing report covering all agencies of the county and spelling out both one-year and ten-year goals for the construction of "affordable housing" units. Most significantly, the local law spells out precise standards and procedures for the location of assisted family housing.

While the local law charges the county executive with general responsibility in specified areas, *Housing Policy* (also an officially adopted document) provides more precise guidelines for implementing this responsibility. A special section of this report, "Summary of Implementing Actions," sets forth major implementation requirements of the housing policy and assigns responsibilities among county agencies. The department of housing and community development is assigned major responsibility for:

The changing urban scene The Department of Housing and Community Development shall establish a Housing Action Section to work in cooperation with the Montgomery County Planning Board, the Housing Opportunities Commission, and other selected agencies to develop strategies and incentives to:

(a) Increase the potential for developing housing units within the central business districts and the transit impact areas

(b) Improve the development potential of the small urban tracts for housing, especially for older households and small family groupings by changing definitions or densities in the Zoning Ordinance

(c) Recommend a development financing program to provide short-term loans for land acquisition, lot development and building construction for housing projects meeting price criteria

(d) Review opportunities for increased efficiency through improving housing design and utilizing latest construction technology . . .

(e) Report annually to the County Executive and the County Council on the state of housing in Montgomery County

The County Council will consider an amendment to the Zoning Ordinance that clarifies the conditions under which single-family residences may be modified to accommodate more than one household.

Source: Montgomery County (Maryland), Department of Housing and Community Development, *Housing Policy for Montgomery County in the 1980's* (Rockville, Md.: Montgomery County Department of Housing and Community Development, 1981), p. 44.

1. Assessing, directing, coordinating, and monitoring the programs that provide housing assistance, grants, loans, services, and information for housing in Montgomery County
2. Developing programs and coordinating activities of other local agencies that address housing issues and needs
3. Establishing a housing action section to work with other county agencies to increase the potential for developing housing units within central business districts and transit impact areas; improve the development potential of small urban tracts for housing by changing zoning definitions or densities; recommend a housing financing program to provide short-term loans for land acquisition, lot development, and building construction for housing projects meeting price criteria; review opportunities for increased efficiency through improving housing design and utilizing the latest construction technology; and monitor housing production to ascertain the effects of existing laws on the price and availability of developable land
4. Establishing a housing finance program in conjunction with the Housing Opportunities Commission and/or the Revenue Authority
5. Recommending use of surplus land for housing purposes
6. Formulating executive regulations that will implement an assisted housing distribution policy
7. Developing and publishing standards for the production, occupancy, and maintenance of all assisted housing so that it is compatible in design, character, and upkeep with that in adjacent communities.

Other housing responsibilities are directly assigned to the Montgomery County Planning Board, the Housing Opportunities Commission, the Office of Management and Budget, the Commission on Human Relations, the Office of Landlord–Tenant Affairs, and the county council. The county council is specifically charged with revising the housing code, which is now administered by two different county agencies: The Department of Housing and Community Development enforces the code for single-family dwellings, while the Office of Landlord–Tenant Affairs enforces the code in multifamily rental housing. While this dual administration has made it possible to have more coordinated and systematic code enforcement, the county sees the need to revise the code to encompass new areas beyond traditional health and safety requirements, including the full maintenance of dwellings and their premises (e.g., grounds and accessory structures, blight, and neighborhood upgrading and preservation). The county is also streamlining its building construction codes, including the promulgation of a development manual that consolidates these requirements in a single process; fees and charges for new construction are also being revised to encourage development by cutting development costs.

Housing organization

Responsibilities for carrying out the county's direct housing functions are divided among three major agencies: the Department of Housing and Community Development, the Housing Opportunities Commission, and the Office of Landlord–Tenant Affairs. Their functions and relationships are shown in Figure 6–2.

Innovative programs

Montgomery County has been a pioneer in developing new housing for families in a range of income groups. For example, under the moderate-priced dwelling unit legislation initiated in 1974 each private developer of a subdivision containing fifty or more units must build a percentage of units to sales prices or rent levels established by the county government. These prices include all costs except land for the production and sale of modest units; land cost is offset by providing the builder with a density bonus—an increase of up to 20 percent in the number of units the land will yield. To date, about 10 percent of the units in these new subdivisions are moderate-priced; the Housing Opportunities Commission is authorized to acquire up to one-third of these moderate-priced units for rental or sale to lower-income families eligible for housing assistance.

In addition, as of July 1980, the county undertook a major initiative to encourage development of affordable housing—the creation of a 4 percent transfer tax on the initial sale of newly converted condominiums; this tax was extended to cooperatives in 1981. The county Department of Housing and Community Development has developed a rental supplement program using these funds. It is designed to foster competition in the development industry to create new housing, of which at least 20 percent must be available to households of modest income. The rental subsidy will be achieved by setting up a dedicated fund for each project, the interest from which will be used to subsidize 20 percent of the total units, with the principal returning to the county after twenty years. Because these units will be set aside for low- or moderate-income families, the entire project is eligible for tax-exempt financing, thus reducing rents for nonsubsidized units as well. In 1982 the county anticipates the initial allocation of about $3 million to stimulate an estimated two hundred new rental units, of which at least forty will be available to low- and moderate-income households. Other uses for this fund are in the planning stages.

Montgomery County, through the Housing Opportunities Commission, was also a pioneer user of tax-exempt mortgage bonds to provide below-market interest rates for home purchases by moderate-income households; two separate bond obligations were marketed in 1980 and 1981.

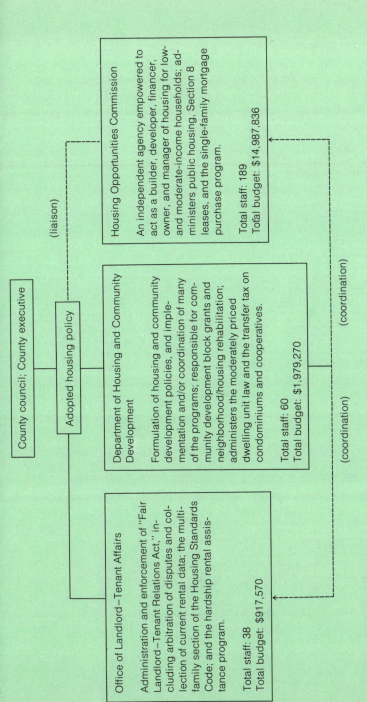

County council; County executive

Adopted housing policy

(liaison)

Housing Opportunities Commission

An independent agency empowered to act as a builder, developer, financer, owner, and manager of housing for low- and moderate-income households; administers public housing, Section 8 leases, and the single-family mortgage purchase program.

Total staff: 189
Total budget: $14,987,836

Department of Housing and Community Development

Formulation of housing and community development policies, and implementation and/or coordination of many of the programs; responsible for community development block grants and neighborhood/housing rehabilitation; administers the moderately priced dwelling unit law and the transfer tax on condominiums and cooperatives.

Total staff: 60
Total budget: $1,979,270

(coordination)

(coordination)

Office of Landlord–Tenant Affairs

Administration and enforcement of "Fair Landlord–Tenant Relations Act," including arbitration of disputes and collection of current rental data; the multi-family section of the Housing Standards Code; and the hardship rental assistance program.

Total staff: 38
Total budget: $917,570

Figure 6–2 Major agencies for direct housing functions, Montgomery County, Maryland.

The Housing Opportunities Commission

The Montgomery County Housing Opportunities Commission (HOC) deserves special attention. It is the largest county housing agency in terms of budget (almost $15 million for fiscal 1982) and number of employees (190). HOC is headed by an executive director who is appointed by the board of the commission. It includes seven divisions encompassing the following programs and activities:

Development: housing financing, purchases, and preservation

Housing management: maintenance, repair, and renovation

Tenant services: counseling, day care, and support services

Finance: budget, payroll, purchasing, and accounting

Housing resources: housing information center, waiting list, Section 8 existing housing, and special rent supplements

Community relations: public information, legislation, and community relations

Administrative services: personnel, equal employment opportunity, data processing, and office space.

HOC manages 1,939 housing units and 1,222 housing leases. It provides special insight into how a separate local housing agency (such as a local housing authority) can become an active partner in the total housing efforts of the city or county government.

HOC is the successor to the Montgomery County Housing Authority, originally established in 1939. The authority was reactivated in 1966 and renamed the Housing Opportunities Commission in 1974, when its powers were expanded to allow the provision of housing and mortgage financing to moderate-income families. The commission is composed of seven members appointed by the county executive and confirmed by the county council for five-year terms.

The commission offers a wide range of housing programs, including information and referral of housing-related citizen inquiries, low-rent public and private-sector housing, tenant counseling and assistance, assistance in locating shelter, and below-market-rate permanent financing for eligible buyers. HOC cooperates with the county in the development of housing policy.

The total HOC budget appears in the comprehensive county budget document, although it is not subject to approval by the county executive or county council. Although there is no legal requirement, HOC also submits its capital improvements program for incorporation in the county's comprehensive improvement program. The HOC board meets periodically with the county executive, and the executive director of HOC serves as chairman of an interagency committee on housing and meets regularly with the county executive. Some indication of the housing involvement of HOC is exemplified in its schedule of operating revenues for fiscal 1982 (see Table 6–1).

While federal funds and tenant rents and charges make up 71 percent of the HOC revenues, a significant 29 percent of revenues comes from other sources; this is in contrast to the operation of most local housing authorities, where revenues are usually 90 percent or more from federal funds and tenant rents.

Another significant factor in the HOC budget is the proportion of staff and budget allocated to housing development; this activity includes eighteen persons (10 percent of the total staffing) and $980,600 (7 percent of the total HOC budget). The staff titles in this division include Mortgage Finance Analyst and Mortgage Finance Underwriter. This again is in contrast to the staffing of most public housing agencies, which have little or no permanent development staff but hire staff or consultants on a project-by-project basis

Table 6–1 Operating revenues for the Montgomery County Housing Opportunities Commission (HOC), fiscal 1982, by source of funds.

Source	Dollars	% of total
Federal funds	$8,155,029	54
State funds	594,903	4
County funds	1,167,364	8
Tenant rents and charges	2,497,670	17
Other HOC operating funds	1,086,439	7
HOC development funds	990,675	7
Private funds	40,316	...
User fees	43,208	...
All other	412,232	3
Total	$14,987,836	100

Source: Montgomery County (Maryland), Housing Opportunities Commission, *Approved Budget for Fiscal Year 1982* (Rockville, Md.: Montgomery County Housing Opportunities Commission, 1981).
Leaders (...) indicate less than 1%.

In the case of HOC, a permanent development staff can be maintained because of the agency's involvement in activities other than those that depend on federal funds.

A final important dimension of the HOC operation is its internal organization. HOC utilizes a "team-oriented" mode of management—a process that allows all employees to participate in planning, organizing, and decision making to meet stated goals. There are five standing teams (management, development, transition, housing programs, and program evaluation) that cut across the seven operating divisions and offices of the agency.

BALTIMORE

The Department of Housing and Community Development (HCD) in Baltimore is a comprehensive, integrated organizational structure where all key local housing functions are grouped under one direction, with important links to local neighborhoods and to private financial and development organizations. Baltimore also demonstrates a key ingredient for performance—making housing a priority concern of the local political leadership, in this case, the office of the mayor.

The current organization for housing and community development in Baltimore was adopted by ordinance in June 1968. It consolidates under one department all the major housing functions of the city. The department not only carries out community development and rehabilitation activity but also administers the building, housing, sanitation, and zoning codes. By virtue of appointment as executive director of the Housing Authority of Baltimore City, the administrator of the HCD has responsibility for the public housing program and the Section 8 leasing program. The administrator also supervises contracts with four private, nonprofit corporations that work with private enterprise in redeveloping the downtown area, attracting and retaining industry, and revitalizing the retail center.

HCD includes an extraordinary range of entities and programs. Four nonprofit corporations link the city government and the business community: Housing Assistance Corporation; Charles Center and Inner Harbor Management Corporation (downtown redevelopment); Baltimore Economic Development Corporation (attracting and retaining industry); and Market Center Development Corporation (revitalizing the retail center).

The Baltimore HCD and the Housing Authority of Baltimore City (a component of HCD) provide a great variety of services and activities, including neighborhood development, social services, public housing management, housing conservation, land development, family relocation, construction, inspection, and finance. Some of these activities are described in the following pages.

Powers and programs of HCD

A program of this scope in this city of over 800,000 population encounters all the serious problems of an older physical structure and economic base. The annual budget of HCD (exclusive of the housing authority) for fiscal 1982 was over $28 million; over three-quarters of these funds came from the city general fund, 23 percent from the federal government, and a small proportion (less than 1 percent) from the state of Maryland. The housing authority adds another budget of $44 million, making a grand total of $72 million. The total staff of HCD is 1,853, including 1,261 employees of the housing authority.

The consolidation of Baltimore's housing functions also provides special opportunities to generate revenues on a local base, relieving the dependence on federal assistance funds. For example, fee schedules ranging from building permits to zoning requests to dispositions of city-owned property can generate substantial local revenues, which can in turn be used for improvement activity. An option pending adoption by the city is the use of city-collected retail business license fees within particular retail business districts; these fees can be returned to business associations within these districts to carry out promotional and improvement activities. The concept of using a similar fee for housing purposes has potential.

Beyond budget numbers, the Baltimore HCD had the following "products" as of early 1981: 16,375 units of public housing; 11,880 subsidized units under other types of assistance, most of them built in conjunction with HCD programs; and 2,306 leases of private housing for low-income families under the Section 8 existing program. Since it began programs of rental housing rehabilitation in 1969, Baltimore has restored 3,294 housing units and adds about 350 each year. Under its weatherization program, more than 8,300 homes received assistance to install storm windows, caulking, weatherstripping, and sometimes insulation.

The Baltimore housing program has a national and international reputation for innovation. It was one of the first cities to undertake urban homesteading (and it created a Baltimore by-product—"shopsteading"). It has locally funded rehabilitation loan and grant programs for residential property owners. The department has gone beyond citywide rehabilitation loans and grants to concentrate special assistance in recycling older buildings for housing uses and in restoring historic structures; it has rehabilitated and sold more than 550 city-owned vacant houses. Most of this rehabilitation activity includes an energy conservation component. Baltimore has also utilized local tax-exempt mortgage bonds to finance low-interest-rate mortgages for eligible families. An informational pamphlet, *27 Services the City provides for you through HCD,* illustrates that whatever a citizen's housing status in Baltimore, he or she is covered by HCD's housing concerns and has access to its services (see Appendix G).

The organization of HCD contributes to program initiatives in several ways:

1. Citizens can identify the one agency that is responsible for housing.
2. The city government looks to a single agency to put together a comprehensive picture of its housing. Needs are identified and priorities are established, and then one agency has the power and resources to expedite the work.
3. HCD can follow a housing initiative from start to finish on a single administrative track. For example, the department (HCD) that realizes the need for low-income housing also examines the plans for new construction, issues the permits, supervises the construction, and rents and manages the housing units, including social services. The department that inspects the housing also arranges rehabilitation loans. The department that establishes urban renewal plans also finds homes for those who must be relocated.

The Baltimore system is defined in broad objectives and relies on flexibility to respond to changing needs and opportunities. Baltimore depends on the capacity of skilled administrators, armed with organizational powers and resources, to mold programs and interventions to meet community needs, in close coordination with political leadership and neighborhood participation.

The structure of the Baltimore HCD is oriented to generic and functional areas rather than to "programs." Thus, although the public housing agency is a distinct legal entity separate from HCD, the HCD administrator (who is also executive director of the authority) can organize public housing resources within the framework of functional requirements. For example, planning for public housing is carried out by the planning section of the HCD structure.

The internal operations of HCD also are geared for flexibility with a minimum of formal procedures and clearances. Thus, ad hoc teams of qualified persons are assembled from across the operating sections to concentrate on special priorities or projects. This offers a capacity to consider several alternative means of attacking problems: the redevelopment specialist's point of view will often be different from the rehabilitation expert's; likewise, the views of the housing inspector, the relocation director, and the public housing director will be different.

Certainly, a major asset of the HCD organization is the ability to relate housing activities to the total city effort of urban renewal and redevelopment. This principle was explored earlier in this book from a national perspective

—the continuing emphasis in national legislation, from 1937 through 1974, on the importance of linking housing to total community development. In Baltimore, one of the strategic tools in achieving this linkage is the power of the HCD to exercise detailed planning in all areas designated as "renewal areas" or "conservation areas." These designated areas currently constitute most of the core areas of the city, as well as some substantial outer city locations. The HCD planning for these areas is subject only to conformance with the city master plan or official detailed plan for that area, prepared by the city planning commission.

The concentrated impact of the many HCD powers and resources can be seen in the following example—the Reservoir Hill area.

The area, site of excellent Victorian rowhouses, had become overcrowded and de-teriorated. In early 1970, Lakeview Tower, the City's first public housing exclu-sively for the elderly, was opened near the lake and extensive planning with the community was undertaken. Several houses in the area were rehabilitated under the Vacant House Program, and put into use as public housing. Parks were built: two blocks were rehabilitated and sold as cooperatives under the LPA Rehab pro-gram. A number of houses were awarded to urban homesteaders, and loans pro-vided to a number of new home-owners. In the same general neighborhood (but in the Madison–Park North Renewal Area) a recreation center, new school, new hous-ing for moderate-income families were constructed. A fine old building, the Norwe-gian Seamen's Home, was rehabilitated into a multi-purpose center with Commu-nity Development Block Grant funds used. Fifteen solar-heated market-rate houses were put under construction.

HCD Divisions involved in the program for Reservoir Hill were: *Planning,* which worked with the community to develop the area plan, and which planned the construction of Lakeview Tower and later an extension to it; *Neighborhood Devel-opment,* which inspected all houses in the area, administered loans and grants, administered the zoning code including rollbacks in density of several houses; *Re-location,* which finds new homes for residents as needed; *Housing Management and Social Work Services,* managing and providing services to residents of both Lakeview Tower and housing renovated under the Vacant House Program; *Con-struction and Buildings Inspection,* supervising construction of Lakeview Tower, and administering all of the total rehabilitation programs; *Land Development,* ac-quiring property as needed for public housing, rehabilitation and parks, and as-sisting developers of new construction; *Information Services,* assisting in assuring public awareness and community participation; *Home Ownership,* administering the urban homesteading program; and *Program Management,* maintaining liaison with the neighborhood and coordinating the scheduling of all activities.[3]

Housing in economic development

The growing trend of linking economic development to housing is well illus-trated in Baltimore. One facet is the Charles Center and Inner Harbor Devel-opment Corporation, a private, nonprofit corporation under the HCD struc-ture. The Charles Center development is a thirty-three-acre project that has created a unified complex of office buildings, hotels, theaters, retail shops, and underground parking garages connected by a system of urban plazas and ground-level and elevated pedestrian ways. An integral part of this development is a residential and shopping complex with four hundred apartments housing residents, none of whom lived in the central downtown area before. Likewise, the Inner Harbor redevelopment project, focused on Baltimore's active seaport and linking it with the business district of downtown, has three residential components.

An additional facet of the economic development–housing linkage came with the federal UDAG program in 1978. Baltimore's five-year capital development program, approved in 1981, includes fifteen UDAG projects, of which eleven incorporate residential development.

Neighborhoods—the key element

The heart of Baltimore's housing functions, however, is not in the central organization and powers of HCD but in the *neighborhood* focus of its structure, programs, and services. When the department was created in 1968, it was working with sixteen neighborhood communities; by 1981, this had grown to sixty. All HCD functions are oriented to neighborhoods. The planning division develops detailed plans and assigns planners and program managers to specific neighborhoods. The neighborhood development division enforces city housing code and zoning ordinances and administers federal, state, and local programs of housing rehabilitation; it operates through five field offices. The program management section of the administrator's office is a liaison between the department and the community; although HCD planners and neighborhood development personnel work directly with community groups, the program managers are involved in all major matters.

HCD also includes within its portfolio the administration of multipurpose centers in fifteen communities; the common element in each is a "mayor's station" or "little city hall," staffed by a representative of the mayor responsible for the general coordination of services throughout the center's target service area. More than thirty different city, state, federal, and private non-profit services are provided, including health, library, social, cultural, and recreational. Every center has been planned with the participation of an established community organization or citizen planning committee; in many instances, program development has been an integral part of urban renewal activity, combining capital and human resources at the neighborhood level. Using CDBG monies, HCD funds a variety of "community support" projects relating to federally financed community development programs, including project area committees, home ownership services, social services, information services, and public housing security.

In addition to the neighborhood activities carried out by HCD, CDBG funds have been used since 1975 to support "special projects" in neighborhoods. Of the $197.3 million of CDBG funds expended by Baltimore between March 1975 and December 1980, 43 percent can be directly tied to neighborhood projects, 3 percent to multipurpose centers, and 18 percent to support services of the Urban Services Agency.[4] The HCD program in 1981 included improvement activities in thirteen neighborhood communities.

Clearly, the involvement of neighborhood residents is not limited to participation in planning for neighborhood improvements. In many instances, residents are directly involved in the provision of services. A particularly promising avenue for citizen involvement is the HCD demonstration in seven neighborhoods through the deputizing of seven volunteers as "citizen inspectors" who inspect and handle all exterior sanitation problems in a specific geographic area. After training, each is responsible for issuing violation notices for unsanitary conditions, maintaining necessary records, processing work orders, and carrying out activities in the same manner as a housing inspector. This program makes possible a housing maintenance system that is beyond the resources of existing HCD inspection staff.

The Baltimore experience

The essence of the Baltimore mode of operation is not so much the organizational structure (although the consolidation of housing powers is a major component) but the "chemistry" among the various actors—the city's housing administrators, the private business community, the resident in the neighborhood. The contacts among these three are not one-time or project-oriented; they are day-to-day and are built into the city government structure. Essentially, the process is one of political leadership centered in the office of the mayor. To orchestrate this multifaceted process, the mayor has formed a mini-cabinet of seven key city officials concerned with city development and improvements, which meets with him on an "on-call" basis. The Baltimore process is dynamic and flexible in responding to changing conditions and opportunities.

PITTSBURGH

The city of Pittsburgh assigns responsibility for housing among two city departments (the Department of City Planning and the Department of Fire, Bureau of Building Inspection) and two separate local agencies (the Urban Redevelopment Authority and the public housing authority). As in Baltimore, the organization has strong ties to local political leadership in the mayor's office.

The changing table of organization

During the years of categorical renewal and residential rehabilitation, the responsibilities for the city of Pittsburgh's housing functions were divided among the Department of City Planning (DCP), the Urban Redevelopment Authority (URA), the housing authority, and the Bureau of Building Inspection.

Major publicly related development activities were primarily in renewal areas and were handled by URA. The housing authority developed and maintained low-rent public housing. The Bureau of Building Inspection handled all building permits and code enforcement. DCP was responsible for all comprehensive planning, neighborhood planning, capital budgeting, and zoning.

With the beginning of the CDBG program in 1975, DCP was given the responsibility of developing the annual CDBG plan and budget and the Housing Assistance Plan. A housing coordinator was added in the mayor's office to orchestrate activities on housing development projects and to work with DCP and URA on the development and implementation of CDBG-funded housing and neighborhood improvement programs.

This structure was difficult administratively. The housing coordinator, lacking staff assistance, had considerable difficulty moving the relevant departments in a consistent direction, and the detailed implementation of programs became problematic. For example, a home repair loan program, developed by the housing coordinator with DCP and URA, was not thought through in detail at the administrative level. No one was perceived as being in complete charge of implementation. Processing applications, which took from six months to one year, became a serious drag on the capacity to make loans to eligible homeowners.

Dismayed with the cumbersome nature of this structure, the city council in 1977 created a cabinet level Department of Housing to oversee the city's overall housing function. The Bureau of Building Inspection was made a part of this new department, and the director of the new department was appointed to the board of the housing authority to facilitate communication between that authority and city government. DCP continued as the CDBG administrator, although policymaking for housing shifted to the new housing department. Through a series of cooperative agreements with URA, the Department of Housing was able to have a direct impact on program development and operations within URA.

The presence of a new department introduced as many questions as it resolved. Viewed by some as an enhancement of the housing coordinator's responsibilities, the department had to define a set of functions for itself that, on the one hand, were not planning, and, on the other hand, were not the actual management of programs by URA.[5]

On the housing development side, responsibility also was ambiguous. Since DCP was responsible for zoning, subdivisions, site planning, and so on, and URA for disposition contracts and enforcement in renewal areas, little room existed for the new department to facilitate housing development. The department found itself involved primarily with developing subsidized housing and acting as a liaison with the home building industry, but it had little to do with the development of market-rate housing.

The administrative system was workable, but it was quite labor-intensive for top management, since many issues and decisions required the attention of top staff from the Department of Housing, DCP, and URA.

After four years with this administrative structure, the mayor reorganized the development functions. In 1982 the mayor, with council approval, consolidated all development functions—housing, renewal activities, and economic development—into the Urban Redevelopment Authority and proposed that the authority be renamed the Housing and Redevelopment Authority.[6] The purpose of the consolidation was to bring all development-related activities into one organization to increase accountability and management of the housing and economic development functions. The Department of Housing and the Department of Economic Development (which was responsible for economic development and commercial improvement programs) were terminated. Roles were clarified between DCP and the revised authority. Figure 6–3 summarizes these changes.

At the beginning of 1982, the city of Pittsburgh had a table of organization for its housing and development programs almost identical, on paper, to that which existed prior to 1970. The Department of City Planning was responsible for overall planning, land use, zoning, capital and CDBG budgeting, and neighborhood planning. The Bureau of Building Inspection became part of the Department of Fire. (Prior to 1970, both had been part of a Department of Public Safety.) Continued liaison between the URA and the separate housing authority was assured by placing the URA executive director on the board of the housing authority.

Obviously, in any city, given the history of experience, personalities, professional strengths and weaknesses, and the general level of satisfaction or dissatisfaction by top elected officials, tables of organization change. In the Pittsburgh case, although the administrative structure went full circle over a twelve-year period, the 1982 organization was based on collective city learning about how functions could best be structured for Pittsburgh in 1982.

The budgets for the four agencies in 1982 total $31.6 million and the total number of employees is 816. The Department of City Planning has a budget of $1.2 million and a staff of 58. The Bureau of Building Inspection of the Department of Fire has a budget of $1.6 million and a staff of 75. The

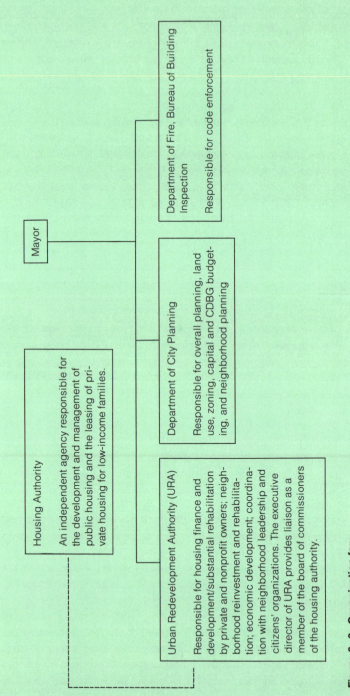

Figure 6–3 Organization for housing, city of Pittsburgh, 1982.

Mayor

Housing Authority

An independent agency responsible for the development and management of public housing and the leasing of private housing for low-income families.

Urban Redevelopment Authority (URA)

Responsible for housing finance and development/substantial rehabilitation by private and nonprofit owners; neighborhood reinvestment and rehabilitation; economic development; coordination with neighborhood leadership and citizens' organizations. The executive director of URA provides liaison as a member of the board of commissioners of the housing authority.

Department of City Planning

Responsible for overall planning, land use, zoning, capital and CDBG budgeting, and neighborhood planning.

Department of Fire, Bureau of Building Inspection

Responsible for code enforcement

Pittsburgh's housing goals The overall goal of the Department of Housing is to take all actions necessary and appropriate to improve housing conditions and choices for residents of the city of Pittsburgh, and to create housing opportunities for potential newcomers.

This overall goal is broken down into twelve goal areas.

1. To create a healthier development environment in the city, making it easier for private builders to construct new and rehabilitate old houses.
2. To develop an effective marketing program to promote Pittsburgh and its neighborhoods as good places to live for current residents and newcomers.
3. To stimulate neighborhood recovery and renewal through appropriate housing reinvestment programs.
4. To protect and improve the existing housing in the city through home repair, maintenance, and code programs.
5. To prevent housing abandonment and to rehabilitate or recommend proper disposition of those units already abandoned.
6. To assist property owners in making their homes more energy efficient.
7. To seek a maximum level of government and private resources to provide good public and privately owned housing for low and moderate income persons.
8. To monitor changing housing needs and conditions through the participation in a long range planning process involving the public and private sectors, and the residents of Pittsburgh's neighborhoods.
9. To encourage full compliance with fair housing laws, and to counter blockbusting, redlining, and other discriminatory practices when they occur.
10. To identify and respond to the housing needs of special population groups, such as women, handicapped, dependent persons, and elderly.
11. To promote housing choice by providing a diversity of financing techniques.
12. To operate a professional and efficient department, responsive to changing circumstances.

Source: City of Pittsburgh, Department of Housing, "Statement of Goals," January 1982.

Urban Redevelopment Authority has a budget of $5.8 million and a staff of 157. The public housing authority has a total budget of $23 million and a staff of 526.

The URA was organized internally to facilitate the integration of the direct housing functions with one another and to assist in the interface between housing and other city government—related functions.

Pittsburgh has had an unusually strong neighborhood preservation and rehabilitation effort, as documented in Chapter 2. It also has been a pioneer in housing finance, as one of the first cities to issue tax-exempt mortgage bonds for single-family housing. The strong interest of the private business community in Pittsburgh's economic revitalization has presented numerous opportunities to integrate housing into mixed-use developments.

Integrating direct housing functions

Integration of the direct housing functions is facilitated because most of the responsibilities for housing are within one authority, the URA, but the task is still administratively and conceptually difficult. One can view the direct housing functions of the city of Pittsburgh in three components: neighborhood conservation and housing rehabilitation, development and management of assisted housing, and response to changes in the housing market. Coordinating these three components requires that certain conditions be in place:

1. The programs developed to facilitate housing rehabilitation and neighborhood improvement must be well administered so that they can actually deliver their product (usually a grant or loan).
2. The neighborhood conservation programs must be developed and implemented in a flexible way, with the capacity to adapt to changing circumstances, based on changing neighborhood housing market conditions.
3. Data about housing market conditions must be available routinely to permit policymakers to adapt programs.
4. Some ability is needed to orchestrate the location of assisted housing to support and be supported by neighborhood improvement efforts.

Neighborhood conservation and rehabilitation programs in Pittsburgh are developed at two levels. The Department of City Planning, as part of its responsibility to monitor neighborhood conditions and changes, suggests broad approaches to neighborhood treatment and recommends areas that appear to be in need of such treatment. URA, in dialogue with DCP, takes this input and shapes specific reinvestment programs for the neighborhoods. URA works with neighborhood leadership, with lenders, real estate agents, and other key actors to implement programs in neighborhoods. In some cases, if the approach requires code enforcement, the Bureau of Building Inspection is brought in to muster the personnel needed for that component of the program.

The development and management of assisted housing is shared among DCP, URA, and the housing authority. DCP is responsible for the broad statement of the areas that are appropriate for assisted housing. URA works with the private profit and nonprofit sectors so that assisted housing is built or rehabilitated in the appropriate areas; the housing authority then develops and manages the public housing in these areas. In all cases, assisted housing developments are small-scale, and, for political reasons, assisted housing for families is extremely difficult to place.

The process for working with neighborhood groups on assisted housing is quite elaborate. Preliminary as well as final drawings are reviewed, and small briefing meetings and formal public hearings are held on each development. The objective of the process, usually involving both DCP and URA, is to arrive at a housing approach that is acceptable to both the developer and the neighborhood.

The city's ability to respond to changes in the housing market is quite good because of routinely reported data on real estate sales prices, price patterns, and mortgage lending activity. Price patterns are a good reflection of changes in neighborhood conditions and are used to make decisions on where to concentrate neighborhood recovery efforts or to determine whether changes in local law are needed to curtail overheated market sectors in some way. Careful analysis of condominium conversion trends in 1979 and 1980, for example, led to the conclusion that intervention was not needed and that the phenomenon was not occurring in sufficient volume to warrant local regulation.

Coordinating these three major housing functions is difficult because the city government cannot control all the activities related to the housing function (HUD controls many), and political considerations sometimes thwart efforts to integrate these functions fully.

Integrating housing with other city functions

The most important vehicle for coordinating development, including housing, is the Mayor's Development Council. Chaired by the mayor's executive secretary (Pittsburgh's equivalent of the appointed chief administrator), the council consists of the top staff person from the departments of city planning, public works, finance, and parks and recreation; the chairman and the executive director of URA; and professional staff of the public parking authority, the port authority (mass transit), and the Regional Industrial Development Corporation.

This group meets weekly to review all major development proposals in the earliest stages and to coordinate the development and implementation of complex proposals among the departments and authorities involved. The council has been extremely important in orchestrating the city's overall development function; the council provides a direct and regular link with the mayor's office for all the key development organizations.

CITY BUDGETING   City capital and CDBG budget decisions are ultimately made by Pittsburgh's nine at-large city council members. However, internal to the administration, a budget review committee, chaired by the mayor's executive secretary and including representatives from the departments of finance and city planning, reviews all requests for capital budget expenditures both to ensure that the budgeted activities make sense in aggregate and to set priorities among the many requests for scarce funds.

CITY OPERATIONS   Perhaps the most problematic issue is coordinating housing with such other city operations as public safety, refuse collection, and maintenance of public property. Conceptually, it makes sense to try to improve these services in an area going through a planned neighborhood recovery effort, and attempts are made to do so. However, the reality of the situation usually is that the operating departments have so little extra capacity that expectations about improved services to complement a housing activity are seldom met. In some respects, the staff responsible for operations of other city functions are so regularly buffeted by requests for improved services that the effort to coordinate with a housing strategy is viewed as a luxury, not a necessity.

In Pittsburgh, various departments and authorities have established structured communications links to integrate the housing function with other city functions. As anyone with experience at the local level knows, however, coordination is a very difficult task and works best when the mayor or city manager and city council expect cooperation among the persons responsible for different functions. In Pittsburgh, where organizatinal theory falls short, reasonableness and good will among the persons involved usually add to the city's ability to carry out its housing function and to see that the housing function relates well to other city functions.

1 Montgomery County (Maryland), Department of Housing and Community Development, *Housing Policy for Montgomery County in the 1980's* (Rockville, Md.: Montgomery County Department of Housing and Community Development, 1981).

2 Ibid., pp. 16–17.

3 Baltimore (Maryland), Department of Housing and Community Development, *Baltimore's Housing and Community Development Programs* (Baltimore, Md.: Department of Housing and Community Development, 1981), pp. 8–9.

4 Ibid., p. 13.

5 The city solicitor had ruled that the city was constitutionally prohibited from making loans or grants directly, but had to do so through the URA.

6 Legal problems prevented this change of name, and the authority remained the Urban Redevelopment Authority.

Appendix A

Housing production incentives for the builder/developer, investor, mortgage lender, and permanent lender

Note: The Economic Recovery Tax Act of 1981 made some significant changes affecting investors in lower-income housing developments, providing additional incentives beyond those described in this appendix, which is based on a 1980 report.

BUILDER/DEVELOPER

Builder/developers are the prime movers in the production process. They conceive the ideas, buy the land, arrange financing, and plan and build projects. Their primary motivation is to make money. With the exception of public housing, developers earn a profit by (1) receiving a fee for their efforts (typically 10 percent of the project's development cost, which often substitutes for the builder's cash equity) and (2) selling the project to passive investors interested primarily in using depreciation deductions to shelter other income.

Typically developers sell subsidized projects to a group of investors (called a syndicated partnership) for about 15 to 20 percent of the mortgage amount. This syndication process is almost essential because it allows the developer to turn over the project and reinvest in other projects. With the exception of public housing, each of the financing alternatives allows syndication to a group of private investors.

INVESTOR

The tax syndication process is the primary attraction for investors and, in turn, acts as a stimulus for housing production.

People who invest in subsidized housing are primarily interested in a tax shelter and the profit if the project appreciates in value. Investors are passive since they do not develop or manage the project but merely buy the investment from the builder/developer and turn the management over to a general partner. The developer of a section 8 project does not generally have sufficient income to take advantage of the considerable tax losses. As a result, the developer converts the available shelter into cash fees by selling equity interests in the project to these passive investors. These ownership interests may be sold to passive investors directly by the developer or through a syndicator or an underwriter. The sale of ownership interests generates cash for the developer to use for the legal and syndication fees, for cash requirements of the construction phase not covered by the mortgage, and for the profit that the developer makes. This mechanism, with its attendant benefits for the developer, is a substantial inducement to develop a section 8 project.

Accelerated depreciation

The most noteworthy tax benefit for section 8 investors is the depreciation of construction cost during the project's operating phase. Depreciation is one of the few expenses against project income that is not a cash expense. The Internal Revenue Code permits several methods by which depreciation can be accelerated over the straight line method. Section 8 has an advantage because the greater financing leverage gives the investor a higher ratio of depreciation losses to equity invested. Because of the greater financing leverage, the interest expense of the project mortgage is higher. Since most financing methods permit 40-year mortgages (as opposed to 20 or 25 years with conventional financing), the interest expense during the first years is greater than for a similarly mortgaged conventional project.

All new rental housing can be depreciated for tax purposes at a rate which is initially twice the normal rate. This method, known as the 200 percent declining balance method, shelters the income generated by the property in the case of private projects and allows section 8 investors to shelter income from other sources with the lower down payments and longer mortgage terms.

Attractive recapture provisions

The Internal Revenue Code also provides other tax benefits to section 8 investors depending on the timing and manner of disposal of a project. When an accelerated depreciation method is used and the project is sold, the excess depreciation is taxed as ordinary income unless the property has been held for a certain period. In the case of low and moderate income housing, no excess depreciation is recaptured if the project has been held for 16 years and 8 months, while all excess depreciation is recaptured if the project is unsubsidized.

Rehabilitation write-off

For investors in multifamily rehabilitation under section 8, the Internal Revenue Code, in section 167(k), provides that any rehabilitation expense can be written off in 5 years rather than the remaining useful life of the project. This section, available only for expenses incurred after 1969, has been credited with stimulating development of a rehabilitation industry since then.

Expected gain upon sale

Investors also participate in section 8 projects because of expected gains when projects are sold. Under older subsidized housing programs (notably the section 236 program) projection of returns on initial investment assumed the projects would be sold for a value equivalent to the mortgage balances. However, returns on investment are likely to be more substantial under section 8 because (1) projects are considered more likely to appreciate in value than in the past and (2) capital gains laws are more favorable.

Tax incentive for continued section 8 private ownership is weak

If the government did not require 20-year or longer contracts, section 8 investors would be highly motivated to sell their projects after only a few years of ownership because the return on investment would be substantial. Although projects would continue to provide good returns after 10 years, the bulk of the tax shelter is exhausted in the first 10 years. Since tax shelter is the primary motivation for investment in subsidized projects, we believe that many owners would be highly motivated to sell or convert to condominiums even at moderate rates of appreciation. Higher appreciation rates, which are bound to occur in some areas, and higher investor tax brackets (which are the norm), result in an even greater incentive to dispose of such investments.

Other tax benefits

The tax on the gain realized from the sale of a federally assisted rental project may be deferred if the project is sold to the tenants, a cooperative, or qualified nonprofit organization and if the seller purchases a similar type of subsidized housing (usually within 1 year from the date of sale of the first project). Moreover, treatment of excess depreciation (as described above) is dated from the date of acquisition of the first project. If the project owner donates the project to a qualified charitable organization, the fair market value rather than the project's depreciated cost may be deducted. The difference in the deduction could be substantial.

Nonprofit investor

Profit-motivated owners are usually passive investors who participate through the syndication process and, as discussed above, are motivated primarily by tax considerations. Nonprofit sponsors, on the other hand, sponsor a development to house needy families or elderly people. These sponsors often involve church-related groups, for example, and are presumably motivated by social concerns. They are allowed 100 percent loans, do not receive any cash returns from the rents, and do not receive deductions for tax purposes.

MORTGAGE LENDER

Most low-income housing assistance mechanisms must have a mortgage lender, although the motivations and goals of these lenders or brokers vary substantially from one alternative to another. The prototype for this discussion is the mortgage lender who provides the financing under the traditional FHA insurance alternative. This lender may be a savings and loan association, a commercial bank, or a mortgage broker. Federal law requires savings and loans to lend a certain percentage of their funds as residential mortgages. Although these banks characteristically opt for single family housing they do finance a substantial amount of multifamily housing. Commercial banks keep some portion of their funds in residential mortgages but do not lend money frequently for subsidized housing. Most FHA multifamily mortgages are placed by mortgage brokers who bring together the borrower and the permanent

lender rather than using their own funds to hold mortgages for a long period. Any of these mortgage lenders may choose to hold multifamily mortgages as investments, but here these lenders are discussed in the role of brokers rather than permanent lenders.

A mortgage banker, mortgage broker, or mortgage lender, as contrasted to a permanent lender, is motivated primarily to earn a one-time fee for placing the loan and perhaps continuing to service the loan (collect payments and deal with the borrowers) for a monthly fee. The one-time fee, which may be 1.5 to 2.5 percent of the mortgage amount, is collected at settlement. The mortgage banker may also earn some initial profit by placing and holding the construction loan. By this description, one can gather that the profit of a mortgage banker is not really dependent on the long-term viability of the loan or the project but rather upon the size of the mortgage and the amount of its loan placement fee. The mortgage lender is really motivated to handle the transaction smoothly and at the least cost so as to maximize profit and enhance its reputation as a loan underwriter. A pattern of bad loans could conceivably result in FHA withdrawing the lender's ability to handle FHA loans.

Functions of mortgage lenders

The principal functions of mortgage lenders are to (1) locate temporary construction funds, (2) arrange for a permanent lender to buy the permanent mortgages (which may mean arranging for GNMA to purchase the loans—see the section on permanent lenders), (3) service the mortgage, (4) evaluate the feasibility of projects, (5) arrange for FHA mortgage insurance, and (6) monitor construction. Each function must be performed to complete the entire development process. But given the fee structure for mortgage lenders, they are (as implied earlier) less likely to adequately perform those functions unrelated to their profit, such as carefully evaluating feasibility and monitoring construction.

For a conventional loan the mortgage lender is exposed to some risk since, if the loan goes bad prior to its placement with a permanent lender, the mortgage lender could take a substantial loss. To avoid such losses on conventional loans the lender will very likely (1) require a higher down payment from the borrower, and (2) arrange for mortgage insurance from a private company. The risk is spread to the borrower and the insurer, but the latter party insures only a certain percentage of the loan. Thus, the lender still stands to lose if the loan goes bad and is, therefore, careful not to lend on an unacceptably risky venture.

With FHA insurance, risk is minimal, since FHA insures 99 percent of the loan. If the borrower defaults, the lender only stands to lose a portion of the profit. So the financial risk to the lender on FHA loans is really nonexistent.

Since FHA theoretically depends on the lender to examine carefully the project for feasibility and since the lender has little to risk, a fundamental principle of risk avoidance is violated. Mortgage lenders should closely watch construction and early project operation. Financial problems of an otherwise sound project can often snowball into financial failures if proper curative steps are not taken. The lack of financial risk with FHA insurance can deter the lender from doing whatever is necessary to cure a problem loan, since it may be more costly for the lender to solve the problem than to assign the loan to HUD, get the loan proceeds, and reinvest in a more profitable venture. This lack of risk-taking on the part of the lender is a serious problem which has plagued FHA-subsidized loans; so far no solution has been found.

SHFAs as mortgage lenders

State housing finance agencies are also mortgage lenders since they arrange the permanent financing (by issuing tax-exempt bonds), lend construction funds to developers, evaluate project feasibility, and monitor construction.

Like private mortgage lenders, SHFAs earn a placement or finance fee for their efforts. However, SHFAs are much more concerned about successful project completion, and therefore carefully monitor the construction process. Construction delays can mean cost overruns and possible default. Such problems can mean either additional bonding or a default to bondholders. In either case, their bond ratings can fall and future bond borrowing could be jeopardized.

LHAs as mortgage lenders

Local housing authorities, or their instrumentalities, also serve as mortgage lenders since they arrange for both construction and permanent lending by either borrowing money from conventional lenders or arranging for the sale of tax-exempt bonds. The difference between FHA insured lenders, SHFA lenders, and LHA lenders is that LHA lenders are not underwriters because they do not evaluate project feasibility. This function is typically carried out by bond underwriters (investment firms) who evaluate the underlying security and then market the bonds.

PERMANENT LENDER

In contrast to mortgage brokers, permanent lenders are interested in a secure long term return on investment. This section describes (1) the permanent lenders under each financing mechanism, (2) the reasons they are motivated to invest in subsidized housing, and (3) the ways in which the motivations differ among alternatives.

FHA-insured lenders

After GNMA purchases FHA insured projects, it sells the mortgages to private lenders at auction. Purchasers are typically mortgage investment firms and, to a lesser extent, insurance companies and pension funds. These investors make money over the long run by borrowing at a lower cost than the return on the mortgages. FHA loans are particularly attractive because of their high insurance against loss.

In the past, many FHA project loans were purchased by the Federal National Mortgage Association, a quasi-government sponsored corporation chartered to help finance housing. FNMA, like other mortgage investors, wants to make a profit.

Bondholders of SHFA financing

Individuals who hold SHFA bonds are motivated to purchase this type of security because of their after-tax return. The average bond rate in 1977, from a sample of SHFA bonds, was about 6.75 percent. If the bondholder is in the 50 percent tax bracket, the return on investment is equivalent to a taxable bond yielding 13.5 percent. Although corporate bonds can match this yield, they generally have much lower investment ratings. This factor alone has allowed a considerable amount of funds to flow into the housing sector through tax-exempt bonds.

Another factor which helps finance projects under SHFAs is that bond denominations are small enough to attract many individual investors. In contrast, purchasers of FHA/GNMA project mortgages are large institutions and their ability to supply funds is limited by the number of firms and the amount of funds each firm can invest.

Bonds can be held by all types of investors, including commercial banks or savings and loan associations that desire tax-exempt securities. Although relatively little activity has occurred under the 11(b) financing method,

many bondholders are actually local financial institutions. These lenders also find the tax-exempt securities lucrative, especially if they are in a high tax bracket.

Mortgage-backed securities attract permanent lenders

Mortgage lenders can issue securities to permanently finance FHA-insured projects they originate; these securities are called mortgage-backed securities (MBS) and are guaranteed by GNMA. The guarantee runs to the investor—the holder of the security certificate—and assures the timely payment of monthly principal and interest. The MBS are so-called "pass throughs," a term which indicates that the mortgage lenders (issuers) pass through to the investors the principal and monthly interest payment on the mortgages.

The majority of MBS are held by mortgage and investment bankers, savings banks, savings and loan associations, pension trusts, and individuals. All these entities invest in securities for five reasons. First, yield (or return on investment) is usually higher than that available from other U.S. investment agency issues and at times better than that available from AAA-rated corporate bonds. Second, the securities are backed with the full faith and credit of the U.S. government; the investor has absolute safety of principal and interest. Third, monthly payments of principal and interest provide a monthly cash flow. Fourth, the MBS are easily traded. Fifth, investors can invest in mortgages without the normal administrative burdens associated with managing a mortgage portfolio.

Federal financing provides permanent public housing funds

Traditionally, tax-exempt bonds were issued by local housing authorities to finance public housing projects. These bonds offer a low before-tax rate of return (never greater than 6 percent), but for very high income investors, yields can be significant. For example, an investor in the 50-percent tax bracket can earn the equivalent of the return on a taxable bond yielding 12 percent. In addition, these securities are absolutely risk-free since they too are backed by the full faith and credit of the federal government. However, public housing bonds have not been issued since 1974, with the government "rolling over" debt by issuing short-term notes with interest rates much lower than 6 percent. Beginning in 1980, the Department of Housing and Urban Development began to provide permanent financing of public housing by selling obligations to the federal financing bank. Unless interest rates on tax-exempt bonds fall considerably, this practice is likely to continue.

Source: Excerpted from U.S., General Accounting Office, *Evaluation of Alternatives for Financing Low and Moderate Income Housing* (Washington, D.C.: Government Printing Office, 1980), pp. 62–72.

Appendix B

MAINTENANCE AND CUSTODIAL

The maintenance function encompasses the routine upkeep of plant and
equipment and the routine and emergency repair or replacement of physical elements of the structures. It includes such activities as routine repair,
emergency repair, periodic maintenance, maintenance requiring special
equipment or expertise (such as eleva-
tors, heating systems, and exterior
lighting), grounds maintenance, and re-
cording/monitoring maintenance conditions.

The custodial function encompasses the routine cleaning and upkeep of a housing development, including such activities as upkeep of
residential public spaces, cleaning of
vacant apartments, upkeep of nonresidential public spaces, cleaning of
grounds and parking areas, solid waste
removal and storage, and operating the
custodial system—e.g., scheduling
and deployment of personnel and monitoring activities.

PURCHASING AND INVENTORY

Purchasing and inventory include buying, storing, and reallocating the material resources for cleaning and maintaining the physical plant. All
expendable supplies, replacement
parts, appliances, tools, and equipment
are secured through this system, as are
the supplies required by the administrative and managerial staff. It includes
the following elements: establishing
purchasing needs, vendor selection,
tracking and accepting deliveries,
identifying current new products and
equipment. It encompasses the following activities: inventory planning, inventory maintenance and accounting,

responding to requests and controlling
outflow, signaling management problems.

MANAGEMENT INFORMATION, FINANCE, AND ACCOUNTING

The management information function
consists of the procedures, facilities,
and staff time whereby quantitative information on the assisted housing operation is assembled, processed, and
disseminated to various levels of the
management system. Its activities include setting management objectives
and monitoring the results, standardizing data, designing reporting forms,
and manipulating data into more integrated and useful formats for decision
making. Not all management information systems will be automated, but
more complex operations will include
use of a computer and will have a computer terminal capacity that permits
managers to call up data when needed.

The finance and accounting function provides the basic scorekeeping
for the entire operation. Financial management concerns the investment of
surplus cash. Accounting generally
refers to the process by which income
and expenses are tracked, using the
standard bookkeeping practices and
HUD's established accounting categories. Also included are accounting activities related to budget preparation.
Specific activities include maintaining
books of accounts and records, providing financial control, and managing
cash flow.

OCCUPANCY

This function includes establishing the
terms of residence, attracting potential
tenants, screening the pool of appli-

cants, and subsequently letting apartments to those found eligible and acceptable and attempting to control occupancy by those who do not meet their obligations as tenants or neighbors. Specific activities include establishing occupancy ground rules in conformance with federal regulations, including lease forms and leasing procedures, income limits and rent schedules, affirmative action and fair marketing, grievance procedures, marketing, waiting lists, and apartment vacancy information. This function also includes applicant screening, apartment preparation, tenant orientation/move-in, income recertification, and legal actions relating to continued occupancy.

GENERAL ADMINISTRATION

General administration is the framework within which all other functions are performed and involves coordinating and regulating the internal operations; generating the resources required and allocating them among the various functional areas and housing sites; and maintaining relations with the local government, HUD, and the public. An important element of this function is developing and coordinating the entire management operation to fulfill contractual obligations with the federal government and with the general-purpose local government, as well as meet provisions of applicable state law in such matters as bidding procedures for contracts and insurance.

PERSONNEL AND TRAINING

This function embraces the recruitment, training, and retention of the required personnel. Specific activities include: job description/recruitment, hiring/firing, compensation/benefits, management of unions/civil service relations, employee evaluation, career ladder/incentives, staff training/opportunities for professional development (including

certification), commissioner training, and tenant training.

PROJECT MANAGEMENT

Project management involves the implementation of various practices and policies as they affect individual sites. It is concerned with the day-to-day operation of housing developments, which primarily means coordinating the activities of a number of other functional areas when they come into the orbit of a given site or set of sites. Specific activities include supervision of site office and site personnel; follow-up on rent collection; oversight of maintenance, custodial staff, and site security; responsibility for time sheets, payroll, and some personnel matters; initiation and/or coordination of apartment move-ins; initiation of requisitions and purchases; and tenant relations and local service referrals.

SECURITY

Security encompasses attempts to reduce crime, antisocial behavior, and vandalism within the housing sites. The main objectives are protection of people and property, and services are generally delivered by a separate cadre of personnel and by special physical arrangement or installations. Specific activities include surveillance and/or personal inspection of all site properties on a regular schedule; handling requests for assistance; coordination and cooperation with local police departments; and work with tenants and community organizations to increase awareness of responsibilities and potential for improved security.

SOCIAL SERVICE

This function deals with activities that meet immediate welfare needs, enhance daily life on a housing site, or help residents become more self-sufficient. It encompasses the delivery of nonhousing services having specific application to the geographic concentration of a needy population under public auspices. Funding for performing these services is not available under federal housing assistance programs. Thus, resources to carry them out must come from local community agencies or from federal assistance from other federal agencies. Typical services include the following:

For the elderly: Congregate or home-delivered meals, adult day care, transportation, homemaker services, information and referral.

For families: Child day care and after-school programs, alcoholism/drug abuse counseling, recreation and summer vacation programs, employment and job development, health and prenatal care, information and referral.

The housing management entity sometimes has a small core social services staff to handle referrals to local social service agencies or to supervise contracts with community agencies or tenant organizations to perform social services if funding is available.

Source: Excerpted and condensed from: Raymond J. Struyk et al., *Case Studies of Public Housing Management: General Design Report,* Working Paper No. 1432–02, prepared for the U.S. Department of Housing and Urban Development (Washington, D.C.: The Urban Institute, 1981).

Appendix C

Ten profiles of alternative approaches to the management of subsidized housing

METROPOLITAN AREA SERVICES

1. Greater Boston Community Development Corporation (1964). A nonprofit housing development corporation that also provides a range of management services. In 1980 it managed almost 500 units of community-sponsored housing, mostly for the elderly, and it is the designated management agent for an additional 208 units under construction.

2. Community Housing Management Corporation, Elmsford, New York (1970). A not-for-profit management company serving primarily nonprofit-owned subsidized multifamily housing in five New York State counties. In 1980 it managed close to 1,500 housing units in thirteen developments, including one condominium and two limited dividend projects.

GEOGRAPHIC, ETHNIC NEIGHBORHOODS

3. Pyramidwest Realty and Management Inc., Chicago, Illinois. A for-profit wholly owned subsidiary of the Pyramidwest Development Corporation (mid-1970s), assumed management of approximately 1,400 HUD-held units in the Lawndale neighborhood, and in 1979 acquired and began rehabilitation of 1,300 of these units. It also manages three privately owned properties.

4. Mount Auburn Good Housing Foundation, Cincinnati, Ohio (1967). A non-profit neighborhood development corporation that has rehabilitated over 300 units of housing for low- and moderate-income families. It has established a for-profit management entity that returns any profits to the neighborhood community. It manages 550 housing units, of which all but 36 are subsidized under Section 221(d)(3) or Section 236.

5. Inquilnos Borocuas En Accion (IBA), Boston, Massachusetts (1968). A non-profit organization whose housing has been developed by a for-profit affiliate, ETC developers. By 1980, IBA and ETC had planned, financed, developed, and were managing 625 housing units in five developments assisted under a variety of federal/state programs.

RESIDENT MANAGEMENT PROJECTS

6. Forest Hills, Ann Arbor, Michigan (1972). A 306-unit housing cooperative financed under Section 236. It has a five-member board of directors, which hires a resident administrator, and a small staff. This management form replaced two different private management firms and has successfully operated the development for six years.

7. Twin Pines Cooperative, Santa Clara, California. An 80-unit Section 221(d)(3) BMIR cooperative, first occupied in 1963. Original management was by private management companies. A board of directors not only determines policy but supervises a staff consisting of a maintenance man, a gardener, and a part-time bookkeeper.

8. Valley Oak Park, Inc., Santa Rosa, California (1970). A 231-unit family rental project sponsored by the North Coast Counties' District Council of Carpenters and financed under Section 236. Management is conducted by an in-house organization with overall policy direction of the sponsoring union

board. It has a general manager and a staff of eight persons.

9. King's Lynn, Lynn, Massachusetts (1976). A 400-unit rental project financed by the Massachusetts State Housing Finance Agency. It is on the site of a former state-aided public housing development. The complex was constructed, and is now managed, with a co-general partnership agreement between a private developer and the residents' council. Each partner appoints two members to a governing board. Day-to-day management is by the private development/management firm. This firm controls 90 percent of the equity in the project, retaining 25 percent and syndicating the rest in limited partnerships. The partnership agreement stipulates that the private developer will provide all financial requirements and that the tenants' organization will receive the remaining 10 percent of the equity, plus the first 1 percent of the allowed 6 percent limited dividend.

MANAGEMENT BY A PUBLIC HOUSING AGENCY

10. Housing Authority of the City of Las Vegas, Nevada. A housing authority that, in addition to its own public housing inventory, manages 582 units of privately owned housing—including a 352-unit development originally financed under Section 236 as an Operation Breakthrough development, completed in 1973. The private general partners who are owners of the project, distressed with vacancies and other problems, contracted with the housing authority. Within eight months, the housing authority had rented all units and was operating the development successfully. The development now regularly pays it owners the standard 6 percent limited dividend, permitted by HUD only when all repairs and other obligations have been met.

Source: Excerpted and condensed from: Margaret Weitkamp and Daniel D. Pearlman, *Alternative Approaches to the Management of Subsidized Housing* (Berkeley, Calif.: National Housing Law Project, Multifamily Demonstration Program, 1981).

Appendix D

Recommendations for state housing actions proposed by the
National Commission on Urban Problems

RECOMMENDATIONS TO PROMOTE ORDERLY URBAN DEVELOPMENT

Recommendation No. 1—Enabling competent local governments to guide urban development effectively

The commission recommends that state and federal agencies take steps to assure that local governments bear primary responsibility for the guidance of urban development, and that they are capable of effectively performing this function.

Recommendation 1(a)—County or regional authority in small municipalities

The commission recommends that state governments enact legislation granting to counties (or regional governments of general jurisdiction, where such governments exist) exclusive authority to exercise land-use control powers within small municipalities in metropolitan areas. Although conditions vary from state to state, it appears that municipalities within metropolitan areas should not have regulatory powers if (1) either their population is less than 25,000 or their area is less than 4 square miles, or (2) in the case of a municipality hereafter incorporated or not now exercising regulatory powers, their population is less than 50,000.

Recommendation 1(b)—State requirement of a local development guidance program

The commission recommends that state governments enact legislation denying land-use regulatory powers, after a reasonable period of time, to local governments that lack a "development guidance program" as defined by state statute or administrative regulations made pursuant to such statute. Powers

denied would be exercised by the state, regional, or county agencies as provided in the statute. The existence and enforcement by the states of such local development guidance program requirements should, after a reasonable period of time, be made a condition of state participation in the federal 701 planning assistance program.

Recommendation 1(c)—Study of government structure in relation to land-use controls

The commission recommends that the Department of Housing and Urban Development require, as a condition of federal 701 grants to states for local planning assistance, the submission of a comprehensive state study of (1) the allocation of planning and land-use control powers and other decisionmaking activities significantly affecting land use within metropolitan areas, (2) the need for regional decisionmaking or regional review of local decisions within such areas, (3) the need for state action to redistribute control powers, and (4) such other matters as may be required to assure more orderly urban development. Such study should be submitted within a reasonably short period after promulgation of the Secretary's requirements and should be published and distributed within the state. Revisions of such studies should be undertaken not less than every 5 years and should report progress made toward implementating recommendations contained in previous studies.

Recommendation 1(d)— Restructuring local planning and development responsibilities

The commission recommends that state governments enact legislation authorizing but not requiring local governments to abolish local planning boards as traditionally constituted.

Recommendation 1(e)—State recognition of local land-use controls

The commission recommends that state governments enact legislation granting to large units of local government the same regulatory power over the actions of state and other public agencies that they have over those of private developers.

Recommendation No. 2— Establishment of state agency for development planning and review

The commission recommends that each state create a state agency for planning and development guidance directly responsible to the governor. The agency should exercise three types of functions: (1) research and technical assistance to localities in land-use planning and control; (2) the preparation of state and regional land-use plans and policies and (3) adjudication and supervision of decisions by state and local agencies affecting land use.

Recommendation No. 3—Assuring greater choice in the location of housing

The commission recommends that governments at all levels adopt policies and implementing techniques for expanding the choice of persons of all income levels in the selection of their homes.

Recommendation 3(a)—Assurance by local governments of housing variety

The commission recommends that state governments amend state planning and zoning enabling acts to include as one of the purposes of the zoning power the provision of adequate sites for housing persons of all income levels and to require that governments exercising the zoning power prepare plans showing how the community proposes to carry out such objectives in accordance with county or regional housing plans, so that within the region as a whole adequate provision of sites for all income levels is made.

Recommendation 3(b)—Multicounty or regional housing plans

The commission further recommends that state governments enact legislation requiring that multicounty or regional planning agencies prepare and maintain housing plans intended to assure that sites are available within each metropolitan area for development of new housing of all kinds and at all price levels. In the absence of a politically responsible multicounty or metropolitan-wide unit, the state should approve such housing plans for each metropolitan area.

Recommendation 3(c)—Collection of regional housing data

The commission recommends that state governments enact legislation directing state or regional planning agencies to prepare and maintain, on a periodic basis, data on the general availability of housing and housing sites for persons of various income levels. The commission further recommends that the Congress provide financial aid to the states to assist them in carrying out these functions.

Recommendation 3(d)—Public acquisition of housing sites

The commission recommends that state governments enact legislation authorizing state, regional, and local agencies to acquire land for present or future use or disposition to provide sites for low- and moderate-income housing.

Recommendation 3(e)— Establishment of state policy on housing near employment centers

The commission recommends that the states adopt resolutions making it official state policy to encourage the provision of housing for employees of all income levels in areas reasonably close to places of employment.

Recommendation No. 4—Unified planning and design of new neighborhoods

The commission recommends that states enact legislation enabling localities to encourage unified planning and design of new neighborhoods and to prevent wasteful and unattractive scattered development. Specifically, the commission proposes the following actions:

Recommendation 4(a)—Restriction of development through holding zones

The commission recommends that state governments enable local governments to establish holding zones in order to postpone urban development in areas that are inappropriate for development within the next 3 to 5 years. Local governments should be authorized to limit development within such zones to houses on very large lots (e.g., 10 to 20 acres), agriculture, and open space uses. The state legislation should require that localities review holding zone designations at least every 5 years.

Recommendation 4(b)—Regulatory process for planned unit development

The commission recommends that state governments enact enabling legislation for, and local governments adopt, provisions establishing a regulatory process for planned unit developments. Such legislation should authorize provisions to vary according to the size of projects (e.g., to permit high-rise buildings or light industry only in projects of more than a specified size).

Recommendation 4(c)—State authorization for planned development districts

The commission recommends that state governments enact legislation enabling local governments to classify undeveloped land in planned development districts within which development would be allowed to occur only at a specified minimum scale. Such statutes should make clear that such minimums could be sufficiently large as to allow only development which created its own environment.

Recommendation 4(d)—Public assistance for land assembly

The commission recommends that state governments enact legislation authorizing local governments of general jurisdiction to use the eminent domain power for the assembly of land needed for large planned unit developments. Such legislation should include a procedure whereby such power can be used to assist private developers to assemble land for approved development. Any such assistance should be conditioned on the conformity of the project with regional plans intended to assure the availability of housing for low- and moderate-income families, and otherwise to insure that the powers are exercised in the public interest.

Recommendation No. 5—Assuring fairness and equality of treatment in the application of standards

The commission recommends that state governments enact legislation establishing clear policies as to the allocation of various costs between developers and local governments. Such legislation should specify the kinds of improvements and facilities for which private developers may be required to bear the costs and the manner in which such obligations may be satisfied, and local governments should not be permitted to deviate from such state policies. As a minimum the legislation should require that developers provide local streets and utilities and dedicate land (or make payments in lieu of dedication) for rights-of-way, utilities, open space, recreation, parks, and schools, provided that such facilities will directly benefit the development and be readily accessible to it.

Recommendation No. 6— Strengthening development controls in developed areas

The commission recommends that states and localities take action to encourage new development in deteriorating built-up areas and to protect built-up areas which now provide a satisfactory living environment and whose protection is in keeping with local plans. Specifically, the commission proposes the following actions:

Recommendation 6(a)— Authorization of planned unit developments in built-up areas

State legislation authorizing the use of planned unit development provisions by localities should extend to situations in which land is assembled in built-up areas, allowing developers the option of obtaining planned unit development review.

Recommendation 6(b)—More effective powers and guidelines regarding variances, rezonings, and nonconforming uses

The commission recommends that the states enact legislation authorizing local governments (1) to impose substantive limitations on the power of boards of appeal to grant variances; (2) to provide effective procedures and aids for the elimination of deleterious nonconforming uses which adversely affect the environment, and (3) to establish formal rezoning policies as a guide to decisions on individual rezonings.

Recommendation No. 7—Use of land purchase and compensative techniques for development control

The commission recommends that states and localities, with the assistance of the federal government, use public land purchase and compensation techniques for the control of development in situations where such approaches

would accomplish better results than traditional police power regulations.

Recommendation 7(a)— Compensative regulation

The commission recommends that the states enact legislation enabling property-owners to compel the purchase of property rights by regulating governments when regulations (or certain types of regulations specified by the statute) would constitute an unconstitutional "taking" of property without just compensation. Land so purchased would then be placed in a public reserve of urban land for present or future disposal and use in accordance with approved plans.

Recommendation 7(b)—State authorization for land banking

The commission recommends that state governments enact legislation enabling state and/or local development authorities or agencies of general purpose governments to acquire land in advance of development for the following purposes: (a) assuring the continuing availability of sites needed for development; (b) controlling the timing, location, type, and scale of development; (c) preventing urban sprawl; and (d) reserving to the public gains in land values resulting from the action of government in promoting and servicing development. At a minimum, such legislation should authorize the acquisition of land surrounding highway interchanges. At such times as development of such land is deemed to be appropriate and in the interests of the region, such land could be sold or leased at no less than its fair market value for private development in accordance with approved plans. Wherever feasible, long-term leases should be the preferred method of disposing of any public land, and lease terms should be set so as to permit reassembly of properties for future replanning and development. Legislation should specify a maximum period that such land may be held by the public before lease or sale.

BUILDING CODE REFORMS

Recommendation No. 3—Adoption of state building codes and mandating building code uniformity in metropolitan areas

The commission recommends the enactment of state legislation providing for the adoption of state building codes dealing with human occupancy, conforming to nationally recognized model code standards developed and/or approved by the proposed National Institute of Building Sciences recommended earlier. We further recommend that such state legislation provide that within 1 year following the adoption of the state code, the provisions of such code shall be applicable without modification throughout each metropolitan area of the state which fails to adopt such nationally recognized standards.

Recommendation No. 4— Strengthening state supervision over building code administration

The commission recommends that states enact legislation providing for (a)

statewide training and licensing programs of local building inspectors, (b) technical assistance to local governments, and (c) statewide appeals mechanisms for reconciling differences arising through code interpretation at the local level.

HOUSING CODE REFORMS

1(a) Adoption of statewide mandatory housing codes by all states

The commission recommends that minimum standard housing code provisions be made applicable to all sections of the nation not now so covered through adoption of statewide mandatory housing codes in the several states.

Source: National Commission on Urban Problems, *Building the American City* (Washington, D.C.: Government Printing Office, [1968]), pp. 236–52, 269–70, 295.

Appendix E

Basic issues in developing state housing policy

People may be unable to obtain the housing they need (or able to obtain it only at a cost that leaves little income for other needs) for one of two basic reasons: (1) the market costs of production—of land, labor, materials and financing—may produce a total housing cost that exceeds their ability to pay; or (2) the mortgage market may fail to produce the needed financing despite the acceptable credit characteristics of the buyer or developer. Each problem deserves separate attention.

Housing costs

Between 1973 and 1979, the cost of home ownership grew by roughly 80 percent, or 17 percent more than the consumer price index as a whole. In 1979 and 1980, median monthly home ownership costs grew at an average annual rate of 17 percent; the proportion of home buyers spending more than 25 percent of their income on housing grew from 38 to 46 percent; and the proportion of first-time home buyers fell from 36 to 18 percent.

This rise in housing costs has been felt most sharply by renters, who comprise fully a third of all households and who typically rent for the simple reason that they are unable to afford either the necessary down payment or the monthly mortgage costs of ownership. This is hardly surprising, for the average renter's income is only slightly more than half that of the typical home-owner. As a result, more than 50 percent of all renters pay more than 25 percent of their incomes for rent. Indeed, the average low-income renter devotes a third of his or her income to housing costs. (As less than one poor family in six is now paying rent in ex-cess of 25 percent of its monthly income and also receiving *any* form of public housing assistance, this can hardly be the result of overly generous federal housing allowances.)

The housing problems facing renters seem certain to increase in the eighties. A growing share of the nation's rental units are lost each year through owner abandonment and condominium conversion. Each of the past several years has seen a new twenty-year low in the number of rental housing units being built. Indeed, very little new unsubsidized rental housing is being built at all, for the simple reason that the existing rental population is seen as undesirable from the perspective of both landlords and developers. Although rents increased dramatically in the decade of the seventies, they have not reached a level that would support either new construction or significant improvements to the rental housing stock. In addition, the federal government has reduced—and now threatens to renounce—its historic commitment to provide quality shelter to the poor and the homeless.

Mortgage interest rates have also played a role in escalating housing costs. For every 1 percentage point increase in the mortgage interest rate, the monthly payment rises about 10 percent. Between 1970 and 1979, the average mortgage rate for new home mortgages rose from 8.45 to 10.77 percent, an increase of 2.32 percentage points. This translates to a 27 percent increase in monthly mortgage payments (this figure is somewhat reduced, of course, through the deduction of mortgage interest from personal income tax liability). At the same time, however, overall monthly ownership costs rose by more than 100 percent. The bulk of this increase is attributable to the extraordinary rise in the average home purchase prices, with other cost components (such as utilities) contributing as well. In 1979 and 1980 interest rates have been much more important in driving up the cost of housing.

From the perspective of its real, after-tax cost, mortgage financing has been extraordinarily cheap for most of the past decade. Nominal interest rates consist of a real rate of interest *plus* an inflation premium intended to ensure that inflation does not wipe out the real value of interest payments to the lender over the life of the loan. Because these premiums were quite low during most of the 1970s, the real cost of borrowing was either zero or negative. Moreover, because interest payments are deductible from taxable income, their money cost can be reduced by as much as 50 percent.

Mortgage market failure

Housing costs are not the only barrier to home ownership or the greater production of multifamily rental units. For a variety of reasons, many people who are ready and able to purchase homes, or to develop multifamily housing rental units, and who have the attributes of creditworthiness that a well functioning capital market requires, are unable to obtain financing. This "failure" in the residential mortgage market can be traced to several sources.

Discrimination

Many people who apply for credit are not evaluated on the basis of their creditworthiness. If they (or the property they want to purchase) possess certain characteristics, the application process frequently grinds to a halt and the loan is denied. These characteristics—including race, sex, and neighborhood— are commonly used by the banking community as a kind of "proxy" for the individual's own credit risk, even though a more thorough analysis (one that is, by definition, more costly to the lender) might well show that the aspiring borrower is entirely creditworthy. Even if the loan is not denied out of hand, the bank will frequently impose terms that do not correspond the borrower's actual default risk. In short, even if discrimination does not entirely preclude the availability of housing finance, it is likely to increase its cost.

Disintermediation

This refers to the process that results in the loss of lendable funds by thrift institutions such as savings and loans, credit unions, and savings banks. By specializing in housing finance, thrift institutions have, over the past thirty years, substantially improved the efficiency of the housing mortgage market. Yet they have also created a major problem pertaining to the overall supply of lendable funds. The portfolios of thrift institutions are dominated by traditional mortgages—fixed-yield investments that require a number of years to pay off (or "amortize"). Many of these mortgages were made years ago at what are now exceedingly low rates of interest—often far below the rate of inflation. When interest rates are rising, thrift institutions cannot compete for the deposits of families and households— their basic source of funds. As a result, people turn to other investments, such as Treasury bills and money market instruments, that closely follow market interest rates.

Usury ceilings

An additional barrier to credit is the state mandated ceilings on the interest rates lenders can set for home mortgages. Originally, these ceilings were created to protect the unsophisticated borrower from financial exploitation by prohibiting loans from being made on excessively unfavorable terms. The exceptionally high interest rates that have prevailed for the past few years—the product of sustained inflation, increased public borrowing, and a somewhat erratic management of the money supply—have made these ceilings a major impediment to credit availability. Because lenders cannot charge interest that is competitive, they channel their funds into open market securities (or their depositors do on their own). The effects of this altered pattern of investment are felt most sharply by less favored mortgage applicants: lenders are unable to charge "riskier" borrowers a relatively higher rate, so they simply curtail the availability of credit. Lenders also compensate for the cap on interest charges by requiring a higher down payment. Both actions are felt most directly by young people, by first-time home buyers, and by low- and moderate-income people entering the home buying market for the first time.

Localism

Local financial institutions usually are the only ones able to originate and service mortgages. The information and transaction costs of mortgage lending are too high for an institution that is geographically distant. Localism in the sources of home financing means that the availability of credit varies greatly among regions and that households (and regions) suffer from a variety of forms of credit rationing with resultant higher interest rates. (While the development of a nationwide secondary mortgage market has reduced the problems that formerly resulted from a sheer shortage of capital, monopoly and noncompetitive banking markets still create major problems for would-be borrowers in rural areas in states without statewide banking.)

Appendix F

The states and urban strategies

INTRODUCTION

When a National Urban Policy was announced by the Carter administration in March 1978, it included a call for a Federal-State Partnership to respond to urban problems. Recognition at the national level of the importance of state governments was long overdue. Reform and modernization at the state level during the past three decades coupled with effective leadership has enabled a number of states to undertake strong initiatives in community assistance.

A number of states are developing comprehensive policies or strategies to deal with the problems faced by their local governments which may serve as models for other states. The National Academy of Public Administration received a research grant from HUD's Office of Policy Development and Research to examine the genesis and character of these state urban strategies and to provide an understanding of how and why states are addressing community needs. The Academy has compared and analyzed ten of these state urban strategies. The states covered are: California, Connecticut, Florida, Massachusetts, Michigan, New Jersey, North Carolina, Ohio, Oregon, and Pennsylvania. In 1979, case studies on each of the states, written by specialists in intergovernmental relations against a common framework, provided the basis for the Academy's comparative analysis.

A "State Urban Strategy" can be defined as an explicit policy framework containing a set of articulated goals and policies with identified programs and activities which can address issues of growth, development or decline affecting the state's communities.

ORIGINS AND POLITICS

The origins of urban strategies are quite parallel. First, state responsibility for problems of growth and the environment were articulated and accepted. Second, a state government capacity in the executive branch to engage in longer-range planning, goal setting and policymaking was created with legislative sanction. Third, state plans evolved from advisory to more influential frameworks for state action. The most significant feature of this evolutionary process is a substantive and political attempt to reconcile concerns for the economy with ecology and to balance the goals of competing interests.

State strategies stemmed largely from action by state legislatures in the late sixties and early seventies, mostly in response to lobbying by environmental groups. The 1977 and 1978 strategies, however, focused more on economic development and were prepared in the state executive branch. The case studies show clearly the importance of the governor in launching these efforts and seeing that they become a serious policy tool.

Electoral politics provide an important impetus to state urban strategies. In several of the states analyzed, an incumbent governor initiated an urban policy exercise because of the demands of a political constituency or to outflank an election opponent. Yet, strategies are motivated not only by political considerations, but also by a substantive desire and necessity on the part of state officials to respond to persistent and popular concerns over the physical and economic quality of life. Analysis of the politics and motivating factors behind the development of state strategies reveals that they have been largely indigenous efforts motivated by internal considerations. They are the exercise by state government of its basic authority in response to objective and political forces.

STRATEGY PARTICIPANTS

Gubernatorial leadership is critical to committing a state to develop and implement an explicit policy on growth and development. There must also be an organizational capacity within state government to manage and implement the process. The importance to the success of a state strategy of a stong central staff agency closely linked to the governor and to the budget process is one of the most significant findings to emerge from these case studies. Among the most important ingredients to an effective strategy are: gubernatorial leadership, organizational capacity, outside support, and capable staff.

State legislatures have exercised considerable influence and authority over strategy initiation and implementation. In several of these case study states, the legislature has helped initiate the strategy process by enacting planning or policy legislation or by mandating growth management/goal-setting procedures. State legislation was critical in providing the executive branch the legal basis and organizational capacity essential to strategy formulation. Generally, legislative involvement has been less direct in the preparation of strategy reports or urban policy documents. Their most important function is, of course, to act upon the governor's recommendations for new programs and policies to implement strategy objectives.

Two types of strategies were identified—*horizontal* and *vertical*. A horizontal strategy concentrates on the co-ordination or redirection of state government policies and state agency decisionmaking. Those states which have relied upon state program coordi-

nation, regulatory approaches, fiscal aid and tax incentives to help their local governments are characteristic of the horizontal approach. A vertical strategy attempts to set policies and processes which would change or guide the actions of local governments as well as state agencies. The states with vertical strategies were focused on growth management and land use and included mandatory or influential processes affecting local government decisions. While each of the strategies we studied addressed some element of both vertical and horizontal coordination or direction, they differ greatly in the degree of attention given the two approaches.

Precisely how local governments participated in the formulation of state strategies depended upon the type of strategy. North Carolina, Oregon, and Massachusetts have adopted vertical strategies, and in those states, participation and involvement of local government officials was formal, continuous and extensive. The horizontal strategies of California, Connecticut, New Jersey, Pennsylvania and Michigan were characterized by local government participation that was less formal and more of an advisory and reactive character.

Regional agency involvement was modest to nonexistent. The states preferred to deal directly with local jurisdictions, rather than working through metropolitan or substate frameworks. As voluntary associations of local government or regional planning councils, their normal role is advisory. In some cases, the state has proposed a stronger regional role and encountered stiff opposition from local governments.

SUBSTANCE AND IMPLEMENTATION

These strategies represent a new way of doing business for state agencies, governors' staffs and legislatures. They are generally more than program initiatives, being instead policy frameworks, new processes, review procedures and guidelines for decisionmaking. As such, they are long-range efforts, not easily implemented with a few pieces of legislation or executive orders. Nor are they implemented with finality; state urban strategies tend to be evolutionary, and to take a long-range view of state policies and programs.

State strategies are generally comprehensive and broad policy statements which cover a wide array of issues facing the state and its communities. They most often begin with a statement of goals, policies or principles which are intended to serve as a general framework for more specific proposals. The goal statements are usually broadly worded and inclusive. In and of themselves, these listings of laudatory objectives provide little indication of the purposes or intents of the strategy. However, there are four major themes which the states are attempting to address: economic development, growth management, urban revitalization, and fiscal reform.

Nine of the ten state strategies give major emphasis to economic development. In fact, all but one accord economic development issues the highest priority. They reflect a growing faith in the power of economic development to solve urban ills—a faith shared by the architects of President Carter's National Urban Policy.

Growth management is also given major attention by six of the ten states, and is the most important area of the Oregon and California strategies. Guiding urban development is the dominant theme in California, while in Oregon protecting prime agricultural lands and establishing urban growth boundaries are the dominant objectives. In Massachusetts and North Carolina, growth or development management is seen as a parallel and supporting theme to economic development. The protection of environmentally sensitive areas and the accommodation of new and continuous

growth is a major theme of the Florida strategy. The Pennsylvania effort relies on growth and investment policies to prevent both urban and rural decline.

All of the strategies addressed the issues of urban revitalization and housing. Two separate phrases are used by the states in describing this area—"urban revitalization" and "community conservation." The former term is understood to mean special recognition of older, declining cities, while the latter term is meant to be inclusive of smaller and less urban communities.

Fiscal reforms to increase the equity of local tax systems and the fiscal capacity of local governments are addressed by the strategies, but are not typically their major emphasis. Major changes in the state-local fiscal system have taken place in the last decade, but mostly outside of these strategies; e.g., educational finance and property tax reform movements.

The states are experimenting with a number of approaches to increase the coordination of functional programs, to develop an increased sensitivity to local needs among state officials, and to reduce the unintended negative consequences of state policies and actions. Program coordination tools adopted or proposed by these states include:

1. Coordinating committees or inter-agency "development cabinets";
2. Budget review processes to ensure conformance with urban policy objectives;
3. Urban or community impact analysis; and
4. State expenditure policies to benefit declining and underdeveloped areas.

CONCLUSIONS

If state strategies are to meet the test of politics, they must be comprehensive and balanced statements of policy. They must be directed toward urban revitalization, farm land preservation, economic development and environmental preservation. They must do so in a way that garners the support of previously competing interest groups and builds a new political coalition.

The federal government, through the HUD 701 planning assistance program, has played an important role in encouraging and assisting state comprehensive planning, yet federal influence over the shape and content of state goals and policies appears to be indirect and limited. While the extent of federal influence over the states in their development of strategies cannot be measured with any precision, it has undoubtedly helped shape some of the policies. It should also be recognized that the states are often influenced by their peers. The publicity that Governors Dukakis and Brown received from the announcement of their urban policies probably had some influence on other chief executives. The National Urban Policy, itself, was not developed in a vacuum, but was the outcome of intensive input and lobbying by associations of state and local governments.

Those who advocate a stronger and more active role for the states have assumed that harnessing and redirecting state powers can yield positive benefits to central cities and distressed communities. A requirement that state officials take into account the impact of their decisions on local communities would be good in itself. Devising frameworks for public capital investment in support of private investment in critical locations would be of immense value.

It is too soon to say whether the states studied here have accomplished any of their objectives. We can conclude, though, that these state strategies are evolving in a comprehensive way and can be expected to provide real pay-offs for urban areas.

Source: Charles R. Warren, *The States and Urban Strategies: Executive Summary* (Washington, D.C.: Government Printing Office, 1980). The research forming the basis of this publication was conducted under a grant by the Office of Policy Development and Research of the U.S. Department of Housing and Urban Development. The substance of such research is dedicated to the public. The author is solely responsible for the accuracy of statements or interpretations contained herein.

Appendix G

City housing services provided through the
Department of Housing and Community Development,
Baltimore

IF YOU OWN YOUR DWELLING

1. Building permits are a means of assuring the health and safety of people in your house when alterations, additions, new construction, repairs, or razing are underway. When a permit is issued (and it is required in almost all of those cases), a building inspector will check the work to insist that it is done in a workmanlike manner that meets the building and zoning codes.

2. Loans for rehabilitation of your home are available under several city, state, and federal programs. They are made for necessary repairs only. The interest rate is lower than is generally available from private lenders, and may vary according to your family size and income. In some cases, loans are available for owners of rental property.

3. Information on energy conservation, including recommendations on your needs for insulation, storm windows, etc., to reduce the need for heating and cooling your home is available.

4. Loans for energy conservation in your home are available for low- and moderate-income homeowners at low interest rates. Applications are made through banks and savings and loans.

5. Weatherization assistance is available free to low-income homeowners. HCD crews install storm windows, caulking, weatherstripping, and sometimes insulation.

6. Emergency repairs under the Rehabilitation Easement Program are available free for very low-income homeowners on a limited basis.

IF YOU OWN OR RENT

7. Housing inspection is a way to help get dwellings safe, clean, in good repair, and not overcrowded. HCD inspects dwellings inside and outside and enforces the housing code in regard to maintenance and sanitation.

8. Assistance for the elderly and handicapped by painting, roofing, and simple carpentry is performed by HCD crews or contractors when housing inspectors find genuine hardships that low-income homeowners are unable to handle.

9. Neighborhood cooperation programs are a means for a community and HCD to work together to correct exterior housing problems. The community association's housing committee receives training, then surveys its area, sending "dear neighbor" letters when it finds violations. When corrections are not made voluntarily, the neighborhood refers the case to HCD for enforcement.

10. Rat eradication includes inspection, education, and sometimes baiting. The inspection section will recommend steps to prevent rat infestation and, when necessary, can issue violation notices. Exterior baiting for rats is done *only* when it will help eliminate the problem. Other remedies must be applied first.

11. Housing clinics are offered periodically to assist tenants or homeowners in matters of housekeeping, sanitation, and legal obligations. Often the educational clinics are offered as a substitute for a housing court fine, but they may be entered voluntarily.

12. Zoning deals with the way property is used. The zoning code is a statement of the uses an owner is permitted to make of his property; all other uses are prohibited. Therefore, zoning is a way of protecting both property

owners and their neighbors. . . . Applications for changes in the way a property is used must be cleared through HCD.

IF YOU RENT

13. Rent escrow is a state law under which, if you believe you have serious fire or safety dangers in your home, you pay your rent to rent court (instead of the property owner) until the hazards are corrected. Inspections made by HCD will help the court decide how the rent money will eventually be used. To use rent escrow, call your attorney or Legal Aid.

14. Housing court may also help if your landlord is failing to provide the heat, gas, hot water, or other services that your rent agreement says you should get. You may have your landlord prosecuted, and your case will be presented by an assistant state's attorney provided by HCD.

IF YOU WANT TO RENT

15. Public housing provides homes for low-income families and for the elderly and disabled. Rents are determined by family size and income, and may not be more than 25% of your income.

16. The Housing Assistance Payments Program (Section 8) pays part of the rent of low-income families or the elderly or disabled. . . . HCD inspects the dwelling, which must be decent, safe, and sanitary and in compliance with the housing code. The rent must be within limits set by the federal government. HCD pays part of the rent and you pay the rest, which can be no more than a quarter of family income for rent and utilities. The program may also be used to pay part of the rent of a unit you live in now.

17. Section 8 new housing is built by developers for rental to low- and moderate-income families and the elderly and disabled. You pay no more than 25% of your income as rent. Information on housing may be obtained through the federal Department of Housing and Urban Development or from HCD.

18. Moderate-income housing, assisted by the federal government, is built in many of Baltimore's community development areas for rental to families (or the elderly or disabled) with incomes slightly higher than the limits of public housing. The rents vary.

IF YOU LIVE IN PUBLIC HOUSING

19. Social services are available to all residents. The services include family counseling, youth services, child development, a senior service center, sheltered and congregate housing, volunteer assistance, recreation, and dental and health screening.

IF YOU MUST MOVE

20. Relocation is a service for people or businesses forced to move because of public improvements, but assistance is also available for anyone seeking a new location. You will receive counseling, help in finding a new place to live or do business, and benefits (such as moving costs and help in paying higher rent) if eligible.

IF YOU'D LIKE TO OWN

21. Home-ownership counseling is provided through the Home Ownership Development Division to people who want to own a home but do not know where to start. Advice is available on the size of the house needed, the amount you can afford, financing, and what various neighborhoods offer.

22. Houses for sale may be purchased through HCD. Some have been rehabilitated by the city. Others are sold "as is" and sometimes need extensive rehabilitation.

23. Urban homesteading makes a house available to you for $1 if you are willing to rehabilitate and live in it over

a two-year period. Loans are generally available to finance the rehabilitation. (Warning! Don't think about the dollar it costs to buy the house; think about the real dollars—often $40,000 to $65,000 —it will cost to rehabilitate.)

24. Financing of a home purchase may be possible through HCD, depending on availability of funds. If you want to buy a house you are renting, you might investigate this program.

IF YOU HAVE (OR WOULD LIKE TO HAVE) A BUSINESS

25. Commercial revitalization is a program under which HCD works with merchants, property owners, and community groups to stimulate small business. In one approach, the city makes public improvements in business districts while business people improve the appearance of their establishments. In the shopsteading program, vacant city-owned storefronts are offered for $100 to people who will rehabilitate and open businesses. Any commercial property owner may apply for long-term, low-interest rehabilitation loans. Help in finding business locations is offered.

IF YOU ARE INTERESTED IN YOUR NEIGHBORHOOD

26. Planning for community development areas is conducted by HCD, working with the community (residents, property owners, business people, any-

one else with an interest in the area). The renewal process provides an opportunity for citizens to help decide the improvements that should be made in their neighborhood.

27. The community development block grant is the money provided every year to Baltimore by the federal government, primarily to make physical improvements. If your neighborhood has an urgent need, and a reasonable and eligible proposal for a special neighborhood project as a means of solving a problem, you should write to the commissioner, HCD.

Mayor William Donald Schaefer
  and the Citizens of Baltimore
Department of Housing and
  Community Development
M. J. Brodie, Commissioner
222 East Saratoga Street
Baltimore, Maryland 21202

Source: Department of Housing and Community Development, *27 Services the City provides for you through HCD* (Baltimore, Md.: Department of Housing and Community Development, 1981). This informational folder, prepared for widespread public distribution, has been slightly abridged. Each of the twenty-seven service descriptions includes a phone number for the specific city office involved; these numbers have been omitted.

For further reference

General references

Fish, Gertrude S., ed. *The Story of Housing.* New York: Macmillan, 1979, 550 pp. Recounts the history of government and private responses to housing needs, decade by decade, from colonial days through the 1970s. Includes a chapter on world housing trends.

Fishman, Richard P., ed. *Housing for All Under Law: New Directions in Housing, Land Use, and Planning Law.* A report of the American Bar Association Advisory Commission on Housing and Urban Growth. Cambridge, Mass.: Ballinger, 1978, 635 pp. Authoritative papers on the interrelationships among local use controls, planning, and housing. Coverage includes such topics as the role of the courts in resolving housing and land use conflicts, inclusionary zoning, the roles of comprehensive planning and housing planning, state and local government roles, and hearings, administrative reviews, and other legal procedures.

National Commission on Urban Problems. *Building the American City.* Washington, D.C.: Government Printing Office [1968], 504 pp. A landmark documentation of the evolution of federal, state, and local housing involvement as of 1968.

Nenno, Mary K. *Housing in Metropolitan Areas: Roles and Responsibilities of Five Key Actors.* Washington, D.C.: National Association of Housing and Redevelopment Officials, 1973. Summarizes studies in the state of Connecticut, the Minneapolis/St. Paul metropolitan area, and Dade County (Miami), Florida. The five key actors are the local government chief executive, the comprehensive planner, the community development administrator, the housing developer, and the housing consumer advocate.

Sternlieb, George, and Hughes, James W., eds. *America's Housing: Prospects and Problems.* New Brunswick, N.J.: Rutgers University, Center for Urban Policy Research, 1980, 562 pp. Presents past trends that have shaped the housing market and present trends that will be altering housing and living patterns.

Periodicals

Housing and Development Reporter, semi-monthly, Bureau of National Affairs, Washington, D.C.

Journal of Housing, bi-monthly, National Association of Housing and Redevelopment Officials, Washington, D.C.

Journal of Property Management, bi-monthly, Institute of Real Estate Management, Chicago, Illinois.

Mortgage Banking, monthly, Mortgage Bankers Association of America, Washington, D.C.

Urban Land, monthly, Urban Land Institute, Washington, D.C.

Additional references

Case, Karl E. *The Role of Housing in Urban Development Strategies.* Prepared for the U.S. Department

of Housing and Urban Development. Cambridge, Mass.: Urban
Systems Research and Engineering, Inc., 1980.

Council on Development Choices for
the '80s. *The Affordable Community: Growth, Change and Choice
in the '80s.* Washington, D.C.: Government Printing Office, 1981,
113 pp.

Federal Home Loan Bank Board.
Reaching Out. A loose-leaf handbook of innovative financing under
the Community Development Investment Fund. Washington, D.C.:
Federal Home Loan Bank Board,
1981, 73 individual project sheets.

Goetze, Rolf. *Understanding Neighborhood Change: The Role of Expectations in Urban Revitalization.*
Cambridge, Mass.: Ballinger,
1979, 162 pp.

Greater Minneapolis (Minnesota) Metro-
politan Housing Corporation. *Cata-
lyst for Urban Change 1971–1980,
Minneapolis.* Minneapolis, Minn.:
Greater Minneapolis Metropolitan
Housing Corporation, 1981, 16 pp.

Levatino-Donoghue, Adrienne. *The Rehabilitation Profession.* Washington, D.C.: National Association of
Housing and Redevelopment Officials, 1979, 140 pp.

Marshall, Patricia, ed. *Citizen Participation Certification for Community
Development.* Washington, D.C.:
National Association of Housing
and Redevelopment Officials,
1977, 204 pp.

Mercer, James L. *Local Government
Organizational Structures for the
Eighties.* Management Information
Service Reports, vol. 12, no. 3.
Washington, D.C.: International
City Management Association,
March 1980, 12 pp.

Michigan State Housing Development
Authority. *Management Agent Processing and Evaluation System for

Authority-Financed Developments.*
Lansing, Mich.: Michigan State
Housing Development Authority,
1980, 15 pp.

_____. *Management Agent Qualifica-
tion Data.* Lansing, Mich.: Michigan State Housing Development
Authority, 1980, 2 pp.

_____. *Specifications for Housing
Management.* Lansing, Mich.:
Michigan State Housing Develop-
ment Authority, 1976, 12 pp.

Montgomery County (Maryland). Department of Housing and Community Development. *Housing Policy
for Montgomery County in the
1980's.* Rockville, Md.: Montgomery County Deparment of Housing
and Community Development,
1981.

President's Commission on Housing.
*Financing the Housing Needs of
the 1980s: A Preliminary Report on
Housing Finance.* Washington,
D.C.: Government Printing Office,
1982, 55 pp.

Public Management Consulting Associates. *An Assessment of the Tacoma, Washington Housing Delivery System and Recommendations
for Improvement: Final Report.* Prepared for the city of Tacoma. Palo
Alto, Calif.: Public Management
Consulting Associates, 1980,
56 pp.

Retsinas, Nicholas P.; Nenno, Mary K.;
and Witte, William. "Community
Development." Chapter 46 in *Productivity Handbook for State and
Local Government,* ed. George J.
Washnis. New York: John Wiley &
Sons, 1980. Includes sections on
measuring productivity in community development and in publicly
assisted housing.

Rigby, Robert, Jr. *The Resident as Resource: A Public Housing Management Demonstration in Jersey City.*
Trenton, N.J.: New Jersey Depart-

ment of Community Affairs, 1982, 97 pp.

Struyk, Raymond J., and Benedict, Marc, Jr., eds. *Housing Vouchers for the Poor: Lessons from a National Experiment.* Washington,

D.C.: The Urban Institute, 1981, 424 pp.

Urban Land Institute. *Mixed Use Developments: New Ways of Land Use.* Washington, D.C.: Urban Land Institute, 1976, 193 pp.

About the authors

Mary K. Nenno is Associate Director for Policy Development, National Association of Housing and Redevelopment Officials (NAHRO). She completed a master's degree in public administration through studies at the Institute of Local and State Government, University of Pennsylvania, and the University of Buffalo. Ms. Nenno was on the staff of the Buffalo Municipal Housing Authority until she joined NAHRO in 1960. At NAHRO, she has served as Assistant Director for Housing, Director of Program Operations, and Director of Legislation, prior to her present position. She is a regular contributor to the *Journal of Housing.*

Paul C. Brophy is Executive Director, Urban Redevelopment Authority, City of Pittsburgh. From 1970 to 1977 he was with ACTION–Housing, Inc., in Pittsburgh, successively as program manager, director of special projects, and executive director. He has been a consultant to several local governments and has written extensively on housing management and neighborhood revitalization. He holds a B.A. from La Salle College and a master's degree in city planning from the University of Pennsylvania.

Michael Barker is an independent writer and financial consultant in Boston and Washington. He was formerly the Assistant Director of the National Governors Association's Council of State Planning Agencies, where he was the general editor of a series of books on state development issues. Mr. Barker started his career as an analyst in the Massachusetts Office of State Planning. He is a graduate of Reed College.

Douglas S. Ford is General Manager, Community Development Department, City of Los Angeles, and Director of the city's Municipal Finance Agency. He has served as administrator of the St. Paul (Minnesota) Housing and Redevelopment Authority and has served as a consultant to local governments in economic development and finance. He holds a bachelor's degree from Claremont Men's College and an M.B.A. degree from the University of California at Berkeley.

Frank Keefe is President of Frank Keefe Associates, Inc., a Boston planning and real estate development firm. He is the originator and project manager for Westland Avenue Apartments and the Bakers Chocolate mill conversion described in this book. Formerly he was Director of State Planning and Chairman of the Development Cabinet for former Massachusetts Governor Michael Dukakis. Prior to that he was City Planning Director in Lowell, Massachusetts, and staff assistant to the Director of Planning and Development of the Port Authority of New York and New Jersey. He holds degrees from Fordham and Oxford Universities and is an adjunct professor at Tufts University and a member of the Visiting Committee of the School of Architecture and Planning at MIT.

G. Terry McNellis is Deputy Director for Housing, City of St. Paul. He was formerly Director of Projects for the St. Paul Housing and Redevelopment Authority, and he has worked extensively in developmental project planning and implementation, particularly in housing. Mr. McNellis attended the University of Minnesota.

William A. Witte is Deputy Director for Housing, Mayor's Office of Housing and Community Development, San Francisco. He was previously with the

U.S. Department of Housing and Urban Development as Executive Assistant to the Assistant Secretary for Housing/FHA Commissioner; and with the National Association of Housing and Redevelopment Officials as Director of Legislative Services and as Director of the Community Development Monitoring Project. He also served as a planner with the Office of Housing and Community Development in Philadelphia. Mr. Witte holds a bachelor of arts degree and a master's degree in city planning from the University of Pennsylvania.

Illustration credits

Chapter 3 Figure 3–5: U.S., General Accounting Office, *Evaluation of Alternatives for Financing Low and Moderate Income Rental Housing* (Washington, D.C.: U.S. General Accounting Office, 1980), pp. 59–60; Figure 3–6: Rosemarie Noonan, "Financial Strategies for Moderate Rehabilitation of Multi-Family Housing Units," *Journal of Housing,* March 1980, p. 152; Figure 3–7: Dakota County Housing and Redevelopment Authority, *Training Manual for Section 8 Rent Assistance Program* (Hastings, Minn.: Dakota County Housing and Redevelopment Authority, 1977), pp. 1–2.

Chapter 4 Figure 4–1: Reprinted with permission from Rolf Goetze, *Understanding Neighborhood Change,* copyright 1979, Ballinger Publishing Company, p. 35.

Chapter 6 Figure 6–1: Montgomery County (Maryland), Department of Housing and Community Development, *Housing Policy for Montgomery County in the 1980's* (Rockville, Md.: Montgomery County Department of Housing and Community Development, 1981), pp. 16–17; Figure 6–2: Derived from: Montgomery County (Maryland), Office of Management and Budget, *Recommended Fiscal Year 1983 Budget* (Rockville, Md.: Montgomery County Office of Management and Budget, 1982); Figure 6–3: Derived from an ordinance adopted by the city council and signed by the mayor in 1982.

Index

Municipal Management Series

Housing and Local Government

Text type
Helvetica Light

Composition
Progressive Typographers, Inc.
Emigsville, Pennsylvania

Printing and binding
R. R. Donnelley & Sons Company
Crawfordsville, Indiana

Paper
Warren Sebago, 55#

Design
Herbert Slobin

'a Bit

e